DECORATIVE
HARDWARE

DECORATIVE HARDWARE

Mark Dittrick
Diane Kender Dittrick

Photographs by David Arky

Illustrations by Mark Dittrick

Hearst Books
New York

Credits:
The hinge shown on page 1 and the lock on page 167 are courtesy
of Kraft Hardware, New York, New York. The photographs
appearing on pages 15 and 271 were taken at The Museum of the
City of New York. The photograph appearing on page 79 was taken
at the Headquarters of the Colonial Dames of America, 417 East
61st Street, New York, New York. The latch shown on page 133 is
courtesy of the Chester Carousel, Chester, New Jersey. The
photographs appearing on pages 149 and 211 were taken at Sleepy
Hollow Restorations, Tarrytown, New York. The photograph
appearing on page 183 was taken in Brooklyn, New York. The
photograph appearing on page 259 was taken at Waterloo Village
Restoration, Stanhope, New Jersey.

Library of Congress Cataloging in Publication Data

Dittrick, Mark.
  Decorative hardware.

  1. Cabinet hardware—Catalogs. 2. Building fittings—
Catalogs. I. Dittrick, Diane Kender. II. Title.
TS887.D57 1982   683   82-12137
ISBN 0-87851-208-X

10   9   8   7   6   5   4   3   2   1

PRINTED IN THE UNITED STATES OF AMERICA

Contents

Acknowledgments

The authors and publishers wish to express their thanks to the sources who have so generously made available for photography the decorative hardware presented in this book. For their extraordinary efforts and for taking time to answer our many technical questions about decorative hardware, a special note of appreciation goes to Stan Saperstein and the staff at Kraft Hardware, Inc.; Philippe R. Bigot and the staff at The Baldwin Brass Center in New York City; Leonard Wolberg, The Merit Brass Collection; Hugo Pfanstiel, H. Pfanstiel Hardware Company; and Alexander Klein, Quincy Manufacturing Company. Special thanks, too, to Sara Bodine, Editor, *Metalsmith*; Fran Jurge-Garvan, Managing Editor, *American Farriers Journal*; and Dimitri Gerakaris, Editor, *Anvil's Ring*. We are deeply grateful to the following individuals for all their help and cooperation: Robert DeLong, Acorn Manufacturing Company; Glenn R. Docherty, Albert Constantine and Son, Inc.; Peter A. Renzetti, The Arden Forge Company; Mahlon Kilgore, Arrowsmith Industries, Inc.; Whitman Ball, Ball and Ball; Bob Patrick, Big Anvil Forge; A. Daniel Danoff and Bob Pryor, Bob Pryor Antiques; Mark E. Bokenkamp, Bokenkamp's Forge; Bill Castor and Ray Girard, The Broadway Collection; Jean Brown, Brookstone Company; Dothan R. Boothe, By-Gone Days Antiques; Barbara Tenaro, Custom Decor, Inc.; Ronald W. Skonning, Erco Manufacturing Company; Larry B. Wood, The Farm Forge; Harvey Grossman, Forms & Surfaces; Peter Segal, Garrett Wade Company, Inc.; Mark Jacobson, Glynn-Johnson Corporation; Mark E. Rocheford, Hammerworks; Kirk Henin, Harris Hardware Sales Corporation; Wynne Broms, Home Hardware, a division of Hammit Industries, Inc.; Barbara Horton, Horton Brasses; Paul Siegel, IDG Marketing Limited, Inc.; Jack Kay, Impex Associates Limited, Inc.; Lalie Kempton, Jaybee Manufacturing Corporation; Craig Kaviar, Kaviar Forge; Arthur Meyers and William Thaler, Kraft Hardware, Inc.; William R. O'Connor, Medeco Security Locks, Inc.; Kathleen Zotter, Michigan Production Grinding Company; Barbara McGrath, Omnia Industries, Inc.; T. J. Kokot, PTI-Dolco/ Simpson Hardware; Ledley Clarke Boyce, Paxton Hardware; Don Stangohr, Period Furniture Hardware Company, Inc.; Wayne Roper, Plexacraft Metals; Lance Cloutier, The Ram's Head Forge; Jay Frost, Renovator's Supply; Steve Gordon, Restoration Hardware; Walt Ritter and Wendy Moss, Ritter & Son Hardware; Ronald H. Kass, Ronald H. Kass Forge; Robert H. Klar, Salmon Falls Forge; Neil Bruckner, Selby Furniture Hardware Company; Vincent Geoffroy, Sherle Wagner International; Bernard Golde, Simon's Hardware, Inc.; Craig Wilson, Ron McKee and Bill Shanahan, Stanley Hardware, a division of The Stanley Works; Steve Kayne, Steve Kayne Hand Forged Hardware; Richard C. Swenson, Swenson's Forge; Arlyne Serot, Terra Sancta Guild; Don Shaw, Tremont Nail Company; Stanley Sternbach, Unique Handicraft Corporation; Leonard Schechter, Urban Archeology; Janet Walters, Urfic, Inc.; Maria T. Fitch, VSI Hardware; Barry Berman, Valley Forgeworks, Ltd.; Denis Daines, Valli and Colombo (USA), Inc.; and George Whinery, Jr., Waddell Manufacturing Company, Inc.

1
Understanding Decorative Hardware

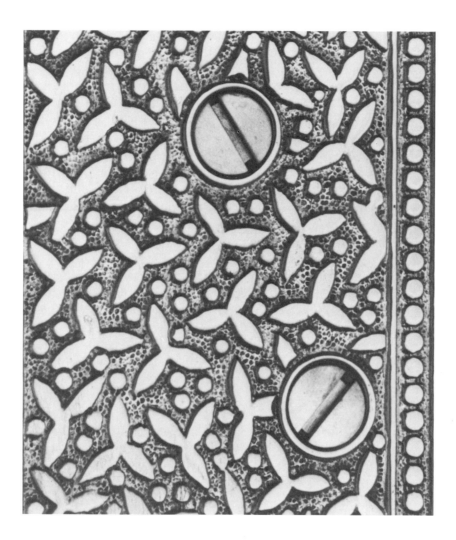

DECORATIVE hardware is interior decorating's stepchild. It's a member of the family. It has to be considered. But it doesn't get nearly as much attention as it deserves.

You might even say it's sort of a Cinderella. Not that any of its siblings—furniture, wall coverings, lighting fixtures, carpets, and such— are particularly ugly, even though they certainly can be, to a startling degree. But few of its sisters work so hard, performing the most mundane chores, and go so woefully unnoticed. What could be the explanation?

Decorative hardware is one of those things you never really have to think about if you don't want to, and that could have something to do with it. Move into an empty house or a vacant apartment and you will probably find it totally equipped with all the necessary architectural decorative hardware: hinges on exterior and interior doors, door knobs and pulls, door bumpers, sash lifts and fasteners, shutter hinges, window locks, push plates and kick plates, door bell buttons, and the like. They were there before you arrived. Then comes the cabinet hardware: the small pulls, knobs and hinges, little latches, locks, and catches. These move in along with the furniture, unheralded hangers-on entering almost out of sight and almost always out of mind.

A blown fuse, or a full-blown power failure, quickly reminds us how much we depend on electricity. And how rapidly our appreciation of water increases when a main breaks or a well goes dry. The importance of decorative hardware is never so vividly brought home by any such swift or dramatic reminders. Just imagine for a moment, though, what would happen if suddenly every piece of decorative hardware in your home were to disappear. Doors would fall out of their frames. Even if they didn't, there would be nothing to grab onto to open them. The same would hold true for drawers—no knobs, locks, hinges, bolts, pulls, hooks, or lifts.

In a world so taken with technological innovation, decorative hardware has very little that's novel to offer. Most decorative hardware performs its work today pretty much the way it worked a long time ago. A knob is a knob, in other words, and the job a knob does so elegantly and simply is hard to improve on. Over the past hundred years or so, the only really significant decorative hardware breakthroughs have had to do with locks. Around the end of the eighteenth century, butt hinges gradually replaced strap hinges. But who noticed? This lack of marvels has undoubtedly added in some measure to our apathy. For gadget fanciers, unfortunately, decorative hardware always has been, and probably always will be, something of a bore.

But to those who appreciate it for what it does functionally and what it can do decoratively, decorative hardware is like a house's jewelry. Like a belt buckle or a coat button, it joins form and function in a nearly perfect partnership. A catch enhances a cabinet and holds its door closed at the same time. A furniture foot with a caster decorates, protects, and provides mobility. A highly polished brass stair carpet holder holds the stair's carpet down while creating a sparkling geometric pattern over the entire length of the staircase. Keeping this duality of purpose in mind is very much a part of developing one's own deeper understanding and appreciation of decorative hardware.

The shame is how little we consider it compared to other elements in an interior. Allowing a carpenter installing a door to select the door's hardware is like letting a carpet layer choose the carpet.

Taking command of one's decorative hardware situation is not much more complicated than acquainting one's self with all or most of the available options. Knowing what there is to choose from and where to get it is the better part of the battle. Sources of decorative hardware, despite its stepchild status, absolutely abound.

Most unknowledgeable nonprofessional decorative hardware buyers make a beeline for their local hardware or housewares store. These stores may differ considerably. Some endeavor to stock an interesting range of not too exotic decorative hardware. Others are content to display a limited line somewhere between the toasters and the snow shovels.

Stores with far more stimulating selections—those that specialize in selling decorative hardware—can be either plentiful or few and far between. It depends, to a large degree, on where one lives. Major urban centers with large decorating and architectural trades usually have several walk-in suppliers supplying architectural and cabinet hardware only. First-time and once-in-a-while retail customers in such shops are almost always outnumbered by professional regulars with a fairly good idea of what they're after, and the atmosphere can be somewhat imposing. But knowledgeable salespeople often surprise with their patience and willingness to offer guidance and help. The real problem in a well-stocked decorative hardware emporium is the amount of merchandise one has to choose from. But for anyone seriously in pursuit of decorative hardware, it can be a most welcome profusion.

Being outside an urban center can have its advantages, if your taste runs toward hardware that's forged by hand. Few blacksmiths set themselves up in the middle of big cities, opting instead for places and spaces where the atmosphere is more conducive to their work. And more and more are setting themselves up every year. Most make articles of decorative hardware for both interior and exterior use as stock items or will make almost anything you can describe in iron exactly to your specifications.

Urban and rural decorative hardware buyers alike can rely entirely on the mails and shop from any one of several mail-order catalogs specializing in decorative hardware items. Having a good idea of what you want in advance is helpful. Many mail-order suppliers specialize in period hardware and the sort of architectural hardware needed for restorations. Furniture periods for anyone other than a museum curator or avid collector of period furniture can be quite confusing. A pull one catalog will call *William & Mary* could be identical with another's *Queen Anne.* Being able to differentiate between Sheraton and Hepplewhite or Empire and Directoire can require extensive study.

If you need to replace something old and can't find a suitable reproduction, you may solve your problem by trying to locate something akin to the original. Hardware from the past, once summarily thrown away, is valuable merchandise for a growing number of antique dealers who resell it to those who value old hardware. The real thing—stripped from elegant old houses or salvaged from buildings torn down—is now becoming more readily available. And unlike shops in which you know what to expect, antique hardware merchants can offer some delightful surprises.

The Materials of Decorative Hardware

Most decorative hardware, both architectural and cabinet, is made from brass, an alloy (''a substance composed of two or more metals intimately mixed and united usually by being fused together and dissolved in each other when molten,'' according to Webster's) of copper (55 to 90 percent) and zinc (10 to 45 percent) and sometimes also small amounts of other metals.

One way to get brass into a desired shape is to cast it: melting the metal, pouring or forcing it into a mold of some sort, and then allowing it to cool and solidify.

In a procedure called sand casting, molten metal is poured into an impression made by a master model in a special mixture of sand and clay or some other binder. Considerable surface detail can be obtained by this method; the finer the sand in the mold mixture, the finer the finished casting. Grinding and polishing the

rough casting removes any mold lines and brings the piece up to the desired level of shine. Incised lines, special textures, and similar surface decorations may be added to castings after they've been cast. A hammer and hand-held punches (short steel rods with variously shaped tips for cutting and indenting) are used in the procedure. Called *hand chasing,* such work can add significantly to the price of an item.

Castings with even greater detail than sand castings can be produced by the lost-wax, or investment, casting process. A very accurate impression or model of the object to be cast is made in wax and then covered with a very fine mud-like, heat-resistant material. When the covering material has dried and hardened, heat is applied, causing the wax to run out of holes left in the coating and leaving a mold into which molten metal can be poured. The solidified casting is removed by destroying the mold. Lost-wax casting is quite costly and decorative hardware made by this method is understandably expensive. Very little decorative hardware today is made this way.

On the opposite end of the casting spectrum from lost-wax casting is die-casting, a technique usually used for manufacturing decorative hardware items and parts only when very large quantities are called for. In this process, there is made a permanent steel mold, or die, into which the liquid metal is forced by the pressure of compressed air or a mechanical plunger. The pressure is released when the casting has solidified, and the die, which is usually in several sections, is separated to release the casting. Most relatively inexpensive, mass-produced cast brass decorative hardware is die-cast, but in Europe, especially in Italy, some exceptionally fine and not so inexpensive decorative hardware is, too.

Brass that's less than liquid can also be turned into many different shapes. Hot brass can be extruded—forced, much like thick toothpaste—through specially shaped openings that give the emerging metal a specific and sometimes quite intricate cross-sectional profile. Door hinges are frequently made in this way; and brass that's to undergo further processing, such as forging, is often first extruded.

Forging is the shaping of metal by hammering. Blacksmiths forge metal, usually iron, by hand and will on occasion work brass on their anvils; but most brass forgings today are produced by modern forging presses. A hot hunk of brass called a billet is placed between two steel dies—one stationary die containing a cavity conforming to the shape of the bottom of the finished forging and one die with a cavity shaped to conform to the top of the forging attached to the underside of a power-driven hammer. The pressure of the descending hammer forces the heated metal into the die cavities and causes it to take on the desired shape. According to one manufacturer of brass forgings, forgings "have 250 percent higher tensile strength, . . . a homogeneous metal structure throughout," and "no surface imperfections, gas holes or voids." However, delicate surface details are captured better in castings. The most successful forgings, therefore, are those that are not excessively embellished.

Because it is a malleable metal, brass can even be formed when totally cold. It can be rolled quite thin into large sheets of what is termed wrought brass, and blanks cut from such sheets can be made to take on complex designs in fairly high relief by hammering, or stamping, them over dies, either by hand or mechanically. The backplates of many Victorian furniture pulls and those of pulls dating as far back as the late eighteenth century were made in this manner. While they may seem fragile compared to castings, stamped brass period reproductions should not be judged too harshly too quickly. It is the cheap casting masquerading as an authentic reproduction of a stamped original that one has to watch out for. And some very sturdy, high-quality decorative hardware is made from heavy-gauge wrought brass.

Another important decorative hardware material is another important alloy of copper: bronze. What makes bronze bronze and not brass is the addition of tin (5 to 25 percent) to the metallurgical mixture. Bronze, which is usually reddish, is generally stronger and more wear-resistant than its naturally yellow-colored cousin, brass. But it is also more brittle. The higher the tin content, the stronger and brittler the bronze. Brittle here should not be taken to mean breakable, only less easily worked when cold. Bronze can be wrought, extruded, forged, and cast.

Iron, the metal that constitutes around 5 percent of the earth's crust, is used—in one of several incarnations—to produce perhaps around that percentage of all decorative hardware. Wrought iron, which we have come to associate with architectural railings, is the raw material of the blacksmith. Wrought iron is almost pure iron and is naturally corrosion resistant. Threads of silicone-rich slag coursing through the metal make it tough and fibrous. It is also ductile and malleable, which makes it also very forgeable. By successively heating it and striking it with a hammer on an anvil, the blacksmith gradually shapes the metal to create pulls, latches, hinges, and all sorts of beautiful utilitarian objects. The black finish traditionally associated with hand forged iron is an oxide scale formed on the surface of the metal during heating. Cast iron, which is hard and brittle and very unforgeable, was once a popular metal for making decorative hardware, especially Victorian hardware. It is used today mostly for making reproductions—especially Victorian reproductions. Steel, the strongest and perhaps the hardest working member of the iron family, can take on many different forms. Thick and flat, it can be a heavy-duty gate hinge plated with zinc and coated with enamel or lacquer to resist rusting. Thin, it can be the stamped metal parts of a tiny roller catch. In an infinite variety of shapes, it can be the working parts and even the springs inside a lock.

Aluminum—cast, forged, wrought, etc.—is frequently used as a light-weight substitute for steel or some other metal. It can be brushed for a dull appearance, polished for a bright one, or plated. Die-cast zinc alloys are common base metals for relatively inexpensive plated decorative hardware items. One such material is called Zamac.

Other materials one can expect to encounter making up either a part or the sum total of many items of decorative hardware include wood, glass, porcelain, various types of plastic, and even rubber. Wooden knobs and pulls, either part wood or all wood, are commonplace. They may be raw and intended to stay that way, raw and awaiting appropriate treatment, or already covered by some sort of decorative or protective coating. Glass, in the form of door and cabinet knobs, may be cast or hand blown, plain, or cut and faceted. Crystal is glass with lead added to it to increase its clarity. The term is often loosely applied, though, to ordinary glass that has been hand blown or cut. The term ceramic covers anything made from clay that has been hardened by firing; porcelain, a distinctly finer form of ceramic material, is very hard, nonporous, naturally white, and translucent and is made from a fine paste that has been fired at a very high temperature. The decorative hardware items most likely to be made of porcelain are door knobs, knob roses and plates, cabinet knobs and pulls, and electrical switch and outlet plates. Porcelain hardware is often decorated with applied (decaled) or hand-painted designs protected by overglazes.

Plastic once suggested cheapness in an article of decorative hardware, but some new plastic materials are putting that notion quickly to rest. Lucite has actually been around for quite a while and as a decorative hardware material has stood the test of time. A more recently developed plastic being used today to make everything from pulls and garment hooks to lock cases, called ABS, is so impact-resistant its more common application is in the fabrication of crash helmets. One interesting advantage plastics have over other decorative hardware materials has to do with color: a colored plastic object is colored through and through, not just on the surface.

If brass is the material most common to decorative hardware, rubber may well be the least. One expects to find it at the end of a door bumper, of course, but some very interesting and beautifully designed decorative hardware that's been on the market for only a short time is made entirely from rubber—a synthetic, polymer rubber called neoprene. What new materials might soon be looming on the decorative hardware horizon is anyone's guess.

Handings

If you could install any lock, lever door handle, or set of hinges on any door, selecting such items would be easy. Unfortunately, there are left-hand lever door handles and there are right-hand lever door handles. Some hinges are right-hand hinges and some are left-hand hinges. Some hinges are reversible. Locks feature even greater

variation. There are left-hand locks with regular bevels and right-hand locks with regular bevels, and left-hand locks with reverse bevels and right-hand locks with reverse bevels. And then there are left-hand locks and right-hand locks with bevels that are reversible, which makes it possible to switch their bevels from regular to reverse and vice versa—which, depending on your point of view and your familiarity with bevels, either simplifies matters or makes them just that much more confusing.

It isn't difficult to see why most decorative hardware buying mistakes not related to matters of taste have to do with what are called ''handings.'' Make such a mistake and select an item that is incorrectly handed for its intended door and that item will, at best, look strange or, at worst, not function at all.

Every door that swings on hinges, from the biggest front entrance door to the humblest cupboard or cabinet door, is either a right-hand door or a left-hand door. Whether a particular door is a right-hand door or a left-hand door depends on the direction it opens in relation to what is assumed to be the outside side of the door and where the hinges are that govern the door's swing. In addition to front doors, cupboard and cabinet doors, room doors, closet doors, and bathroom doors are affected.

Butt door hinges with numerous knuckles (the aligned prominent cylinders through which a narrow rod, or pin, is passed to join two sides of a hinge together) can be used to attach one edge of a door to one side of a door frame (see figure 1) or to attach the other edge of the same door to

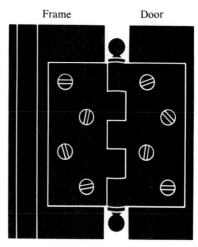

Frame   Door

FIGURE 1

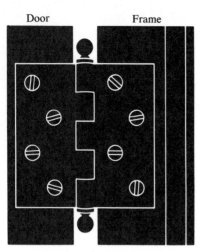

Door · Frame

FIGURE 2

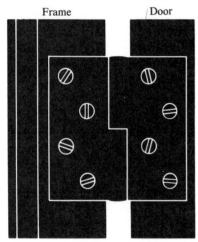

Frame · Door

FIGURE 3

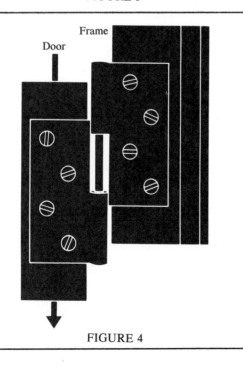

Door · Frame

FIGURE 4

the other side of the frame (see figure 2). Hinges like these are reversible, or not handed. A two-knuckle lift-off hinge is an example of a hinge that *is* handed and not reversible. A two-knuckle lift-off hinge can be used to attach one edge of a door to a door frame (see figure 3) but not the other edge of that door to the other side of the frame. A door hung with wrongly handed lift-off hinges will, with the help of gravity, unhinge itself and wind up on the floor (see figure 4).

Door knobs, because they are essentially round with no discernible left or right to them, are not handed. But lever door handles, which are by their nature not symmetrical, are *sometimes* handed. A lever door handle with a distinct top and bottom is handed. Such a handle pointing properly to the right (see figure 5) is a right-hand handle.

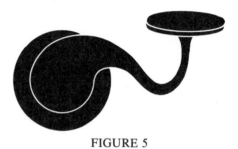

FIGURE 5

The same lever door handle in a left-hand version (see figure 6) would point to the left.

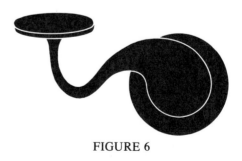

FIGURE 6

You could, in a pinch, replace a right-hand handle with a left-hand handle, but the appearance of the replacement might be quite inappropriate (see figure 7).

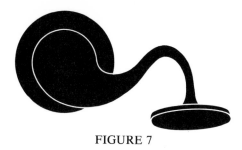

FIGURE 7

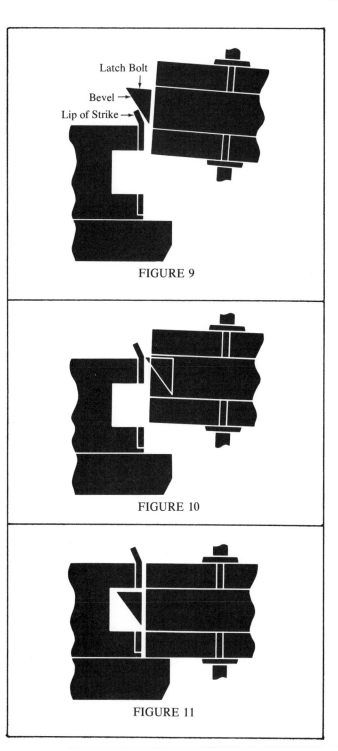

Latch Bolt

Bevel →

Lip of Strike →

FIGURE 9

FIGURE 10

FIGURE 11

A lever door handle that is exactly the same top and bottom viewed horizontally is reversible (see figure 8) and, therefore, not handed—unless the manufacturer hid the set screw holes out of sight at the "bottom" of the shank.

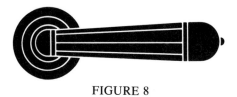

FIGURE 8

Installing a lever door handle that is handed only because of where its set screws are upside down would not effect its functioning, and maybe no one but you would ever notice the unsightly set screws.

A lock with exactly the same functional apparatus on the inside and on the outside would be reversible and not handed. A lock with different locking and unlocking features on opposite sides—which describes the vast majority of locks—would be handed. Then there are bevels. One feature most locks have in common is a latch bolt, also called a live bolt. Latch bolts are spring actuated and have heads that are slanted, or beveled, on one side and straight on the other. When a door with a lock with a latch bolt closes, the beveled side of the bolt meets the lip of the strike in the door jamb (see figure 9), retracts against the pressure of its spring as it rides along the strike (see figure 10), and then shoots out, propelled by the force of the spring, into the recess of the strike (see figure 11) when the door is completely closed. In order for this sequence to happen, the beveled side of the latch bolt must be facing the jamb and its strike. If the bevel were facing the other way, the straight side of the bolt would impinge against the strike and the door wouldn't be able to close. The direction the latch bolt is facing—the bevel of the lock, in other words—is, therefore, quite important. Different doors take different locks, with latch bolts facing in one direction or the other.

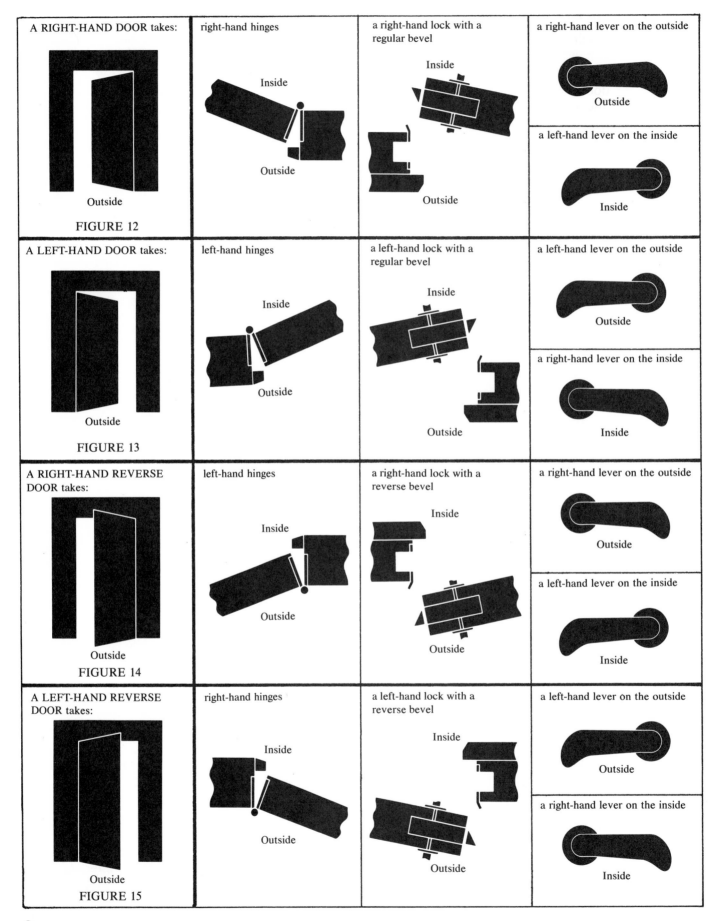

A RIGHT-HAND DOOR takes:	right-hand hinges	a right-hand lock with a regular bevel	a right-hand lever on the outside
	Inside / Outside	Inside / Outside	Outside
Outside — FIGURE 12			a left-hand lever on the inside — Inside
A LEFT-HAND DOOR takes:	left-hand hinges	a left-hand lock with a regular bevel	a left-hand lever on the outside
	Inside / Outside	Inside / Outside	Outside
Outside — FIGURE 13			a right-hand lever on the inside — Inside
A RIGHT-HAND REVERSE DOOR takes:	left-hand hinges	a right-hand lock with a reverse bevel	a right-hand lever on the outside
	Inside / Outside	Inside / Outside	Outside
Outside — FIGURE 14			a left-hand lever on the inside — Inside
A LEFT-HAND REVERSE DOOR takes:	right-hand hinges	a left-hand lock with a reverse bevel	a left-hand lever on the outside
	Inside / Outside	Inside / Outside	Outside
Outside — FIGURE 15			a right-hand lever on the inside — Inside

Fortunately, there are some fairly simple rules you can follow to determine whether a door is a right-hand door or a left-hand door and what hand hinges, levers, or lock it takes. When looking at a door in order to determine the hand of the door, always *stand facing the door on the outside* side of the door.

- The outside of a front entrance door is the street, sidewalk, or (for an apartment) the common hall side.

- The outside side of a closet door is the hall side.

- The outside side of a room door is the hall side.

- The outside side of a bathroom door is the side outside the bathroom.

- The outside side of a cupboard or cabinet door should be obvious.

Some doors are regular and some are reverse doors:

- A door with hinges on the *right* that opens *in* (see figure 12) is a *right-hand door*.

- A door with hinges on the *left* that opens *in* (see figure 13) is a *left-hand door*.

- A door with hinges on the *right* that opens *out* (see figure 14) is a *right-hand reverse door*.

- A door with hinges on the *left* that opens *out* (see figure 15) is a *left-hand reverse door*.

The right-handedness or left-handedness of a door is determined by the location of the hinges in relation to the viewer. Therefore:

- A door opening *in*, or *away* from you, when you are looking at it from the outside is a regular door, simply either a right-hand door or a left-hand door.

- A door opening *out*, or *toward* you, when you are looking at it from the outside is a reverse door, either a right-hand reverse door or a left-hand reverse door.

Installing Decorative Hardware

Putting decorative hardware in place properly so that it will do what it's supposed to do, and do it without looking odd, is sometimes easy and sometimes not.

Perhaps the easiest decorative hardware item to install is the electric wall plate. Assuming an outlet or switch is already in place, all that's involved is matching up the plate's screw hole or holes with those in the outlet or switch mounting before screwing in the screws.

Other plate types—push and kick plates, name plates, house numbers (which are plates of sorts), for instance—are almost as easy. Some measuring, marking, drilling of holes, and screwing on is all that's necessary. Plates around knobs and lever door handles situate themselves and just have to be kept straight as they're screwed into place.

Door knockers can be large and weigh a lot but installation is usually fairly simple. A couple of holes carefully placed and drilled part way or all of the way through the door to accommodate whatever bolts or fasteners are required or provided take care of the most difficult part of the job.

To find the ideal placement for a door bumper or holder, hold the bumper or holder at the most likely location on the wall or floor with one hand while moving the door up to it with the other hand and then make the necessary corrections in placement to affect the optimal meeting.

Cabinet knobs are all simple installations. Some have fixed screws that allow you to screw them in wherever you want them. Others have fixed bolts that accept nuts that twist on from the other side of whatever they're applied to. And some have holes drilled part of the way into them that accommodate screws or bolts also applied from the other side. Thru-screw knobs have screws, as their name implies, running right straight through them.

Pulls attach in essentially the same way that knobs do, but usually in at least two locations. Proper horizontal or vertical positioning is, therefore, an added factor. Pulls also normally have two lengthwise measurements: an overall, which covers the distance from end to end, and a boring (see figure 16), which tells you the

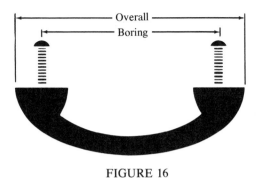

FIGURE 16

distance between two points of application. If you are at all interested in replacing an old boring pull with a new one, you may have to shop around to find a new pull with a boring that matches up with the old one.

A knob or lever handle is kept in its place on a spindle (see figure 17), a long square bar that usually runs straight through a door from one side of it to the other. Inside the door, the central section of the spindle fits snugly through a square hub that operates a spring-actuated latch bolt. Both ends of the spindle are generally threaded, as are the shafts running into the shanks of knobs and levers. (The most common spindle threading is 20 threads to the inch.) To put a knob or lever door handle on the end of a spindle, simply screw it on, and continue screwing until it reaches the door or the intervening rose or plate. A normal installation, of course, would find you threading a corresponding knob or lever onto the other end of the spindle on the other side of the door.

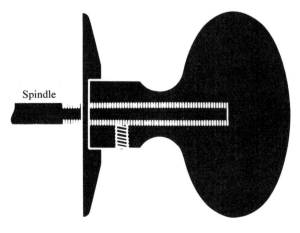

Spindle

FIGURE 17

Different spindle sizes and types are available for different purposes. Spindles with different hub dimensions allow for connecting old knobs and levers to new locks, and vice versa. Stops on one side of the hub are sometimes employed on spindles to prevent its unauthorized removal from the outside side of an exterior door. Swivel spindles permit the deactivation of one knob or lever on one side of a door while leaving the corresponding knob or lever unaffected. A short spindle, called a split spindle, connects a knob or lever to a lock hub when there is no knob or lever to connect up to on the opposite side of a door.

Lever door handles, which for decades have been commonplace on the Continent, were quite rare in North America until relatively recently. According to decorative hardware merchants, lever door handle popularity is growing rapidly and knobs are often being replaced by levers.

One does not just replace a door knob with a lever handle, though, without taking into consideration at least two important factors, one purely esthetic and the other quite practical. Lever door handles were originally used on doors with relatively narrow stiles (the outer upright sections of panelled or glass-paned doors). A knob positioned in the middle of such a narrow stile would leave little clearance between it and the door frame for one's hand and knuckles. A lever handle pointing away from the door frame poses no such problem. Placing a lever on a wide stile where a knob once was, far away from the door frame, simply looks peculiar. On the more practical side, most lock innards simply aren't designed for the stresses placed on them by a lever. The principal problem is the latch spring or springs. The repeated use of a lever, which exerts far greater force than a knob, and the constant stress of keeping the lever in its proper horizontal attitude eventually take their toll on latch's springs, causing them to lose their elasticity. The result after a while is an unesthetically droopy lever handle.

The answer is a latch bolt especially designed for a lever, one with a spring or springs that can take the wear and tear meted out by a lever and also bring it back to the horizontal again and again with little effort. Most latches with springs strong enough to take a lever have narrow backsets (as they properly should), but wide backset versions, specifically designed for knob-to-lever conversions, are now readily available.

Replacing a lever with a knob, assuming there is sufficient knuckle clearance, is not always advisable either. If the replaced lever was off-center near the door frame on a wide stile, the knob replacing the lever would be off-center on the stile as well, which would look even worse than a mis-positioned lever. And if the latch the lever operated had springs strong enough to handle the lever, it would also be powerful enough to make turning the spindle with a mere leverageless knob quite difficult. Switching from a knob to a lever (or from a lever to a knob) is best accomplished by starting from scratch—new latch, new door, the works.

Replacing a Schlage-type single-unit cylinder and knob set with a spindle-mounted knob or lever set or installing the latter in a door drilled for the former presents another sort of problem. A hole in a door that had, or was intended to have, a cylinder lock and knob set fitted into it is around 2⅛ inches in diameter. Spindle-mounted knobs and levers don't require anywhere near this much room, and the roses normally placed between them and a door are usually not much more than 2¼ inches or so in diameter—and usually somewhat smaller for levers. Roses of this size are virtually useless on a 2⅛ inch-drilled door. You could use an oversized rose, one specifically made for this purpose that's large enough to cover the hole up and then some so there is sufficient room beyond the perimeter of the outsized hole for screwing in screws. Such mammoth roses seldom look right with a normal-sized knob, and they always look ridiculous when combined with a lever. There is, fortunately, a better way.

There exists a special adaptor (see figure 18) that is designed to fit into existing 2⅛-inch openings. The adaptor plates are just a little bit bigger than the hole and lipped around their edges so they will set a bit into the hole. They are held tightly together, one on each side of the hole, by two long screws. Holes in the centers of the plates permit the passage of a spindle. A short threaded tube extending from the spindle hole accepts a standard screw-on concealed screw rose that at 2¼ inches easily covers the plate. Simply insert a spindle and screw on a lever or knob.

There are scores of different hinge types and

FIGURE 18

almost as many installation variations, far too many to cover at all comprehensively here. There is one very basic hinge application, though, that's well worth a closer inspection—mortising a classic loose-pin butt door hinge into a door frame and a door.

Hanging a door on butt hinges begins with selecting hinges that are the right size for the door. A hinge designed for a large door will look inappropriate on a small one. The knuckle of the hinge would protrude in an unsightly way and the screw holes nearest the knuckle might be too close to the front of the door jamb to support the screw. Too small a hinge, on the other hand might not hold the door adequately.

Most interior doors (closet doors, room doors, etc.) are 1⅜ inches thick. Most exterior doors (a front entrance door, for example) are 1¾ inches thick. If you know your door's thickness and can measure the thickness of the molding that projects beyond the face of the jamb, you can calculate the proper hinge width (measure across the hinge opened flat) by using the following simple formula:

Twice the door thickness + the trim size − ½ inch = the hinge width

If the door you are hanging is 1⅜ inches thick and the trim projects 1¼ inches, for example, your calculation would look like this:

2¾ inches + 1¼ inches − ½ inch = 3½ inches

The next step is deciding where to place the hinges. For doors of average size, the rule of thumb is: the top hinge should be 7 inches from the top of the door frame and 11 inches from the floor. If a third hinge is deemed desirable, it should be placed halfway between the other two.

Place the door into the frame and wedge the bottom to lift the door enough to allow at least a ⅝-inch clearance between the bottom of the door and the floor. There should also be at least 1/16 inch between the top of the door frame and the door. Carefully mark the position of each hinge on both the jamb and the door. Then remove the door from the frame and place it on two saw horses or some other suitable surface.

If you are using a hinge that is the right width, place the leaf that's to go on the door ¼ inch from what is, in relation to the way the knuckle is pointing, the back of the door. Mark all around the edge of the leaf with a pencil (see figure 19). Check to be sure that the loose pin will be in the ''up'' position when the door is finally hung.

Next, make deep cuts with the end of a chisel all around the pencil mark, keeping the bevel of the chisel always facing in (see figure 20).

Make feather cuts up and down the area to be mortised (see figure 21), spacing them around ¼ inch apart and cutting just deep enough for the mortise depth desired.

Place the cutting edge of the chisel parallel to the edge of the door and remove the scored wood to the proper depth (see figure 22).

Place the hinge leaf into the mortise to check the depth and adjust it if it isn't deep enough.

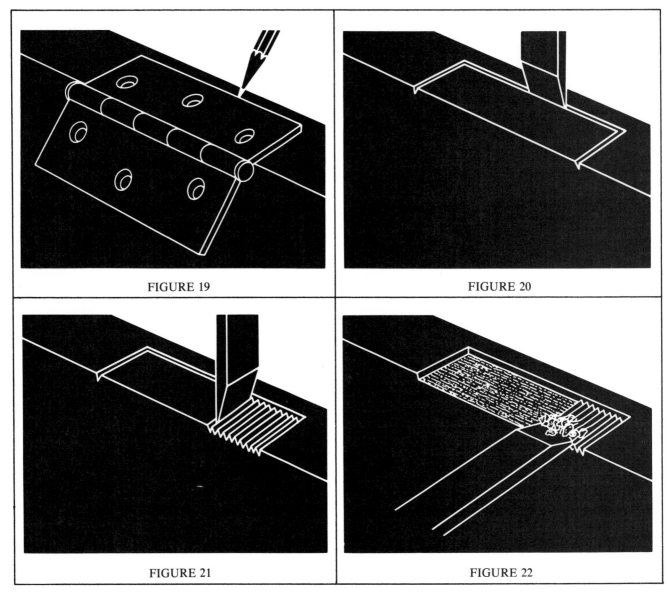

FIGURE 19

FIGURE 20

FIGURE 21

FIGURE 22

Mark starter holes with an awl or nail in the centers of the hinge holes and then, making sure the hinge is straight, screw in the screws (see figure 23).

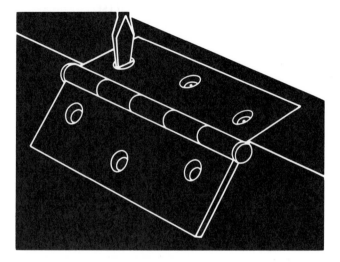

FIGURE 23

When both hinges have been installed, remove the pin from the top hinge, and place the jamb leaf up to the spot marked near the top of the jamb earlier. Bring the hinge out so that it is about ⅜ inch from the stop molding and look to see whether all of the knuckle barrel appears to clear the projecting trim. If it does, line the leaf up straight and proceed to mark and mortise and screw it on. Then install the other leaf and hang the door.

Having mastered the mortising of a hinge leaf, you are equipped for deeper emplacements involving lock strikes, small cabinet locks that half-mortise in like a deeply implanted hinge leaf, flush bolts, and flush pulls. Full mortise locks call for deep, four-walled mortises. Most new large door locks, both surface and mortise types, come packaged with detailed installation instructions. For further information regarding lock installation, see *Popular Mechanics Home Security Handbook* (Hearst Books, 1982).

2
Cabinet Knobs & Pulls

T HE oldest of all the many different forms of decorative hardware may very well be the cabinet knob. On display in New York's Metropolitan Museum of Art there is a beautiful toiletry case that was fashioned around the time of Egypt's XI Dynasty (2134 to c. 2000 B.C.). It features a slide-out drawer and a slide-off lid, each of which sports a dainty and sophisticated knob. During the intervening three thousand years, knobs have changed very little, and variations in knobs today involve materials,

color, pattern, shape, and size. If the knob isn't the earliest element of decorative hardware, it certainly is the simplest.

Second in terms of antiquity is probably the pull. Unlike the knob, though, the pull has undergone some interesting transitions. The first pull might have been a short hunk of rope affixed at both ends to some primitive lid or door. Today, there are simple bar pulls, bail pulls, ring pulls, drop pulls, recessed pulls, flush pulls, flush ring pulls, bin pulls, and more.

Selecting a knob or pull for a particular place or piece of cabinetry is only to a degree a matter of choice. A Chippendale highboy or chest-on-chest, for example, would be absolutely the wrong place for a Victorian bail pull. On such a piece of furniture a Chippendale bail pull and only a Chippendale bail pull—real or, more likely, a reproduction—will do. Appropriateness must also be considered. Obviously, a heavy, ornate, and highly polished knob suitable for a cabinet at Versailles would not be suitable for a simple country spice cabinet.

Some Cabinet Knob & Pull Terms

Backplate. Any plate that serves as a mount for a knob or pull and intervenes between it and the cabinetry it is attached to.

Bail. The pivoting drop handle portion of a bail pull.

Bail Pull. A type of drawer pull originating around the time of William and Mary (1689–1702) characterized by a wide, ∪-shaped, pivoting handle—the bail—held against the furniture by cotter pins (in the earliest forms) or nut-secured posts (in later forms) which may or may not also extend through a decorative backplate or rosettes.

Ball and Spear Pull. A hand-forged pull with mounting plates shaped like balls with single spear points projecting from them; very similar to an onion pull.

Bean Pull. A hand-forged pull with lima bean-shaped mounting plates.

Bin Pull. A pull originally used on storage bins during the Victorian era, characterized by a projecting handle in the shape of a shallow horizontal hood.

Drop Pull. Any pull whose main feature is a hanging pendant.

Flush Pull. Any pull mortised into a door or drawer, with no part projecting beyond the surface.

Flush Ring, or **Flush Ring Pull.** Any pull mortised into a door or drawer, having a drop ring that folds flat into a recessed cup.

Heart Pull. A hand-forged pull with heart-shaped mounting plates.

Onion Pull. A hand-forged pull with mounting plates resembling a sprouting onion.

Oval Pull. A type of bail pull popularly used on furniture of the type designed by Thomas Sheraton (1751–1806) and George Heppelwhite (d. 1786), characterized by a thin, oval brass backplate stamped to produce a deep design that frequently features a raised pictorial pattern.

Recessed Pull. Any pull either completely or partly mortised into a door or drawer.

Ring Pull. Any pull whose main feature is a hanging ring.

Rosette. A small round backplate with a hole for receiving the screw, post, or other fastening holding one side of a pull.

Rosette Pull. A bail pull with rosette backplates on either side of the pull.

Spade Pull. A hand-forged pull with mounting plates shaped like spade blades.

Thru-Screw Knob. Any knob with a hole through it to receive a mounting screw.

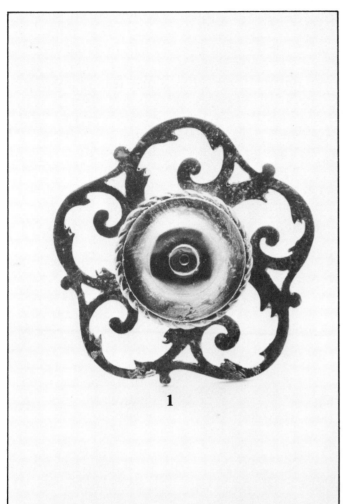

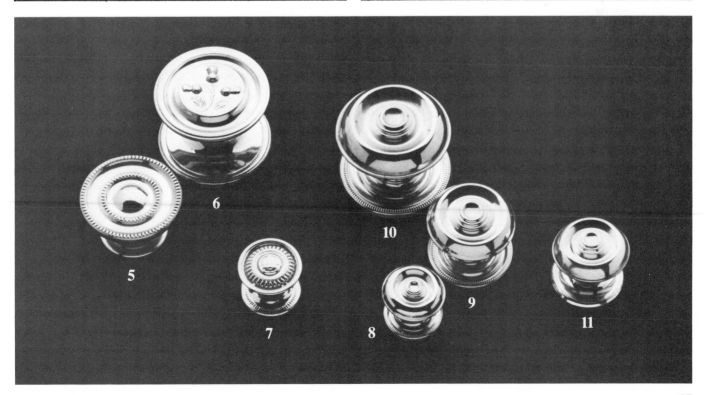

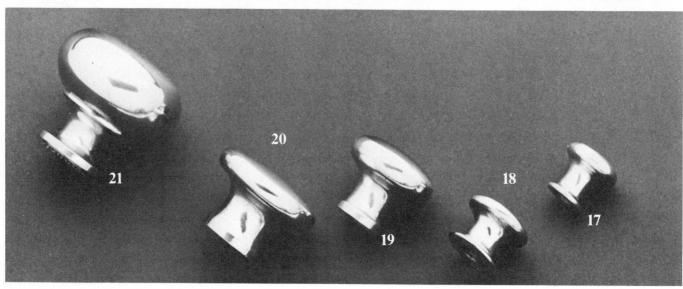

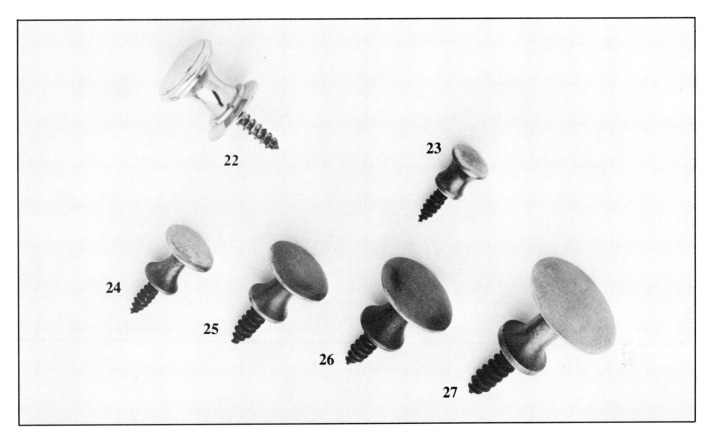

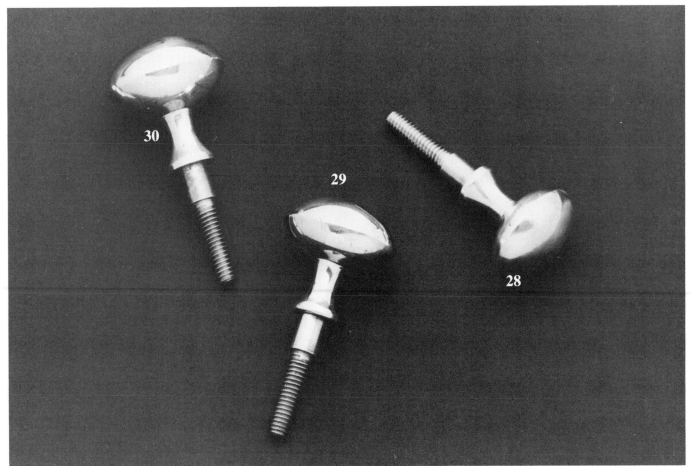

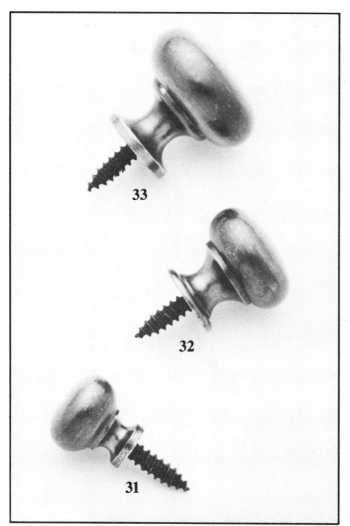

33

32

31

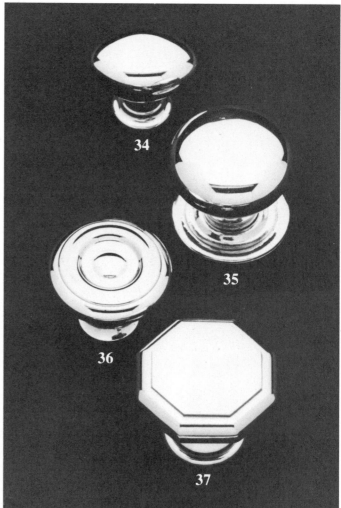

34

35

36

37

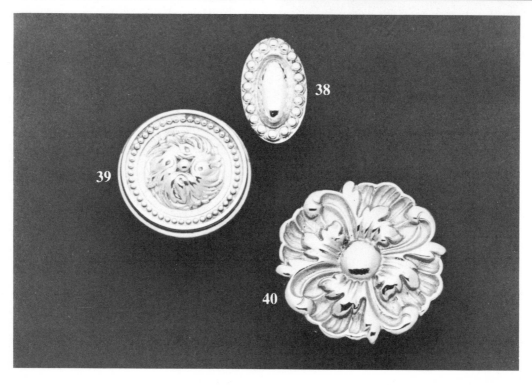

38

39

40

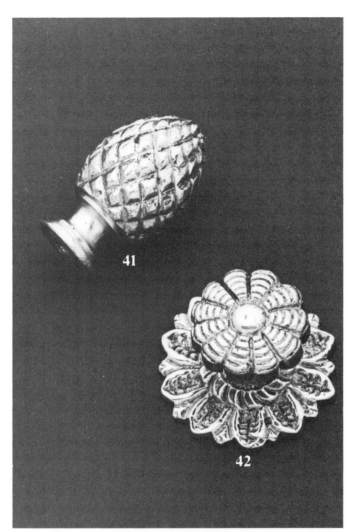

41

42

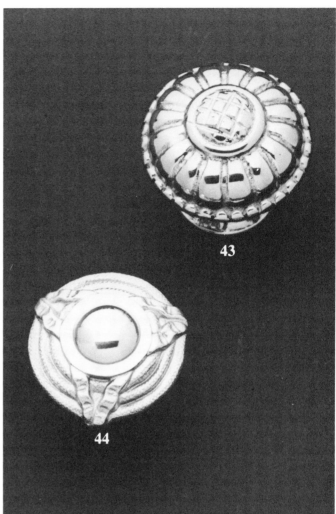

43

44

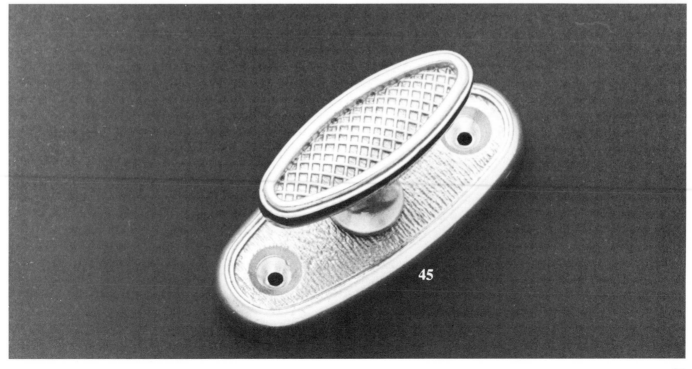

45

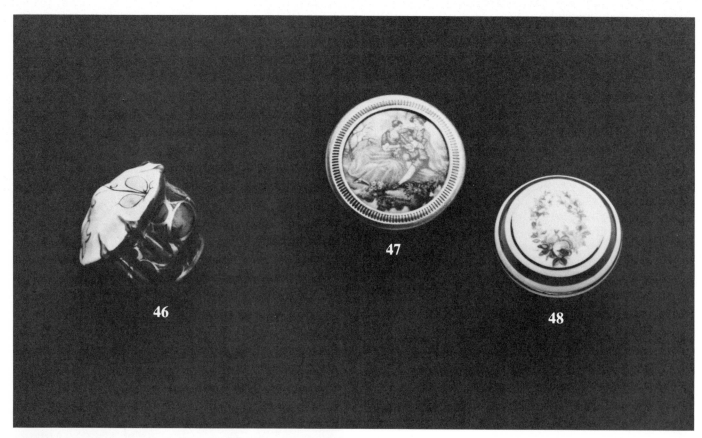

46

47

48

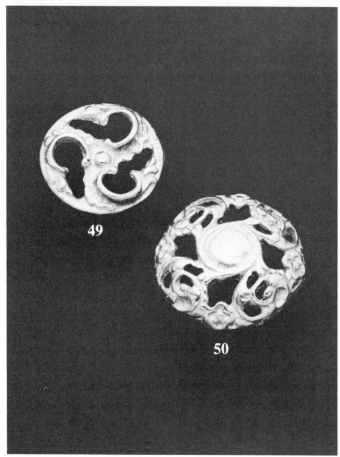

49

50

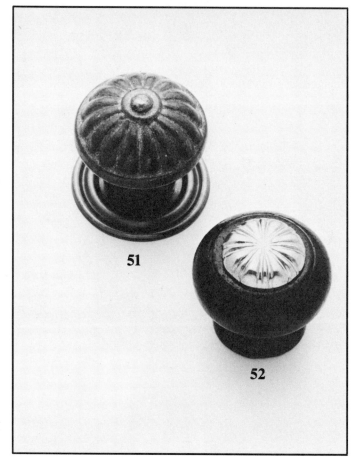

51

52

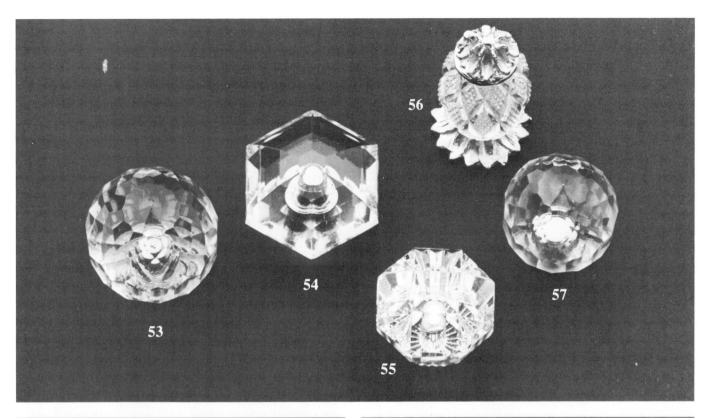

56

54

53

55

57

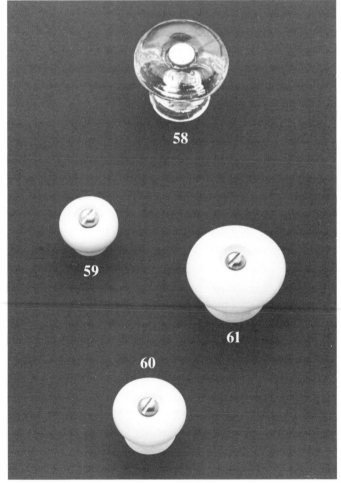

58

59

61

60

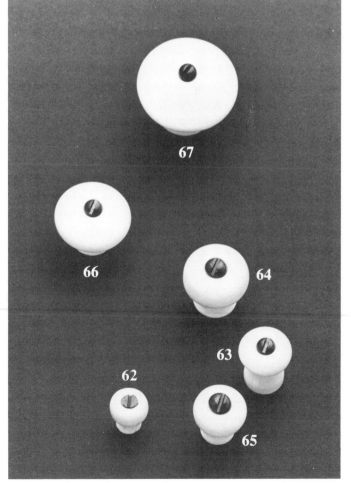

67

66

64

63

62

65

23

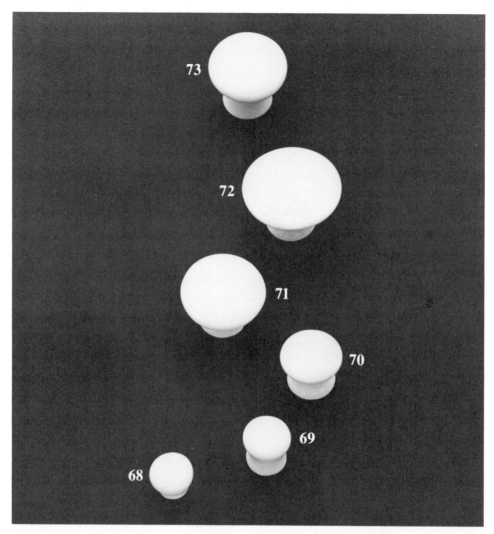

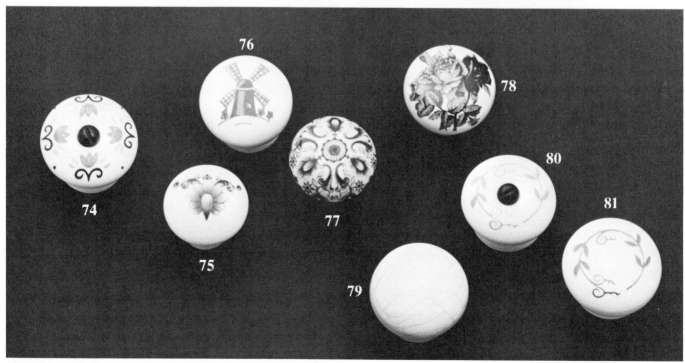

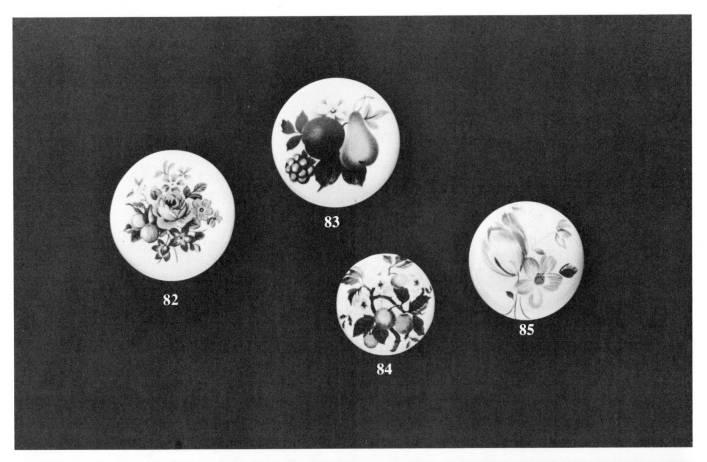

82
83
84
85

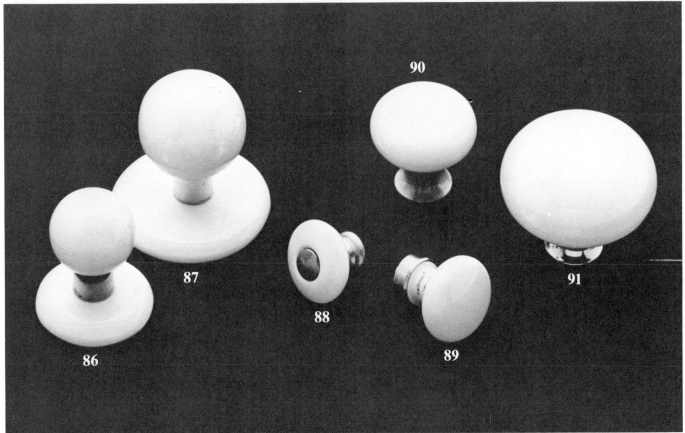

86
87
88
89
90
91

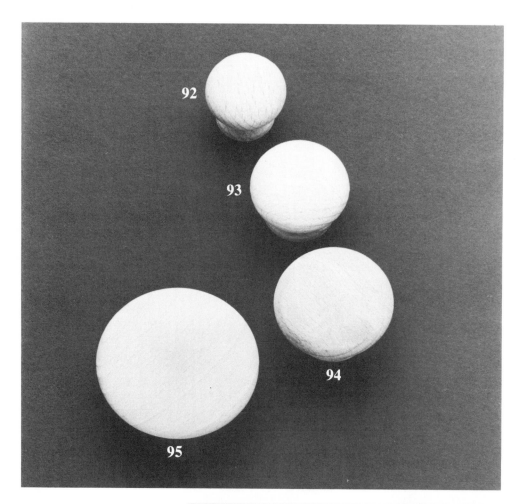

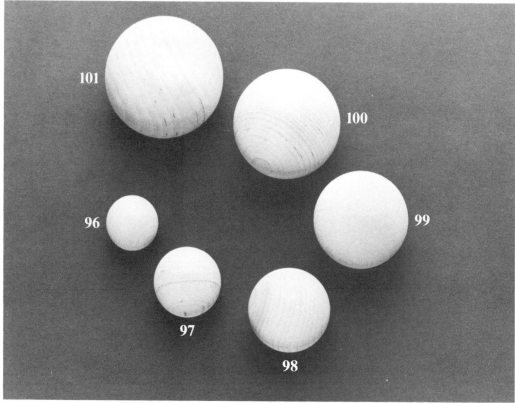

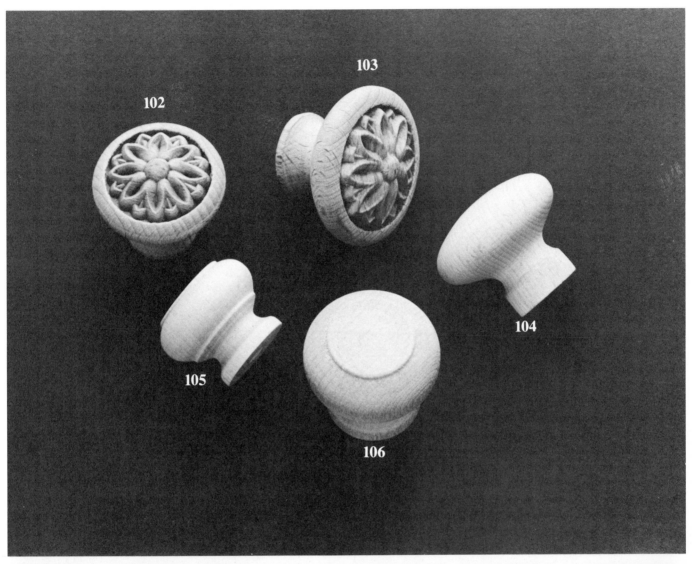

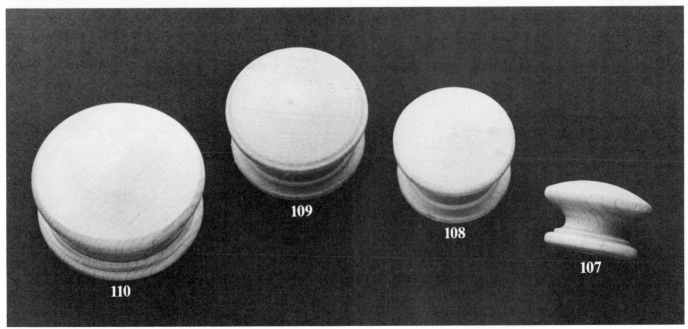

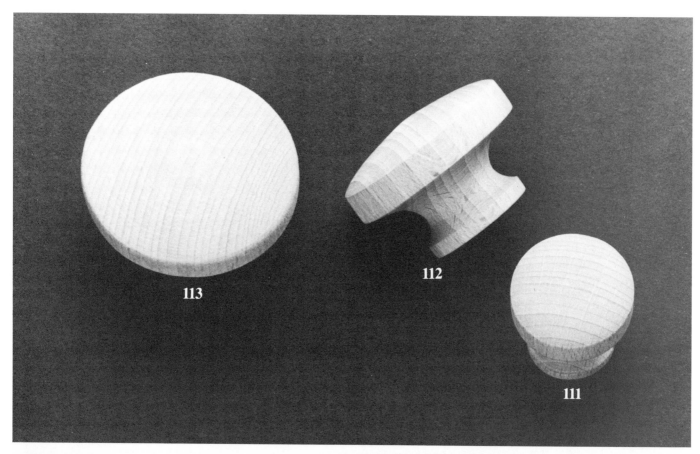

113

112

111

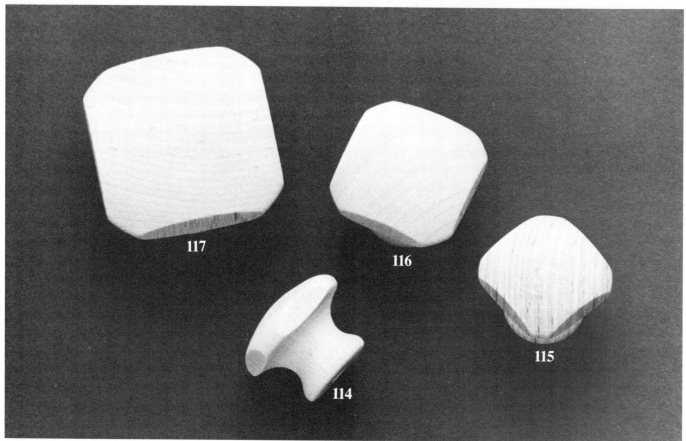

117

116

115

114

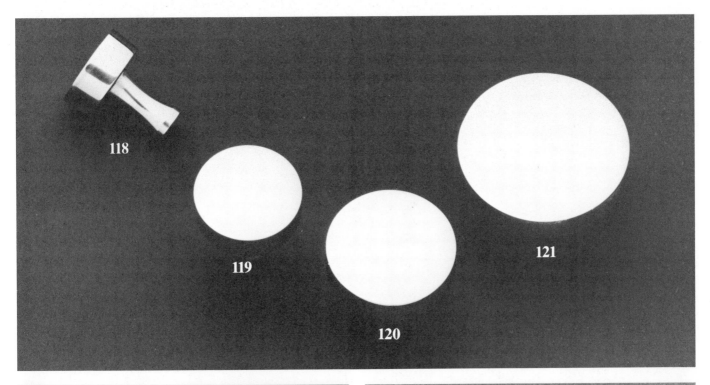

118

119

120

121

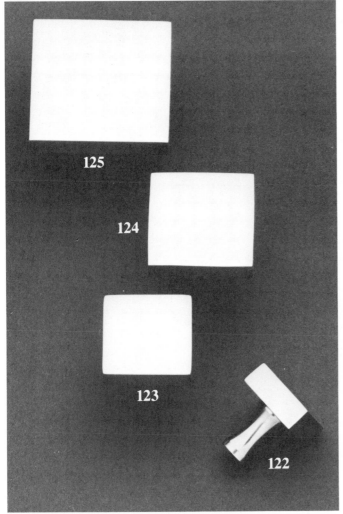

125

124

123

122

127

126

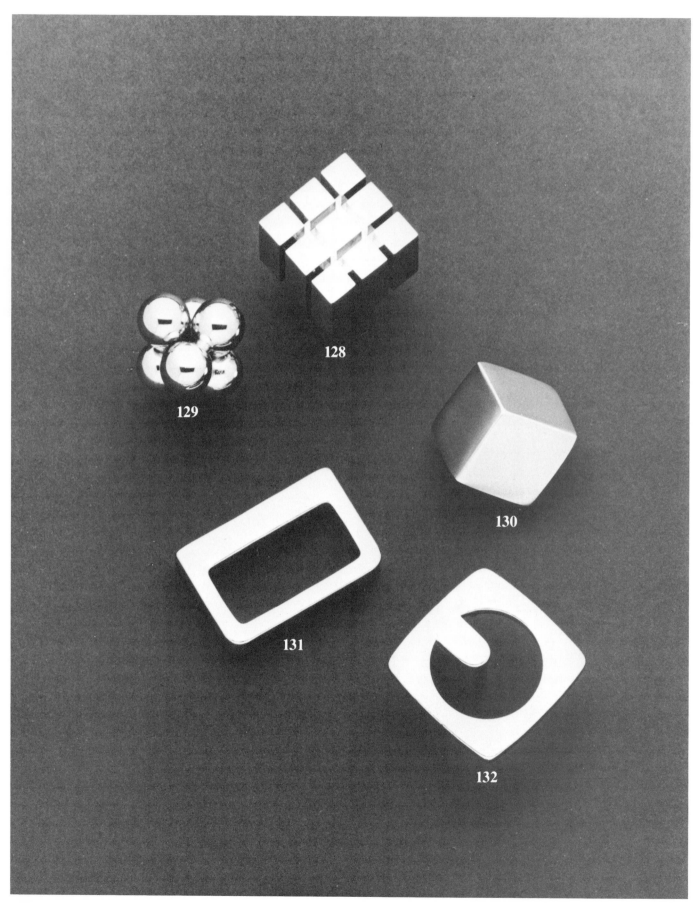

128

129

130

131

132

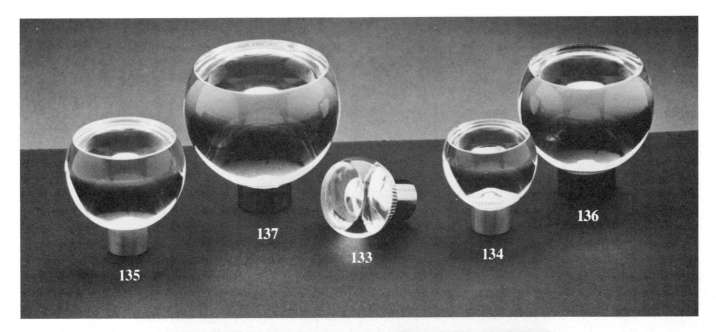

137 133 134 136
135

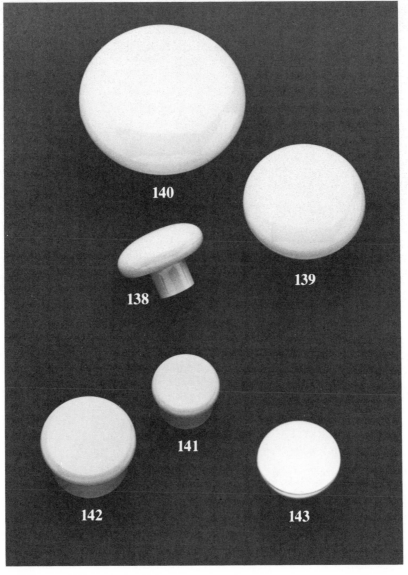

140
139
138
141
142 143

144

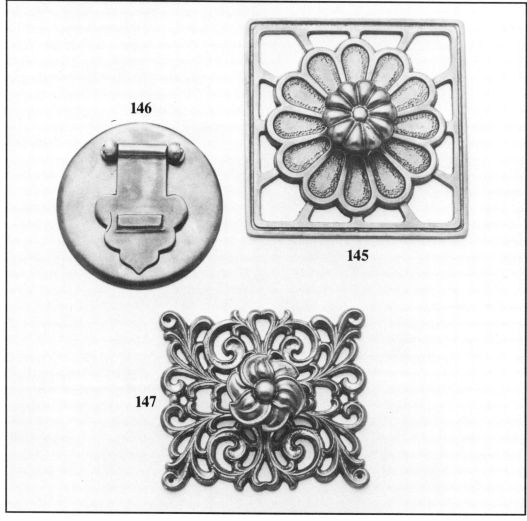

146

145

147

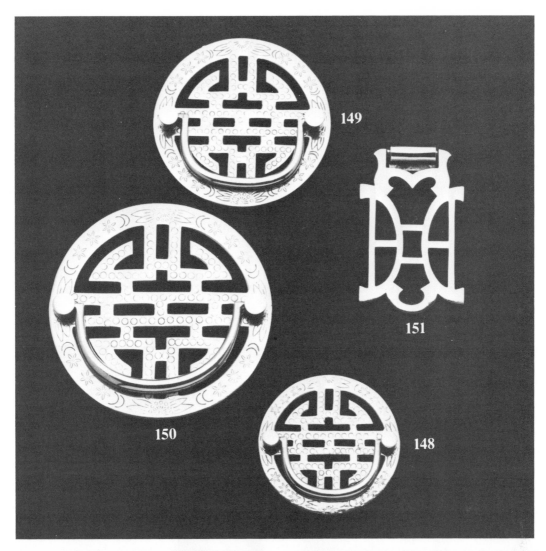

149

151

150

148

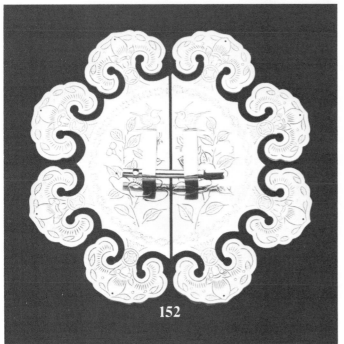

152

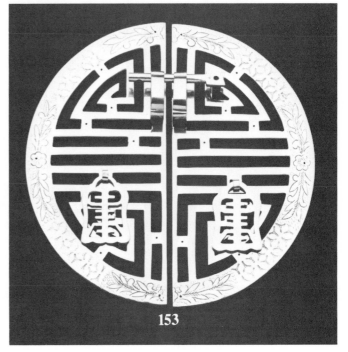

153

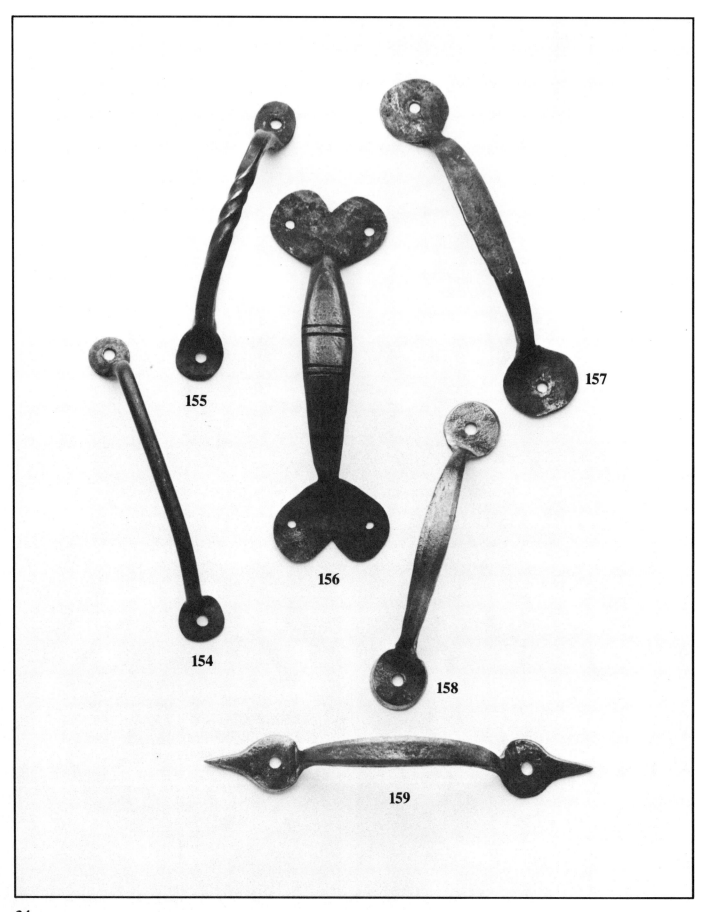

155

157

156

154

158

159

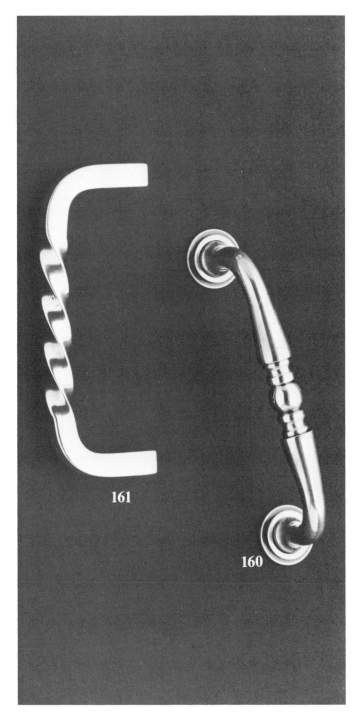

161

160

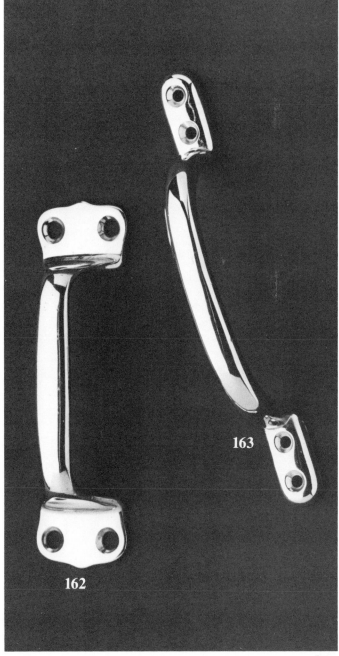

162

163

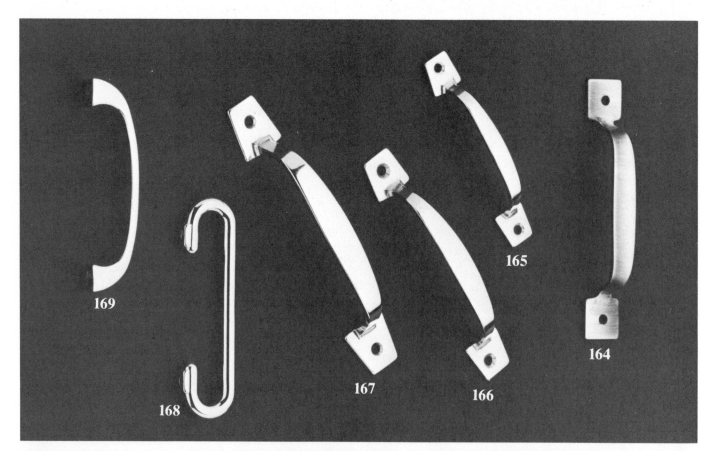

169

168

167

166

165

164

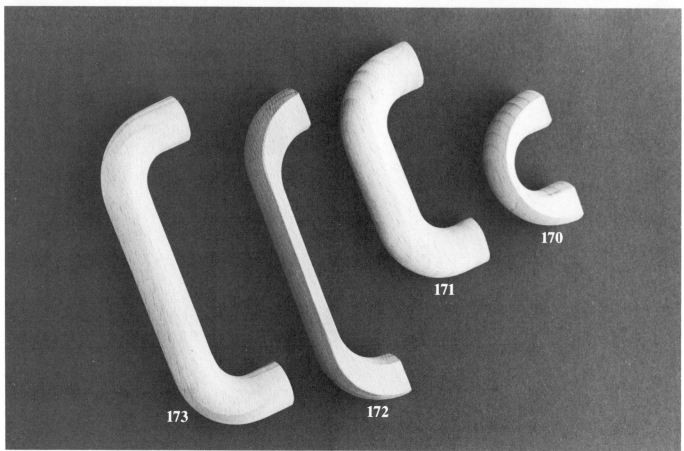

173

172

171

170

175   176   177   178   174

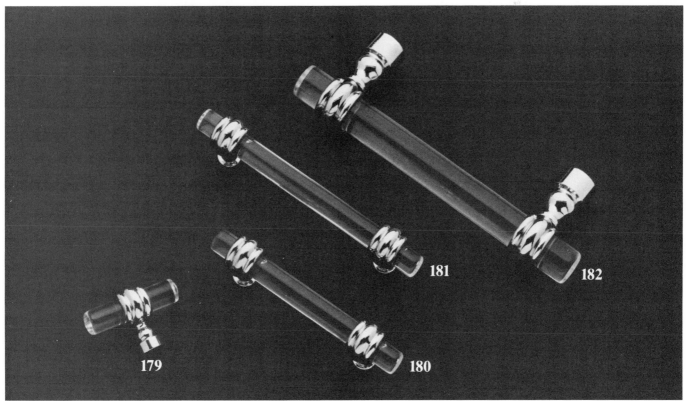

179   180   181   182

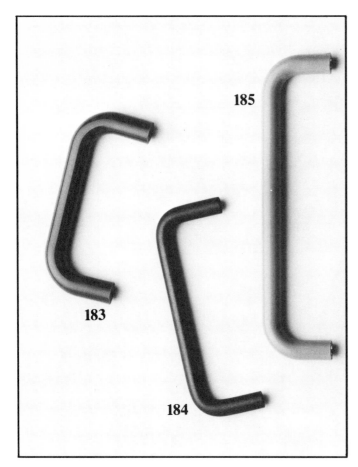

183

185

184

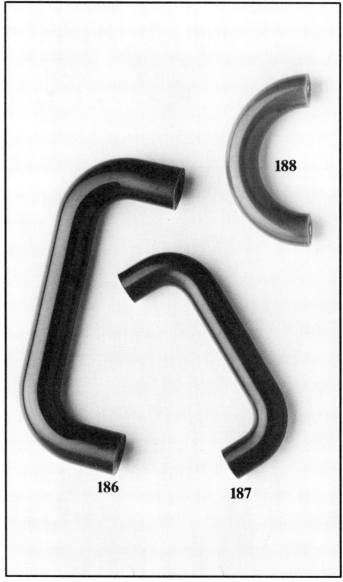

188

186

187

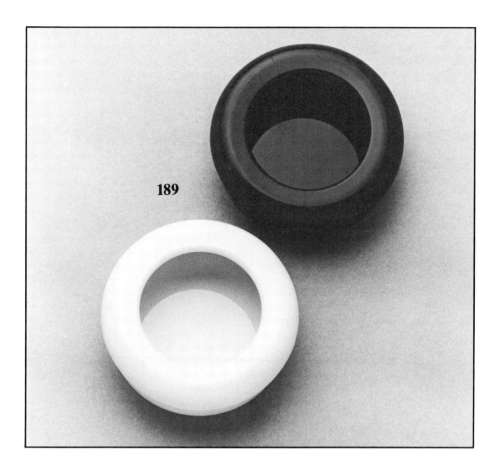

189

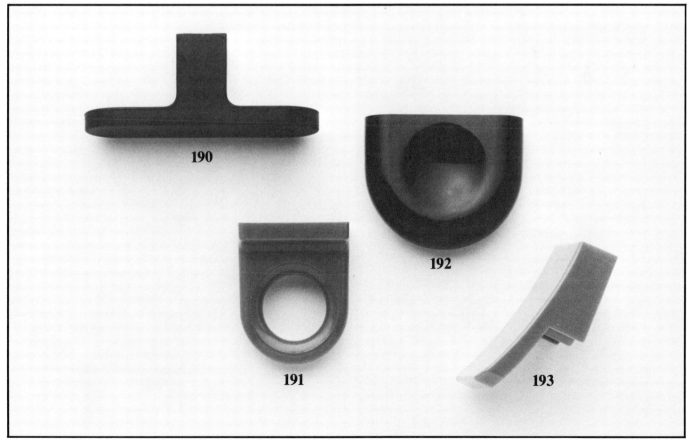

190

192

191

193

Drawer & Bin Pulls

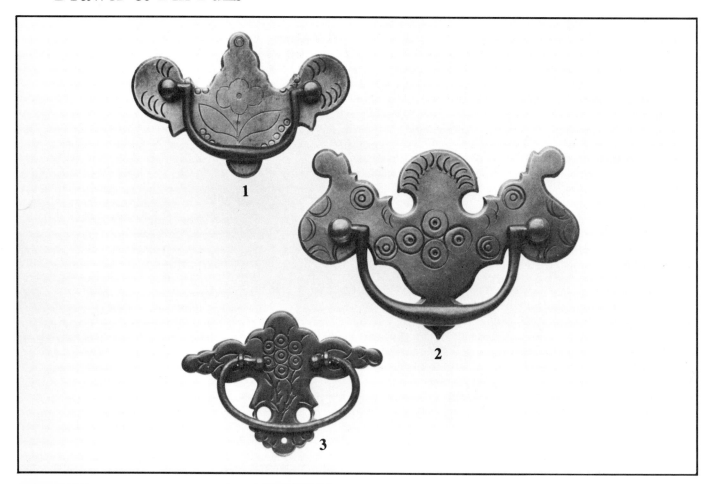

1

2

3

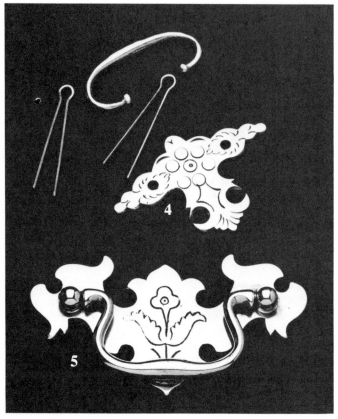

4

5

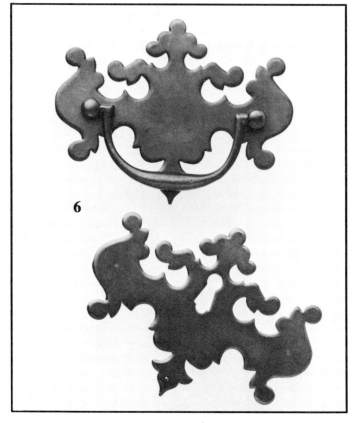

6

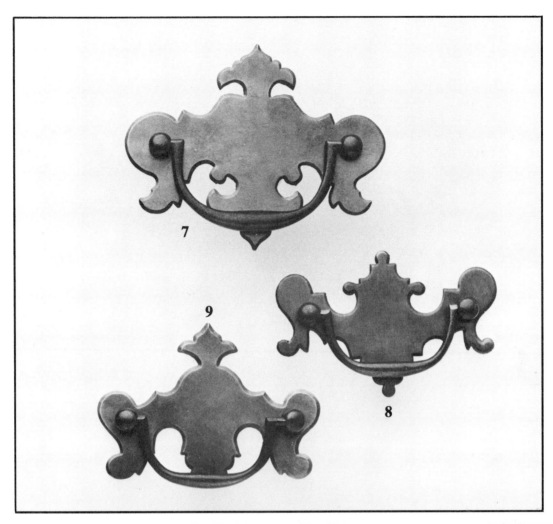

7

9

8

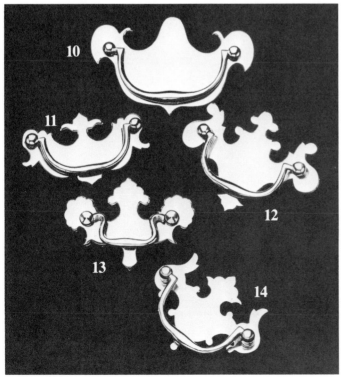

10

11

12

13

14

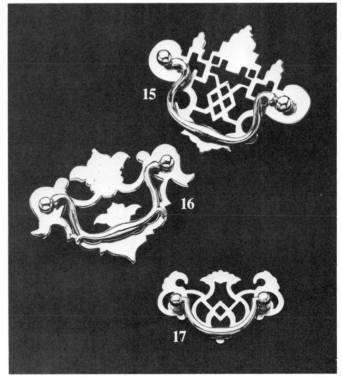

15

16

17

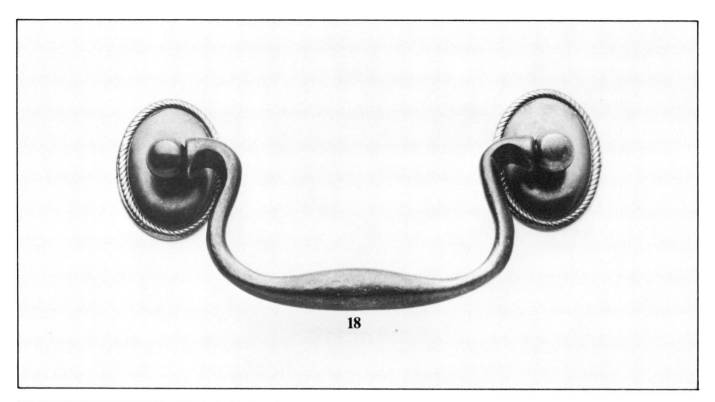

18

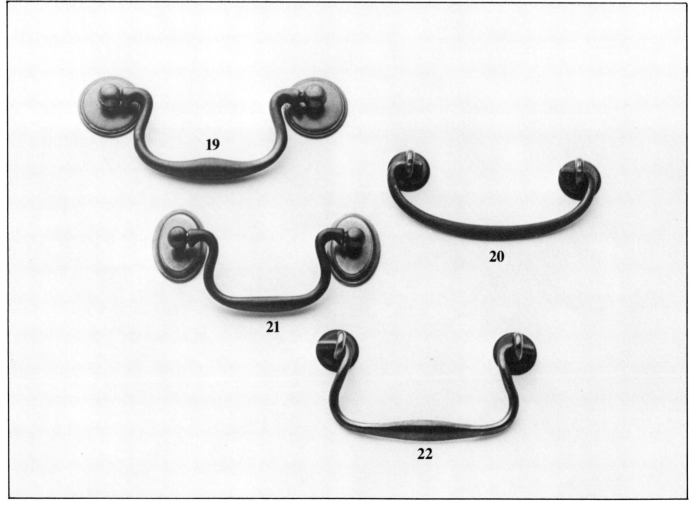

19

20

21

22

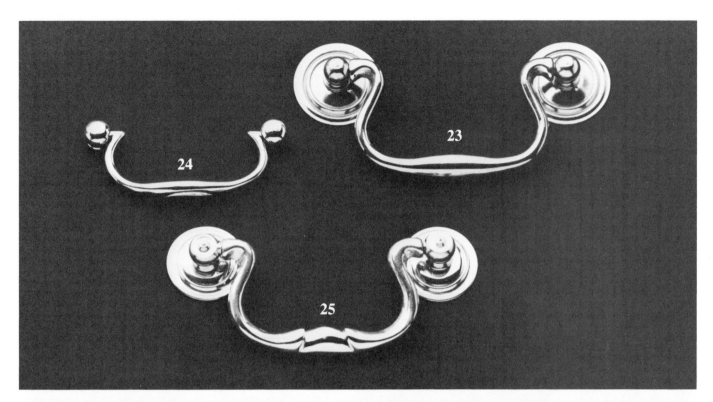

24

23

25

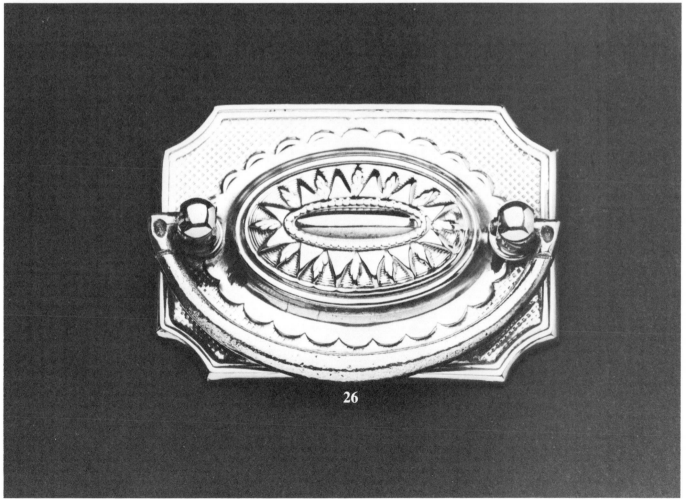

26

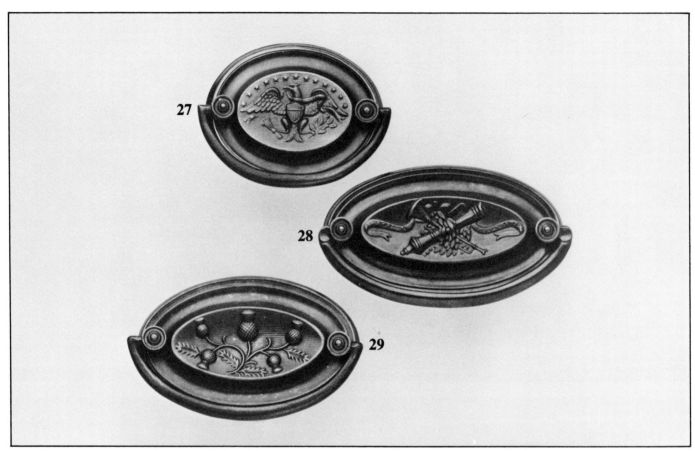

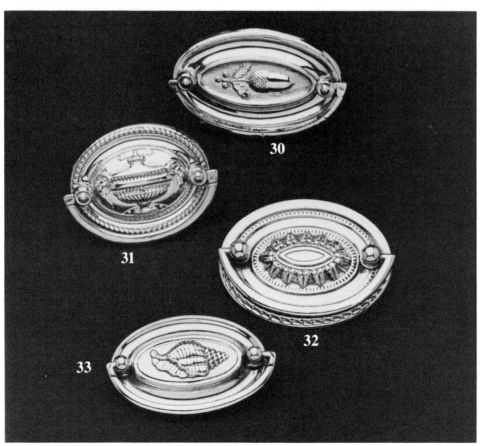

44

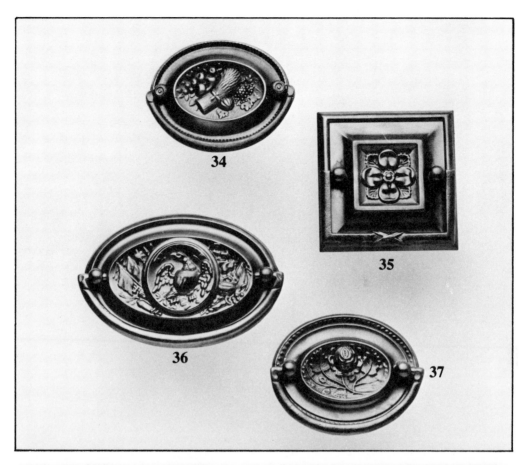

34

35

36

37

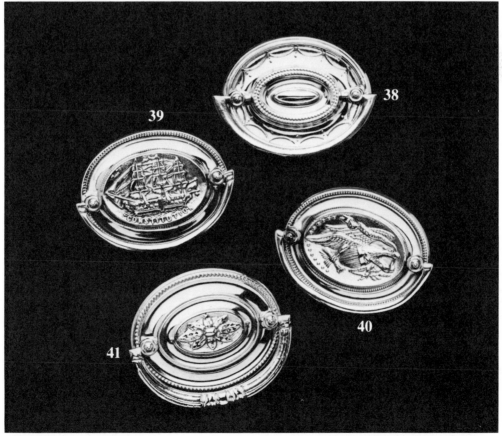

38

39

40

41

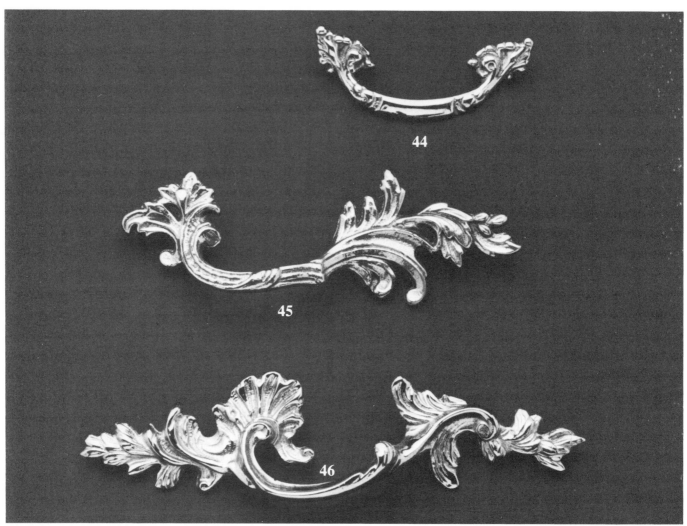

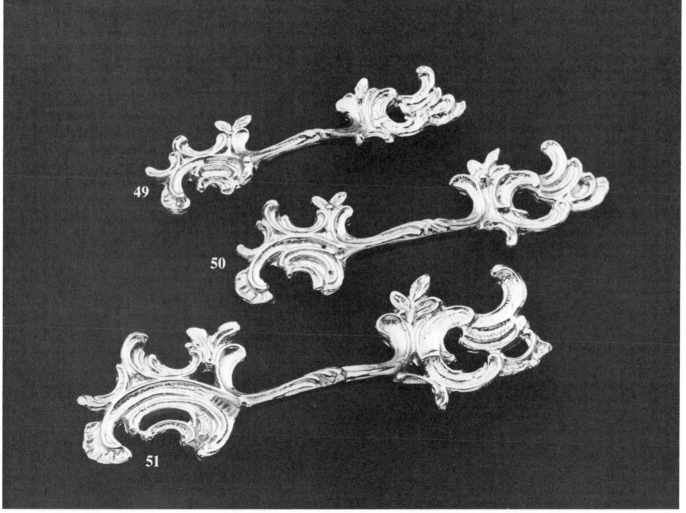

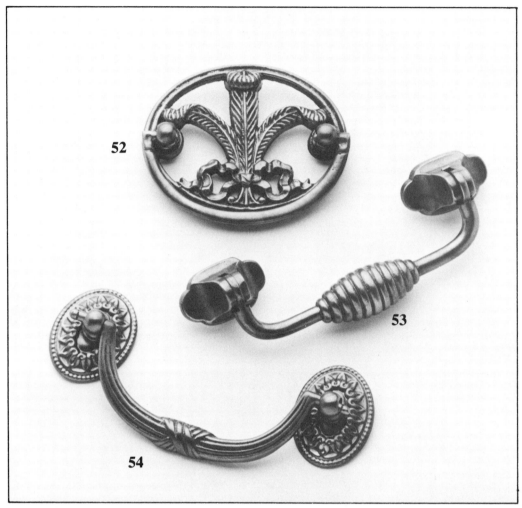

52

53

54

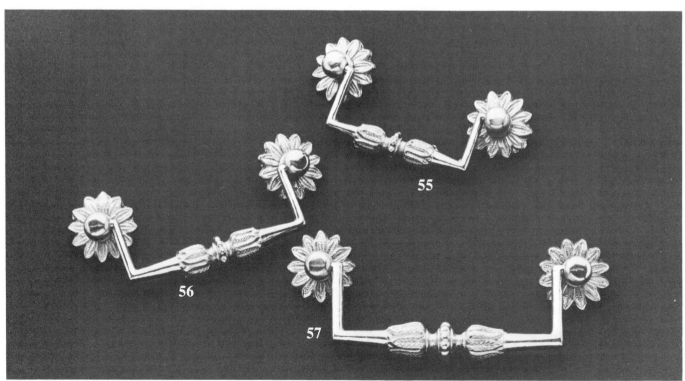

55

56

57

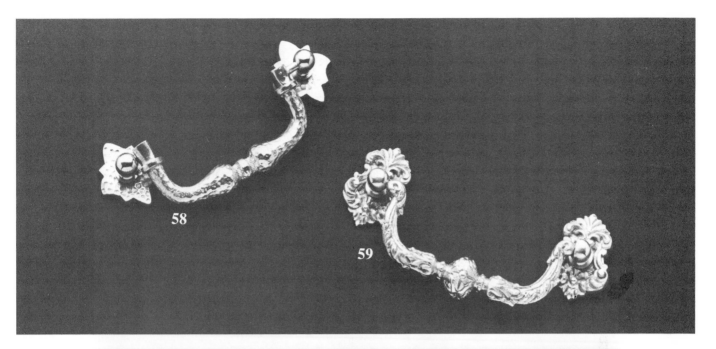

58

59

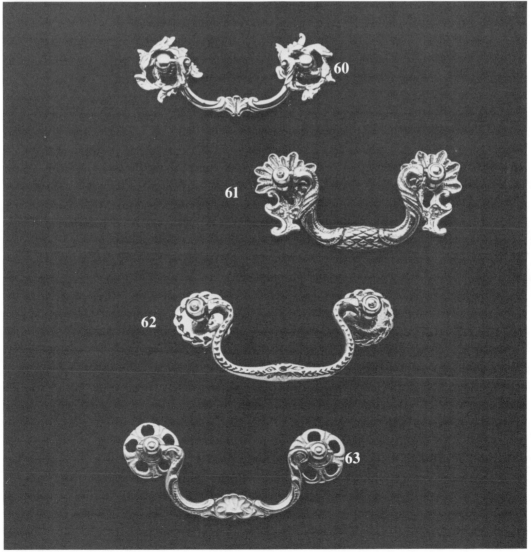

60

61

62

63

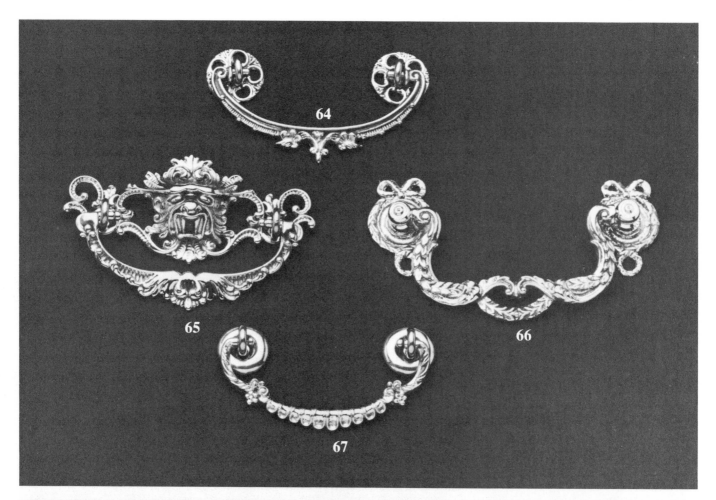

64

65

66

67

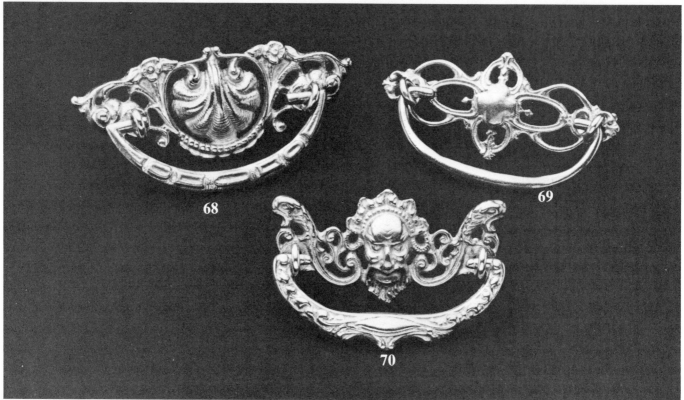

68

69

70

50

71

72

73

74

75

76

77

78

79

85

86

87

88

89

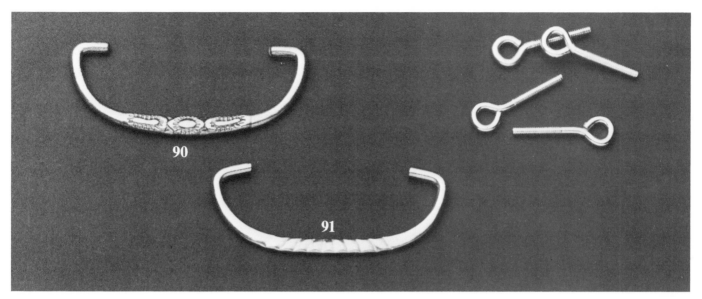

90

91

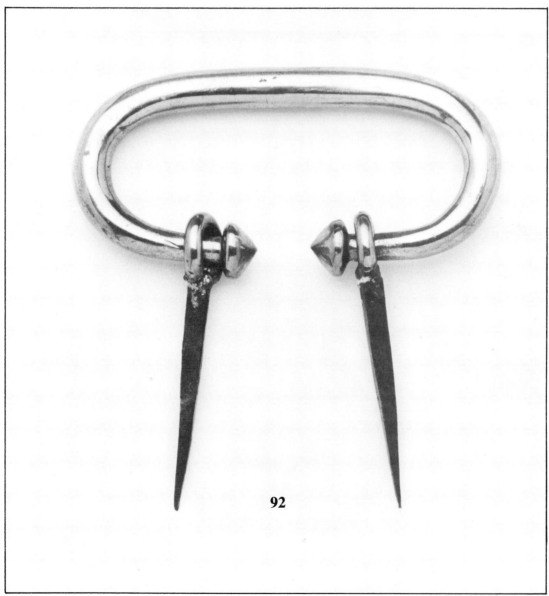

92

93

94

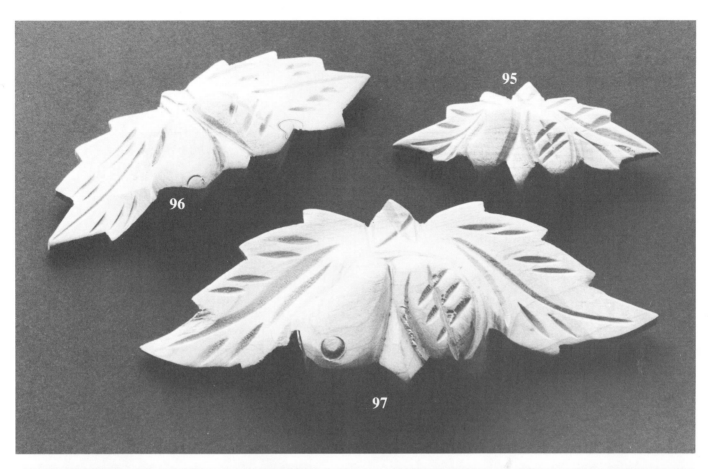

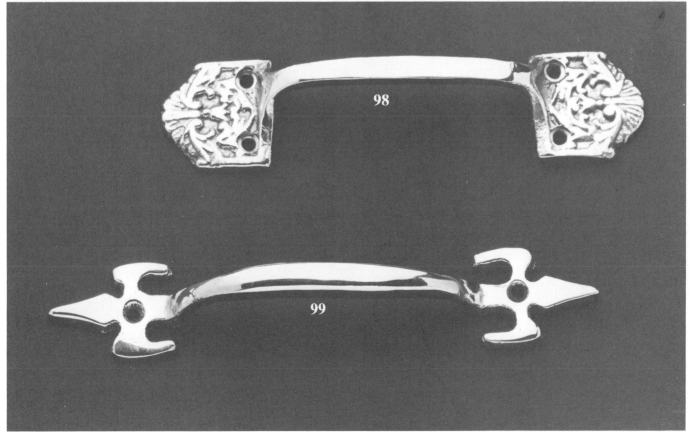

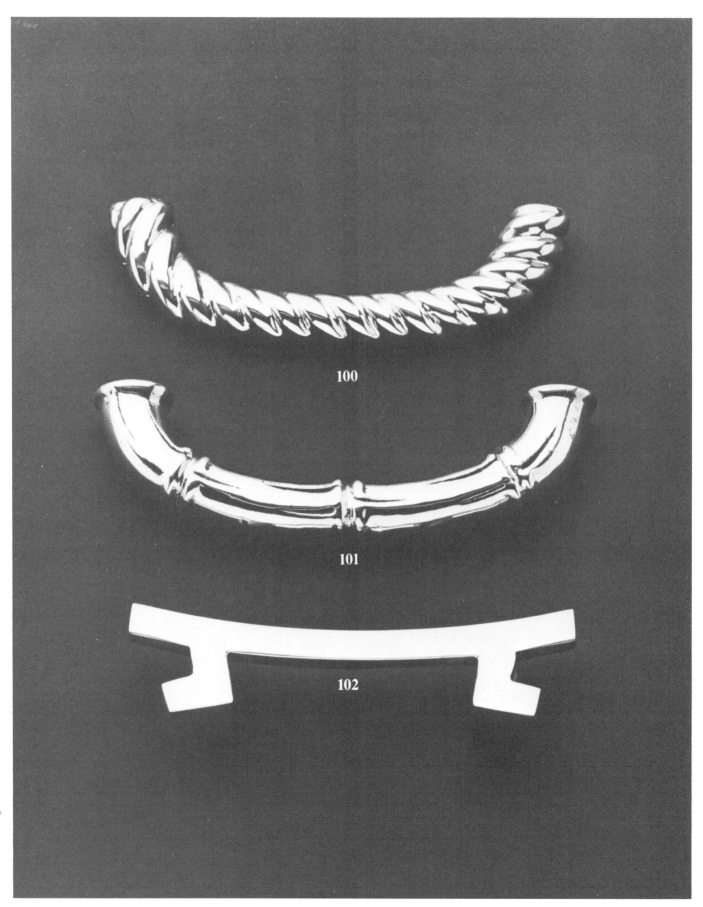

100

101

102

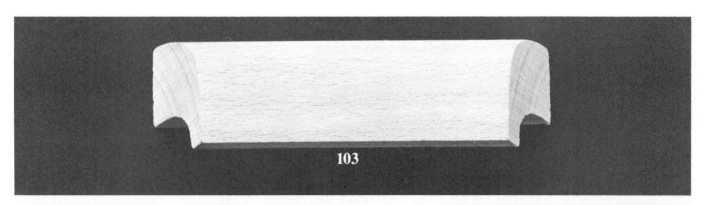

103

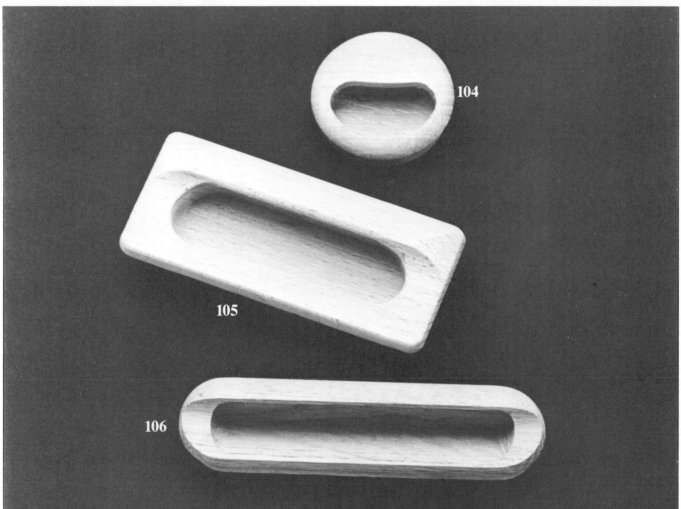

104

105

106

107

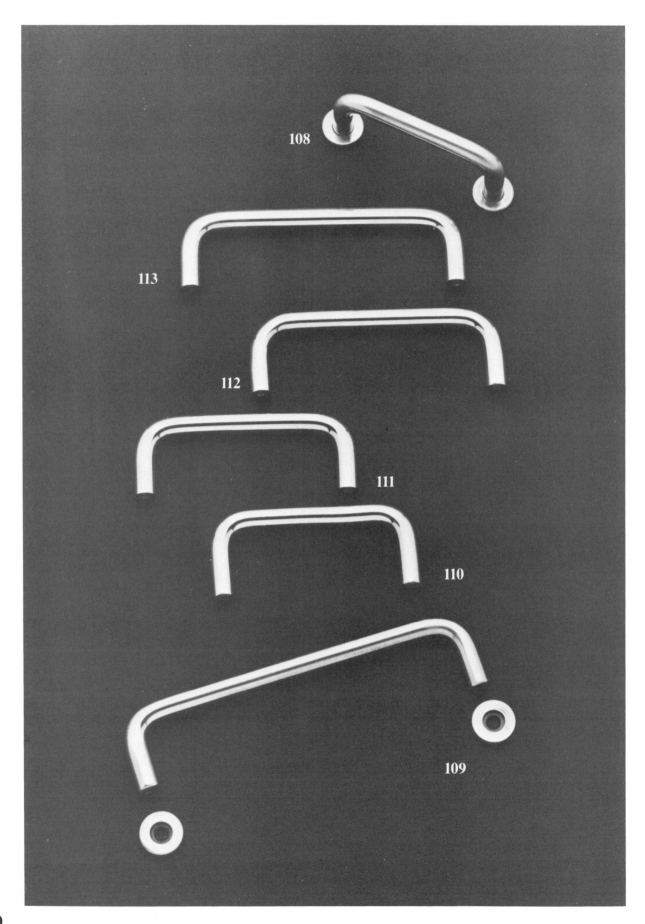

108

113

112

111

110

109

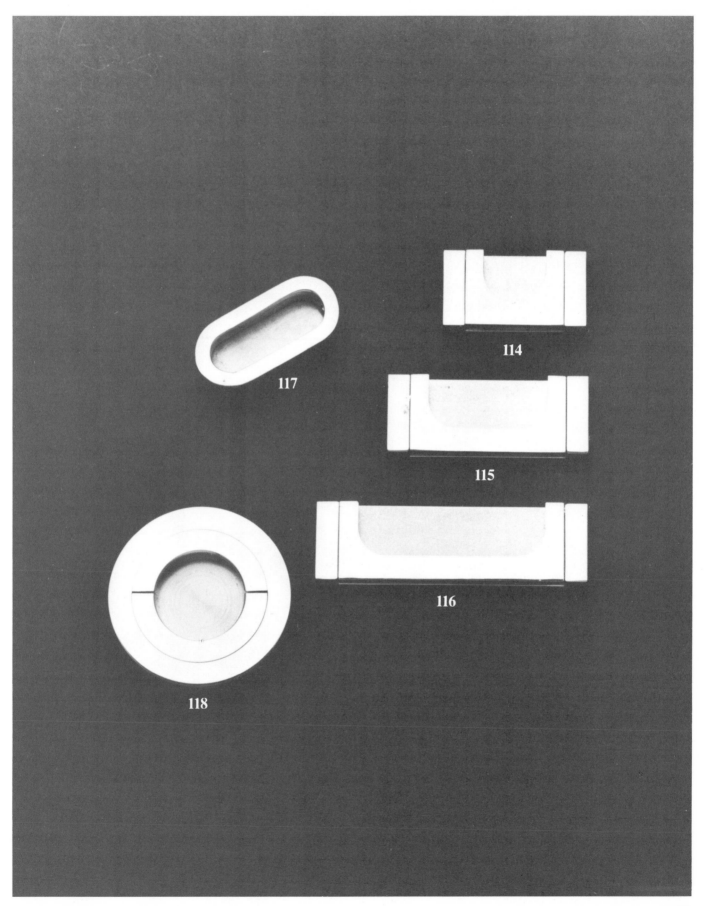

117

114

115

116

118

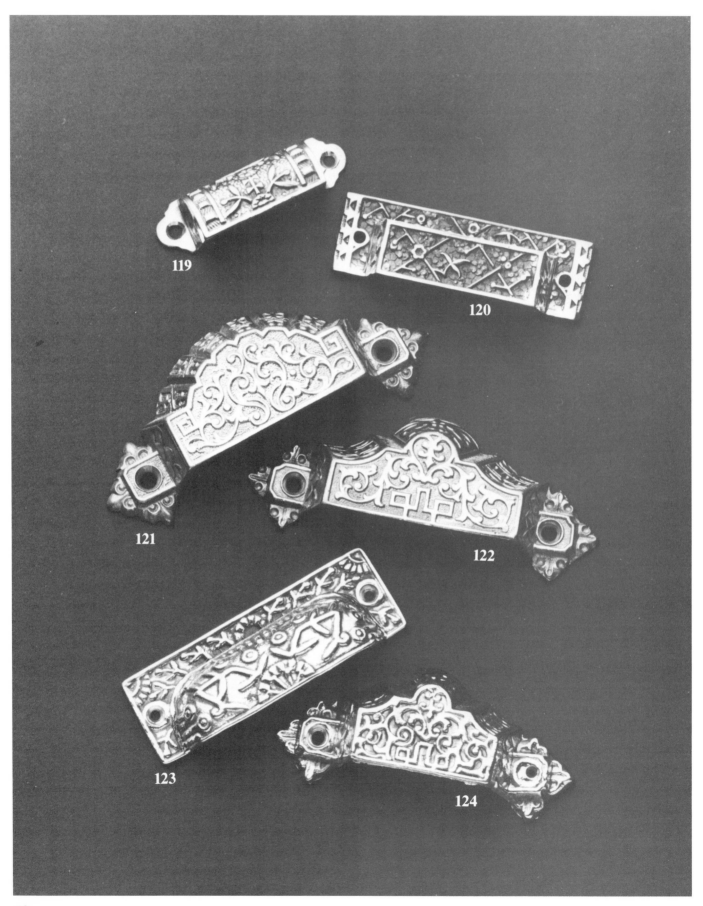

119

120

121

122

123

124

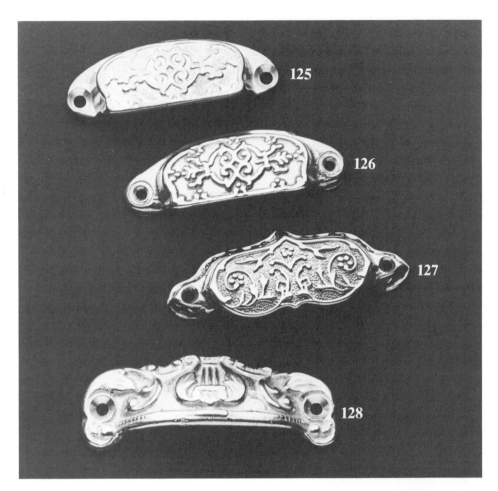

125

126

127

128

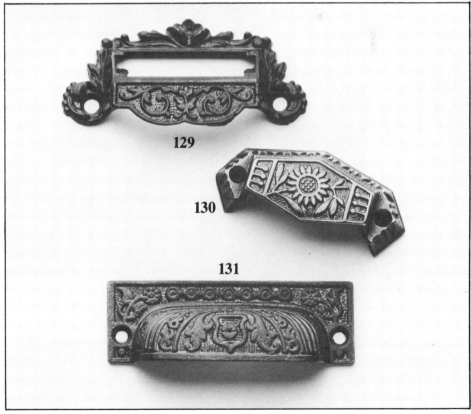

129

130

131

63

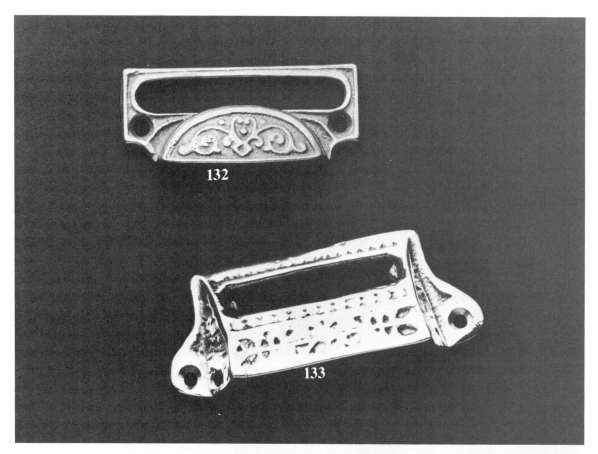

132

133

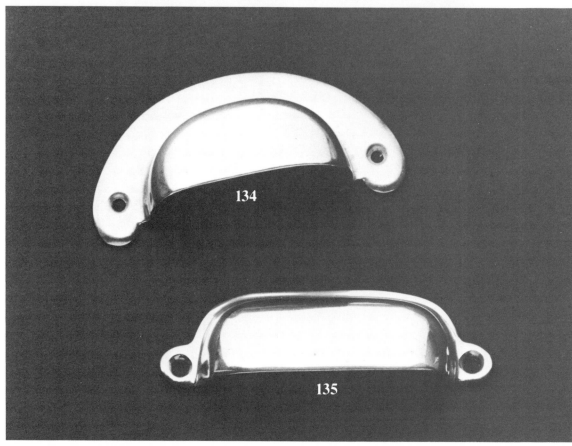

134

135

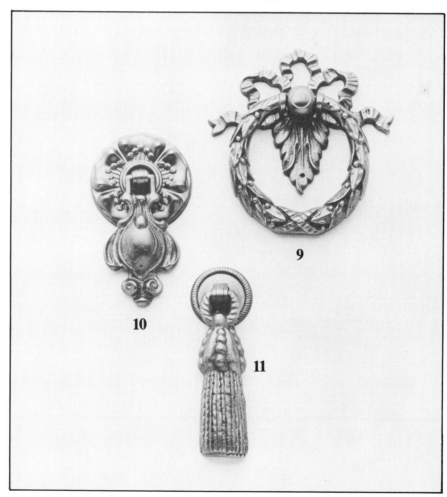

13

12

14

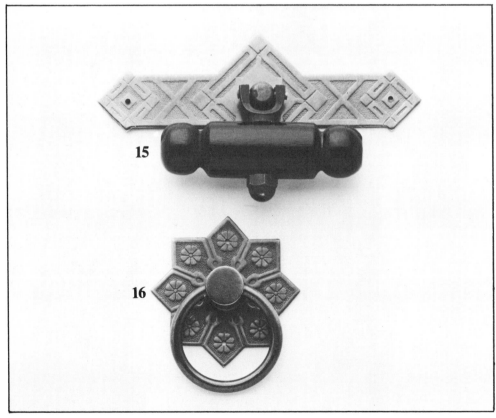

15

16

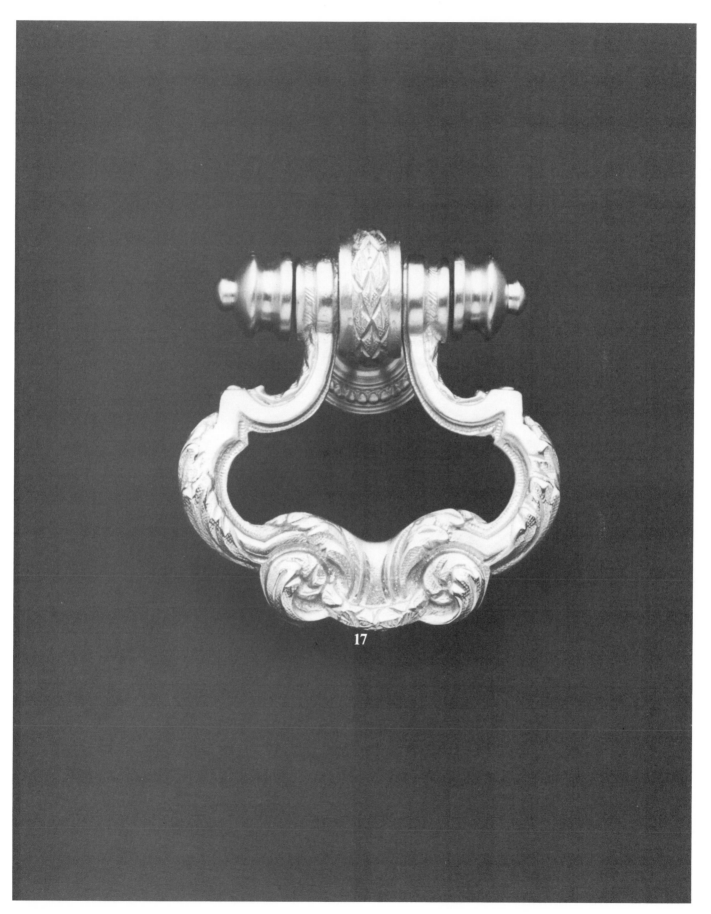

17

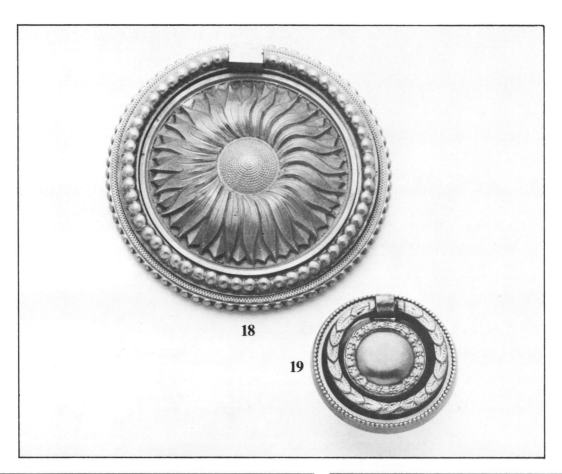

18

19

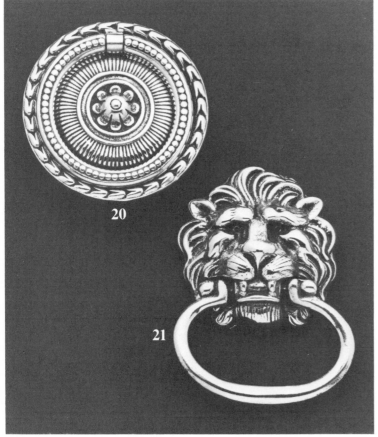

20

21

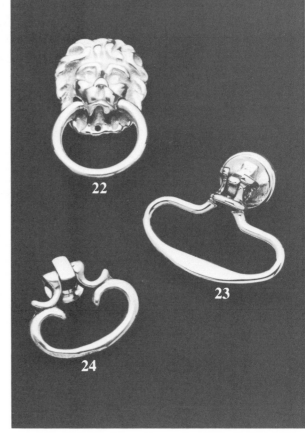

22

23

24

25

26

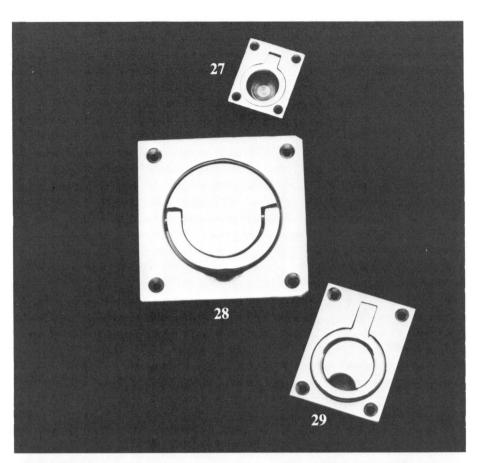

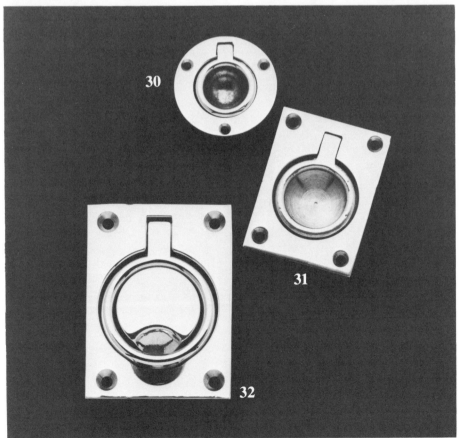

Cabinet & Cupboard Knobs & Pulls

1 Cabinet knob and filigree backplate
Mark E. Bokenkamp, Bokenkamp's Forge
Hand forged iron, antique tin plate finish
Knob diameter: 1⅛", backplate diameter: 2⅛"

2 Cabinet knob and backplate (Sheraton)
Horton Brasses
Stamped brass
Knob diameter: 2", backplate diameter: 2"

3 Cabinet knob and backplate (Sheraton)
Horton Brasses
Stamped brass
Knob diameter: 2", backplate diameter: 2"

4 Cabinet knob and backplate (Empire)
Period Furniture Hardware
Stamped brass
Knob diameter: 1⅜", backplate diameter: 1½"

5 Cabinet knob (Sheraton)
H. Pfanstiel
Solid brass
Diameter: 1¾"

6 Cabinet knob and backplate (Sheraton)
Ball and Ball
Stamped brass
Knob diameter: 2", backplate diameter: 2"

7 Cabinet knob and backplate (Sheraton)
Ball and Ball
Stamped brass
Knob diameter: 1", backplate diameter: 1"

8–10 Cabinet knobs and backplates (Sheraton)
Paxton
Stamped brass
Knob diameters: 1", 1½", and 2", backplate diameters: 1", 1½", and 2"

11 Cabinet knob and backplate (Sheraton)
Ball and Ball
Stamped brass
Knob diameter: 1¼", backplate diameter: 1¼"

12–16 Cabinet knobs
Baldwin
Solid, hot-forged brass
Diameters: ¾", 1", 1¼", 1½", and 1¾"

17–21 Cabinet knobs
The Merit Brass Collection
Solid brass
Diameters: ½", ¾", 1", 1¼", and 1½"

22 Desk interior knob
Period Furniture Hardware
Solid brass
Diameter: ⅝"

23–27 Desk interior knobs
Horton Brasses
Solid brass
Diameters: ⅜", ½", ⅝", ¾", and ⅞"

28–30 Cabinet knobs
Ball and Ball
Solid cast brass
Diameters: 1¼" × 1", 1½" × 1³⁄₁₆" and 1⁹⁄₁₆" × 1¼"

31–33 Cabinet knobs
Horton Brasses
Solid brass
Diameters: ¾", 1", and 1¼"

34 Cabinet knob
Baldwin
Solid, hot-forged brass
Diameter: 1¼" × ¾"

35 Cabinet knob and backplate
The Broadway Collection
Solid brass
Knob diameter: 1¼"

36 Cabinet knob
Baldwin
Solid, hot-forged brass
Diameter: 1¼"

37 Cabinet knob
Period Furniture Hardware
Solid brass
Diameter: 1¼"

38 Cabinet knob
H. Pfanstiel
Solid brass
Diameter: 1¼"

39 Cabinet knob
Baldwin
Solid, hot-forged brass
Diameter: 1½"

40 Cabinet knob
H. Pfanstiel
Solid brass
Diameter: 2"

41 Cabinet knob
Impex Associates
Solid brass
Diameter: ⅞"

42 Cabinet knob and backplate
Impex Associates
Solid brass
Knob diameter: 1", backplate diameter: 1½"

43 Cabinet knob
Kraft Hardware
Solid brass
Diameter: 1½"

44 Cabinet knob
Sherle Wagner International
Solid brass
Diameter: 1⅜"

45 Cabinet knob and backplate (Louis XIV)
H. Pfanstiel
Solid brass
Knob length: 1¾", backplate length: 2½"

46 Cabinet knob
Sherle Wagner International
Porcelain, hand painted
Diameter: 1⅜"

47 Cabinet knob
Period Furniture Hardware
Porcelain and brass, applied pattern
Diameter: 1½"

48 Cabinet knob
Baldwin
Limoges porcelain, applied pattern and gold
Diameter: 1½"

49 Cabinet knob
Ritter & Son
Solid brass
Diameter: 1⅛"

50 Cabinet knob
Ritter & Son
Solid brass
Diameter: 1½"

51 Spool cabinet knob and backplate (Victorian)
Horton Brasses
Cast brass
Knob diameter: 1¼", backplate diameter: 1¼"

52 Cabinet knob (Victorian)
Horton Brasses
Black painted wood and brass
Diameter: 1¼"

53 Cabinet knob
Home Hardware
Crystal with brass insert
Diameter: 1½"

54 Cabinet knob
Home Hardware
Crystal with brass insert
Diameter: 1½"

55 Cabinet knob
Home Hardware
Crystal with chrome insert
Diameter: 1⅜″

56 Cabinet knob
Sherle Wagner International
Cut crystal and brushed chrome
Diameter: 1⅛″

57 Cabinet knob
Period Furniture Hardware
Crystal with brass shank
Diameter: 1⅛″

58 Thru-screw cabinet knob
Restoration Hardware
Handblown glass
Diameter: 1⅛″

59–61 Thru-screw cabinet or shutter knobs
Plexacraft Metals
Porcelain
Diameters: ⅝″, ¾″, and 1¼″

62–64 Thru-screw cabinet knobs
Restoration Hardware
Ceramic
Diameters: ⅜″, ⅝″, and ⅞″

65–67 Thru-screw cabinet knobs
Horton Brasses
Porcelain
Diameters: ¾″, 1″, and 1⅜″

68 Spice knob
Plexacraft Metals
Porcelain
Diameter: ⅝″

69–71 Cabinet knobs
Horton Brasses
Porcelain
Diameters: ¾″, 1″, and 1⅜″

72, 73 Cabinet knobs
Plexacraft Metals
Porcelain
Diameters: 1½″ and 1⅛″

74 Thru-screw cabinet knob
Period Furniture Hardware
Porcelain, applied design
Diameter: 1½″

75 Cabinet knob
The Broadway Collection
Porcelain, applied design
Diameter: 1½″

76 Cabinet knob
Period Furniture Hardware
Porcelain, applied design
Diameter: 1½″

77 Cabinet knob
Baldwin
Limoges porcelain and brass, applied design
Diameter: 1¼″

78 Cabinet knob
Omnia Industries
Porcelain, applied design
Diameter: 1⅜″

79 Cabinet knob
Period Furniture Hardware
Porcelain, crazed glaze
Diameter: 1½″

80 Thru-screw cabinet knob
Period Furniture Hardware
Porcelain, applied design
Diameter: 1½″

81 Cabinet knob
Period Furniture Hardware
Porcelain, applied design
Diameter: 1½″

82 Cabinet knob
Period Furniture Hardware
Porcelain, applied design
Diameter: 1½″

83 Cabinet knob
Period Furniture Hardware
Porcelain, applied design
Diameter: 1½″

84 Cabinet knob
The Renovator's Supply
Porcelain, applied design
Diameter: 1¼″

85 Cabinet knob
Restoration Hardware
Australian porcelain, hand-painted design Diameter: 1⅜″

86 Cabinet knob and backplate
Plexacraft Metals
Porcelain knob and backplate, brass shank
Knob diameter: 1″, backplate diameter: 1½″

87 Cabinet knob and backplate
Plexacraft Metals
Porcelain knob and backplate, brass shank
Knob diameter: 1¼″, backplate diameter: 2″

88 Thru-screw cabinet knob
Paxton
Ceramic with brass shank
Diameter: 1″

89 Cabinet knob
Period Furniture Hardware
Porcelain with brass trim
Diameter: 1¹/₁₆″

90 Cabinet knob
Plexacraft Metals
Porcelain with brass shank
Diameter: 1¼″

91 Wardrobe knob
Plexacraft Metals
Porcelain with brass shank
Diameter: 1¾″

92–95 Cabinet knobs
Home Hardware
Wood
Diameters: 1″, 1¼″, 1½″, and 2″

96–101 Spherical cabinet knobs
Waddell
Wood
Diameters: 1″, 1¼″, 1½″, 1¾″, 2″, and 2¼″

102, 103 Cabinet knobs
Period Furniture Hardware
Polished beechwood
Diameters: 1⁵/₁₆″ and 1⅝″

104 Cabinet knob
Period Furniture Hardware
Polished beechwood
Diameter: 1⅝″

105, 106 Cupboard knobs
Horton Brasses
Wood
Diameters: 1¼″ and 1½″

107–110 Cupboard knobs
Horton Brasses
Wood
Diameters: 1¼″, 1½″, and 1¾″

111–113 Cabinet knobs
Period Furniture Hardware
Polished beechwood
Diameters: 1¼″, 1⅝″, and 2⅛″

114–117 Cabinet knobs
Jaybee
Wood
Diameters: 1″, 1″, 1¼″, and 1¾″

118–121 Cabinet knobs
Kraft Hardware
Solid brass
Diameters: 1″, 1¼″, 1½″, and 2″

122–125 Cabinet knobs
Kraft Hardware
Solid brass
Diameters: 1″, 1¼″, 1½″, and 2″

126, 127 Cabinet knobs
Kraft Hardware
Solid brass
Diameters: 1″ and 1¼″

128 Cabinet knob
Sherle Wagner International
Polished chrome
Overall size: 1″ × 1″ × ¾″

129 Cabinet knob
Sherle Wagner International
Polished chrome
Diameter: 1″

130 Cabinet knob
Sherle Wagner International
Brushed chrome
Diameter: 1¼″

131 Cabinet knob
Omnia Industries
Polished chrome
Overall length: 1⁹⁄₁₆″, boring: 1¼″

132 Cabinet knob
Omnia Industries
Polished chrome
Diameter: 1⁵⁄₁₆″

133–137 Cabinet knobs
Plexacraft Metals
Lucite
Diameters: 1″, 1¼″, 1½″, 1¾″, and 2″

138–140 Cabinet knobs
IDG Marketing
ABS plastic (white, red, yellow, brown or blue)
Diameters: 1¹⁷⁄₃₂″, 2⅛″, and 3″

141, 142 Cabinet knobs
Omnia Industries
Plastic (available in a variety of colors)
Diameters: 1³⁄₁₆″ and 1⅝″

143 Cabinet knob
Stanley Hardware
Cast Zamac, aluminum finish
Diameter: 1½″

144 Cabinet knobs with split openwork backplate
Period Furniture Hardware
Solid brass
Backplate overall: 6½″ × 5½″

145 Cabinet knob and backplate
Period Furniture Hardware
Solid brass
Backplate: 4½″ × 4½″

146 Oriental cabinet pull
Period Furniture Hardware
Solid brass
Diameter: 3¼″

147 Cabinet knob with openwork backplate
Period Furniture Hardware
Solid brass
Backplate: 3½″ × 4″

148–150 Oriental cabinet pulls
Kraft Hardware
Solid brass
Diameters: 3″, 4″, and 5″

151 Oriental cabinet pull
Period Furniture Hardware
Solid brass
Length: 4″, width: 2½″

152 Oriental split plate cabinet pull
Kraft Hardware
Solid brass
Diameter: 7½″

153 Oriental split plate cabinet pull
Kraft Hardware
Solid brass
Diameter: 8″

154 Cabinet pull
Steve Kayne, Steve Kayne Hand Forged Hardware
Hand-forged iron
Overall length: 5″

155 Cabinet pull
Steve Kayne, Steve Kayne Hand Forged Hardware
Hand-forged iron
Overall length: 4¾″

156 Heart cabinet pull
Steve Kayne, Steve Kayne Hand Forged Hardware
Hand-forged iron
Overall length: 6″

157 Bean cabinet pull
Steve Kayne, Steve Kayne Hand Forged Hardware
Hand-forged iron
Overall length: 5¾″

158 Ball cabinet pull
Mark E. Rocheford, Hammerworks
Hand-forged iron
Overall length: 5″

159 Ball and spear cabinet pull
Mark E. Rocheford, Hammerworks
Hand-forged iron
Overall length: 6″

160 Cabinet pull
Baldwin
Solid forged brass
Boring: 3″

161 Cabinet pull
Baldwin
Solid forged brass
Boring: 3″

162 Cabinet pull
The Merit Brass Collection
Cast brass
Overall length: 4″

163 Cabinet pull
Period Furniture Hardware
Solid brass
Overall length: 4⅞″

164 Cabinet pull
Acorn
Steel, pewter finish
Overall length: 4¾″

165–167 Cabinet pulls
Omnia Industries
Polished chrome
Overall lengths: 3¾″, 4¾″, and 5½″

168 Cabinet pull
Omnia Industries
Polished chrome
Overall length: 3⅞″, boring: 2½″

169 Cabinet pull
Stanley Hardware
Polished chrome
Boring: 3″

170 Cabinet pull
Period Furniture Hardware
Polished beechwood
Boring: 1¼″

171 Cabinet pull
Period Furniture Hardware
Polished beechwood
Boring: 2½″

172 Cabinet pull
Period Furniture Hardware
Polished beechwood
Boring: 3¾″

173 Cabinet pull
Period Furniture Hardware
Polished beechwood
Boring: 3¾″

174–178 Cabinet knobs and pulls
H. Pfanstiel
Plastic (clear, white, red or black) and brass
Overall lengths: ¾″, 1″, 4″, 6″, and 8″; knob diameters: 1″, pull diameters: ¾″

179 Cabinet pull
Simon's Hardware
Lucite and chrome
Length: 2″

180–181 Cabinet pull
Simon's Hardware
Lucite and chrome
Overall lengths: 4½″ and 5½″, borings: 3″
and 4″

182 Cabinet pull
Simon's Hardware
Lucite and chrome
Overall length: 7″, boring: 5″

183 Cabinet pull
Forms & Surfaces
Nylon (available in a wide range of
colors)
Boring: 3″

184 Cabinet pull
Stanley Hardware
Black, gold, aluminum, or brown finish
Boring: 3½″

185 Cabinet pull
Omnia Industries
Plastic (available in a wide range of
colors)
Boring: 5″

186 Cabinet pull
Kraft Hardware
Nylon
Boring: 5″

187 Cabinet pull
IDG Marketing
ABS plastic (white, red, yellow, brown,
or blue)
Overall length: 3⅛″, diameter: ¹⁹⁄₃₂″

188 Cabinet pull
IDG Marketing
ABS plastic (white, red, yellow, brown,
or blue)
Overall length: 4⁵⁄₁₆″, diameter: ¹⁹⁄₃₂″

189 Recessed cabinet pulls
Forms & Surfaces
Nylon (available in a wide range of
colors)
Diameter: 2½″

190 Cabinet pull
Forms & Surfaces
Soft neoprene, black
Length: 2½″, projection: 1″

191 Cabinet pull
IDG Marketing
ABS plastic (white, red, yellow, brown,
or blue)
Projection: 1½″

192 Cabinet pull
Forms & Surfaces
Soft neoprene, black
Boring: 1³⁄₁₆″, projection: 1⅜″

193 Cabinet pull
IDG Marketing
ABS plastic (white, red, yellow, brown,
or blue)
Length: 1⅞″, width: ¹⁵⁄₁₆″, projection: 1¼″

Drawer & Bin Pulls

1 Drawer pull (William and Mary and
Queen Anne)
Horton Brasses
Solid brass, hand chased
Overall: 3⅛″ × 2″; borings: 2″, 2¼″, or
2½″
(Matching escutcheon available.)

2 Drawer pull (William and Mary and
Queen Anne)
Horton Brasses
Solid brass, hand chased
Overall: 4″ × 2½″; borings: 2½″, 2¾″, 2⅞″,
3″, or 3¼″
(Matching escutcheon available.)

3 Drawer pull (William and Mary and
Queen Anne) with cotter pin fittings
Horton Brasses
Solid brass, hand chased
Overall: 2⅞″ × 2″, boring: 1¼″
(Matching escutcheon available.)

4 Drawer pull (William and Mary and
Queen Anne) with cotter pin fittings
Ball and Ball
Sand-cast brass, hand chased
Overall: 2¾″ × 1⅞″, boring: 1⁵⁄₁₆″
(Matching escutcheon available.)

5 Drawer pull (William and Mary and
Queen Anne)
Period Furniture Hardware
Cast brass
Boring: 3″

6 Drawer pull (Chippendale) and
matching escutcheon
Horton Brasses
Solid brass
Overall: 3⅜″ × 4⅜″; borings: 2¾″, 2⅞″, 3″,
3¼″, or 3½″

7 Drawer pull (Chippendale)
Horton Brasses
Solid brass
Overall: 4⅛″ × 3¼″; borings: 2¾″, 2⅞″, 3″,
or 3¼″
(Matching escutcheon available.)

8 Drawer pull (Chippendale)
Horton Brasses
Solid brass
Overall: 2¼″ × 3½″; borings: 2½″, 2¾″,
2⅞″, or 3″
(Matching escutcheon available.)

9 Drawer pull (Chippendale)
Horton Brasses
Solid brass
Overall: 3½″ × 2½″; borings: 2¼″, 2½″, or
2¾″
(Matching escutcheon available.)

10 Drawer pull (Chippendale)
Ball and Ball
Solid brass
Overall: 4⅜″ × 2⅝″, boring: 3¼″
(Matching escutcheon available.)

11 Drawer pull (Chippendale)
Ball and Ball
Solid brass
Overall: 3¼″ × 2″, boring: 2⅝″
(Matching escutcheon available.)

12 Drawer pull (Chippendale)
Ball and Ball
Sand-cast brass
Overall: 3¾″ × 2¾″, boring: 2¾″
(Matching escutcheon available.)

13 Drawer pull (Chippendale)
Period Furniture Hardware
Cast brass
Overall: 3⅛″ × 2¼″, boring: 2″

14 Drawer pull (Chippendale)
The Broadway Collection
Solid brass
Boring: 2½″

15 Drawer pull (Queen Anne)
Ball and Ball
Sand-cast brass
Overall: 4⅜″ × 3¼″, boring: 3¼″
(Matching escutcheon available.)

16 Drawer pull (Queen Anne)
Ball and Ball
Sand-cast brass
Overall: 4⅛″ × 2⅞″, boring: 3″
(Matching escutcheon available.)

17 Drawer pull (Queen Anne)
The Broadway Collection
Solid brass
Boring: 1⅞″

18 Rosette pull (Chippendale)
Horton Brasses
Solid brass
Rosette: 1½″ × 1⅛″; borings: 3¼″, 3½″,
3⅝″, 3¾″, 3⅞″, 4″, or 4¼″

19 Rosette pull (Chippendale)
Horton Brasses
Solid brass
Rosette diameter: 1″; borings: 2¼″, 2½″,
2¾″, 2⅞″, or 3″

20 Rosette pull (Chippendale)
Horton Brasses
Solid brass
Rosette diameter: ¾″, boring: 3″

21 Rosette pull (Victorian)
Horton Brasses
Solid brass
Rosette: 1″ × 1⅜″; borings: 2¼″, 2½″, 2¾″, 2⅞″, or 3″

22 Rosette pull (Victorian)
Horton Brasses
Solid brass
Rosette diameter: ¾″, boring: 3″

23 Rosette pull
The Broadway Collection
Solid brass
Boring: 3″

24 Bail pull (Chippendale)
Ball and Ball
Sand-cast brass
Boring: 2⅜″

25 Rosette pull (Chippendale)
Ball and Ball
Cast brass
Rosette diameter: 1¹⁄₁₆″, boring: 3″

26 Drawer pull (Hepplewhite)
Period Furniture Hardware
Stamped brass
Boring: 2″

27 Drawer pull (Hepplewhite)
Horton Brasses
Stamped brass
Boring: 2¼″

28 Drawer pull (Hepplewhite)
Horton Brasses
Stamped brass
Boring: 3″

29 Drawer pull (Hepplewhite)
Horton Brasses
Stamped brass
Boring: 2¾″

30 Drawer pull (Hepplewhite)
Ball and Ball
Stamped brass
Boring: 2½″

31 Drawer pull (Hepplewhite)
Ball and Ball
Stamped brass
Boring: 2″

32 Drawer pull (Hepplewhite)
Period Furniture Hardware
Stamped brass
Boring: 2¼″

33 Drawer pull (Hepplewhite)
Period Furniture Hardware
Stamped brass
Boring: 2¼″

34 Drawer pull (Hepplewhite)
Horton Brasses
Stamped brass
Boring: 2″

35 Drawer pull (Hepplewhite)
Period Furniture Hardware
Stamped brass
Boring: 1¾″

36 Drawer pull (Hepplewhite)
Period Furniture Hardware
Stamped brass
Boring: 3″

37 Drawer pull (Hepplewhite)
Period Furniture Hardware
Stamped brass
Boring: 2″

38 Drawer pull (Hepplewhite)
Ball and Ball
Stamped brass
Boring: 2½″

39 Drawer pull (Hepplewhite)
Ball and Ball
Stamped brass
Boring: 1⅝″

40 Drawer pull (Hepplewhite)
Ball and Ball
Stamped brass
Boring: 2½″

41 Drawer pull (Hepplewhite)
Ball and Ball
Stamped brass
Boring: 2⅜″

42 Drawer pull (French type)
Period Furniture Hardware
Cast brass
Overall length: 4¼″, boring: 2½″

43 Drawer pull (French type)
Period Furniture Hardware
Cast brass
Overall length: 6¾″, boring: 3″

44 Drawer pull (French type)
Ball and Ball
Cast brass
Overall length: 3¼″, boring: 2⅜″

45 Drawer pull (French type)
Kraft Hardware
Cast brass
Overall length: 5½″, boring: 2½″

46 Drawer pull (French type)
Kraft Hardware
Cast brass
Overall length: 7″, boring: 2½″

47 Drawer pull (French type)
Period Furniture Hardware
Cast brass
Overall length: 4⅛″, boring: 2″

48 Drawer pull (French type)
Ball and Ball
Cast brass
Overall length: 7″, boring: 3″

49–51 Drawer pulls (French type)
Kraft Hardware
Cast brass
Borings: 2″, 2½″, and 3″

52 Oval openwork bail pull
Period Furniture Hardware
Cast brass
Length: 2½″, width: 2″

53 Rosette pull
Period Furniture Hardware
Cast brass
Boring: 3⅛″

54 Rosette pull
Period Furniture Hardware
Cast brass
Boring: 3″

55–57 Rosette pulls (Louis XVI)
Kraft Hardware
Cast brass
Borings: 2¾″, 3¼″, and 3⅞″

58 Rosette pull
H. Pfanstiel
Cast brass
Boring: 3¼″

59 Rosette pull
H. Pfanstiel
Cast brass
Boring: 3⅝″

60 Rosette pull
Ball and Ball
Cast brass
Rosette diameter: 1¼″, boring: 2⅞″

61 Rosette pull
Ball and Ball
Cast brass
Rosette: 1¼″ × 1¾″, boring: 3″

62 Rosette pull
Ball and Ball
Cast brass
Rosette diameter: 1³⁄₁₆″, boring: 3½″

63 Rosette pull
Ritter & Son
Cast brass
Rosette diameter: 1″, boring: 3″

64 Rosette pull (Victorian)
Restoration Hardware
Cast brass bail, stamped rosette
Boring: 3″

65 Drawer pull (Victorian)
Paxton
Cast brass
Overall length: 4⅜″, boring: 3″

66 Rosette pull
Ball and Ball
Cast brass
Rosette: 1¼″ × 2″, boring: 4″

67 Rosette pull (Victorian)
Restoration Hardware
Cast brass bail, stamped rosettes
Boring: 3″

68 Drawer pull (Victorian)
Ritter & Son
Cast brass
Boring: 3″

69 Drawer pull (Victorian)
Ritter & Son
Cast brass
Boring: 3″

70 Drawer pull (Victorian)
Ritter & Son
Cast brass
Boring: 3″

71 Drawer pull (Chinese Chippendale)
Period Furniture Hardware
Cast brass
Overall length: 3½″, boring: 2½″

72, 73 Rosette pulls (Chippendale)
Kraft Hardware
Cast brass
Borings: 3″ and 4″

74 Drawer pull (Victorian)
The Renovator's Supply
Cast brass bail, stamped backplate
Overall length: 3⅝″, boring: 3″

75 Drawer pull (Victorian)
The Renovator's Supply
Sand-cast brass
Overall length: 5⅛″, boring: 3″

76 Drawer pull (Victorian)
Horton Brasses
Cast brass bail, stamped backplate
Overall length: 4³/₁₆″, boring: 3″

77 Drawer pull (Victorian)
Horton Brasses
Cast brass bail, stamped backplate
Overall length: 4½″, boring: 3″

78 Drawer pull (Victorian)
Horton Brasses
Cast brass bail, stamped backplate
Overall length: 5″, boring: 3″

79 Drawer pull (Victorian)
Horton Brasses
Cast brass bail, stamped backplate
Overall length: 4¼″, boring: 3″

80 Drawer pull (Victorian)
Ritter & Son
Cast brass bail, stamped backplate
Boring: 3″

81 Drawer pull (Victorian)
Ritter & Son
Cast brass bail, stamped backplate
Boring: 3″

82 Drawer pull (Victorian)
Paxton
Cast brass bail, stamped backplate
Boring: 3″

83 Drawer pull (Eastlake)
Restoration Hardware
Cast brass bail, stamped backplate
Boring: 3″

84 Drawer pull (Eastlake)
Paxton
Wrought brass
Overall length: 4¼″, boring: 3″

85 Drawer pull (Victorian)
Horton Brasses
Solid brass
Overall length: 3¾″, borings: 2½″ or 3″

86 Drawer pull (Victorian)
Horton Brasses
Solid brass
Overall length: 4¼″, boring: 3″

87 Drawer pull (Victorian)
Horton Brasses
Solid brass
Overall length: 4½″, boring: 3″

88 Drawer pull (Victorian)
Horton Brasses
Solid brass
Overall length: 3¾″, boring: 2½″

89 Spool cabinet pull (Victorian)
Horton Brasses
Solid brass
Overall: 2″ × 1⁵/₁₆″

90 Bail set
The Renovator's Supply
Die-cast brass
Overall length: 3½″, boring: 3″

91 Bail set
The Renovator's Supply
Die-cast brass
Overall length: 3¾″, boring: 3″

92 Antique drawer pull (English, late 18th century)
Bob Pryor Antiques
Forged brass
Overall length: 4½″, boring: 2″

93 Drawer pull
Bob Patrick, Big Anvil Forge
Hand-forged iron
Overall: 3½″ × 2¾″

94 Drawer pull
Steve Kayne, Steve Kayne Hand Forged Hardware
Hand-forged iron
Overall length: 6¼″ × 2¾″

95–97 Carved wooden drawer pulls
Paxton
Maple
Overall length: 3″, 5″, and 7″

98 Drawer pull
The Renovator's Supply
Cast brass
Length: 6″

99 Drawer pull
Custom Decor
Sand-cast brass
Length: 6½″

100 Drawer pull
Kraft Hardware
Cast brass
Boring: 4⅛″

101 Drawer pull
Kraft Hardware
Cast brass
Boring: 4½″

102 Drawer pull (Oriental)
Kraft Hardware
Cast brass
Overall length: 4½″, boring: 2⅞″

103 Drawer pull
Home Hardware
Wood
Boring: 2½″

104 Recessed drawer pull
Forms & Surfaces
White oak
Diameter: 2″

105 Recessed drawer pull
Period Furniture Hardware
Polished beechwood
Length: 4½″

106 Recessed drawer pull
Forms & Surfaces
White oak
Length: 4¾″

107 Drawer pull
The Broadway Collection
Porcelain, applied design
Boring: 3″

108, 109 Drawer pulls with base plates
Baldwin
Solid brass
Borings: 2½″ and 5″, base diameters: ⅝″
(Bases prevent the small diameter of the pulls from imbedding into soft surfaces.)

110–113 Drawer pulls
Period Furniture Hardware
Solid brass
Borings: 2¾″, 3″, 3½″, and 4″

114–116 Flush drawer pull
Period Furniture Hardware
Solid brass
Lengths: 2″, 3″, and 4″

117 Flush drawer pull
The Merit Brass Collection
Cast brass
Overall: 1″ × 2³⁄₁₆″, mortise depth: ⁷⁄₁₆″

118 Flush ring pull
Kraft Hardware
Solid brass
Diameter: 2½″

119 Bin pull (Victorian)
Ritter & Son
Cast bronze
Boring: 2⁵⁄₁₆″

120 Bin pull (Victorian)
Ritter & Son
Cast bronze
Boring: 2¾″

121 Antique bin pull (Victorian)
Urban Archeology
Cast bronze
Boring: 3⅝″

122 Antique bin pull (Victorian)
Urban Archeology
Cast bronze
Boring: 3½″

123 Bin pull (Victorian)
The Renovator's Supply
Die-cast brass
Boring: 3¼″

124 Bin pull (Victorian)
The Renovator's Supply
Die-cast brass
Boring: 2¾″

125 Bin pull (Victorian)
Ritter & Son
Cast brass
Boring: 2¾″

126 Bin pull (Victorian)
The Renovator's Supply
Die-cast brass
Boring: 3″

127 Bin pull (Victorian)
Paxton
Cast brass
Boring: 4″

128 Bin pull (Victorian)
Ritter & Son
Cast brass
Boring: 3⅜″

129 Antique apothecary drawer pull (Victorian)
Urban Archeology
Cast iron
Boring: 2½″

130 Kitchen drawer pull (Victorian)
Horton Brasses
Cast brass
Overall: 1¼″ × 2⅞″

131 Kitchen drawer pull (Victorian)
Horton Brasses
Cast brass
Overall: 1³⁄₁₆″ × 3⁹⁄₁₆″

132 Apothecary drawer pull (Victorian)
Ritter & Son
Cast brass
Boring: 2¼″

133 Apothecary drawer pull (Victorian)
The Renovator's Supply
Die-cast brass
Overall: 3¾″ × 1½″

134 Bin pull
Restoration Hardware
Stamped brass
Boring: 3″

135 Bin pull
The Merit Brass Collection
Cast brass
Overall: 3⅝″ × 1⅛″

Drop Pulls & Ring Pulls

1 Drop pull (William and Mary and Queen Anne) with cotter pin fittings
Horton Brasses
Solid brass
Overall: 1⅛″ × 2¼″

2 Drop pull (William and Mary and Queen Anne) with cotter pin fittings
Horton Brasses
Solid brass
Overall: 1⅜″ × 2½″

3 Drop pull (William and Mary and Queen Anne) with cotter pin fittings
Horton Brasses
Solid brass, hand chased backplate
Overall: 2¼″ × 2¾″
(Matching escutcheon available.)

4 Drop pull (Victorian)
Horton Brasses
Cast brass
Overall: 1½″ × 2¾″

5 Drop pull (William and Mary and Queen Anne)
Ball and Ball
Solid brass
Drop length: 1⅝″, backplate diameter: 1¹⁄₁₆″

6 Drop pull (William and Mary and Queen Anne)
Ball and Ball
Sand-cast brass
Drop length: 1⅜″, backplate diameter: 1⅛″

7 Drop pull (William and Mary and Queen Anne)
Ball and Ball
Sand-cast brass, hand-chased backplate
Drop length: 1¾″, backplate diameter: 2⅛″

8 Drop pull (William and Mary and Queen Anne)
Ball and Ball
Sand-cast brass, hand-chased backplate
Drop length: 1½″, backplate diameter: 1⅝″

9 Ring pull
Period Furniture Hardware
Cast brass
Ring diameter: 2″

10 Ring pull
Period Furniture Hardware
Solid brass
Drop length: 2″, backplate diameter: 1½″

11 Ring pull
Period Furniture Hardware
Solid brass
Drop length: 2⅜″

12 Drop pull (Victorian)
Paxton
Black painted wood and brass, stamped
backplate
Drop length: 3¼″, backplate diameter:
1½″

13 Drop pull (Jacobean)
Period Furniture Hardware
Cast brass
Backplate diameter: 1¾″

14 Drop pull (Victorian)
Horton Brasses
Black painted wood and brass, stamped
backplate
Overall: 1½″ × 3¼″

15 Drop pull (Victorian)
Horton Brasses
Black painted wood and brass
Overall: 2⅜″ × 4¼″
(Matching escutcheon available.)

16 Ring pull (Victorian)
Horton Brasses
Solid brass
Overall: 1⅞″ × 2¼″

17 Drop pull
Sherle Wagner International
Solid brass, gold plated
Overall: 2¾″ × 3″

18 Ring pull (Neoclassical)
Kraft Hardware
Cast brass
Diameter: 3⅝″

19 Ring pull (Neoclassical)
Period Furniture Hardware
Brass, wrought plate and cast ring
Diameter: 1⅞″

20 Ring pull (Neoclassical)
Period Furniture Hardware
Cast brass
Diameter: 2¾″

21 Ring pull (Neoclassical)
Period Furniture Hardware
Cast brass
Overall: 3½″ × 2⅝″

22 Ring pull
Ball and Ball
Solid brass
Backplate diameter: 1¼″, ring diameter:
1½″

23 Ring pull
Baldwin
Forged brass
Overall: 2″ × 1¾″

24 Ring pull
The Broadway Collection
Solid brass
Ring diameter: 1½″

25 Ring pull (Neoclassical)
Kraft Hardware
Cast brass
Ring diameter: 1½″

26 Ring pull (Neoclassical)
Period Furniture Hardware
Cast brass
Diameter: 5″

27 Flush ring pull
The Merit Brass Collection
Cast brass
Overall: 1¼″ × 1½″, mortise depth: 7/16″

28 Flush ring pull
Baldwin
Solid, hot-forged brass
Overall: 3½″ × 3½″

29 Flush ring pull
The Merit Brass Collection
Cast brass
Overall: 1⅞″ × 2½″, mortise depth: 7/16″

30 Flush ring pull (Neoclassical)
Baldwin
Solid, hot-forged brass
Diameter: 1¾″

31 Flush ring pull (Chippendale)
The Merit Brass Collection
Cast brass
Overall: 1⅞″ × 2½″, mortise depth: 9/16″

32 Flush ring pull (Chippendale)
Baldwin
Solid, hot-forged brass
Overall: 2½″ × 3 5/16″

3

Door Knobs, Levers & Pulls

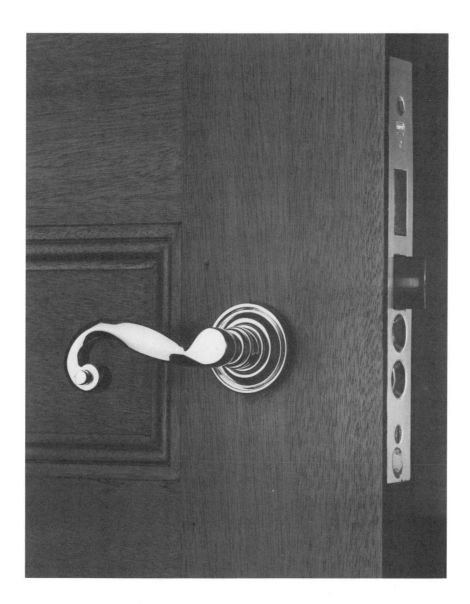

Like all decorative hardware, door knobs and lever door handles serve two purposes—one functional and one decorative. But unlike most other decorative hardware, door knobs and lever door handles also do double duty on the functional side.

A door knob or lever door handle is first of all something for your hand to grab onto when you want to open or close a door. If a handhold was all that was needed, though, some simpler sort of handle or grip would just as easily do.

What makes door knobs and lever door handles special is their ability to turn. A turned door knob or lever in turn turns a spindle that rotates a hub that activates a spring that retracts a latch bolt that permits a door to be opened. Without the second part of the job performed, the first would be superfluous.

Doors without latch bolts are normally interior doors with some sort of catch operated by key or by hand and usually need no more than a simple pull.

A cross between the turning door knob or lever door handle that rotates a hub and the simple pull that makes for a grip on a door with a simple locking function is the thumblatch: a pull with a thumbpiece that moves up and down a bar that either lifts a simple latch on the other side of the door or connects up to a latch bolt retracting mechanism inside a lock. If you don't like levers and have had enough of knobs, you may want to consider a thumblatch.

Some Door Knob, Lever & Pull Terms

Cup Escutcheon. A combination door plate and flush pull used on sliding doors with sliding door locks and having a keyhole as a feature of its recessed part.

Door Edge Pull. A pull mortised into the edge of a door that slides into a pocket.

Door Plate. Any plate that serves as a mount for a door knob or lever door handle and intervenes between it and the door.

Drop Ring. A door knob variation that features a rotating drop ring handle whose shank attaches to a bolt-activating spindle and drops into a recessed cup when not in use.

Dummy Knob, or **Dummy Lever.** Any door knob or lever door handle that serves simply as a pull and is not attached to a bolt-activating spindle.

Flush Cup Pull. Any door pull mortised into a sliding door so that no part of it projects above the surface.

Knob Set, or **Lever Set.** Two matching door knobs or lever door handles with a spindle between.

Offset Pull. Any pull whose handle angles off to one side. Pulls offset to the right are used on right-hand doors and pulls offset to the left are used on left-hand doors.

Rose. A small round backplate that serves as a mounting for a door knob or lever door handle and intervenes between it and the door.

    Concealed Screw Rose. A two-part rose consisting of a covering rose applied to a threaded projection on an underplate that is attached by means of visible screws to a door.

    Surface Mounted Rose. Any rose with exposed mounting screws.

Shank. The generally cylindrical base of a knob or lever door handle that contains a hole for receiving a spindle.

Spindle. A narrow square bar usually threaded at both ends that connects communicating door knobs or lever door handles and operates a latch bolt.

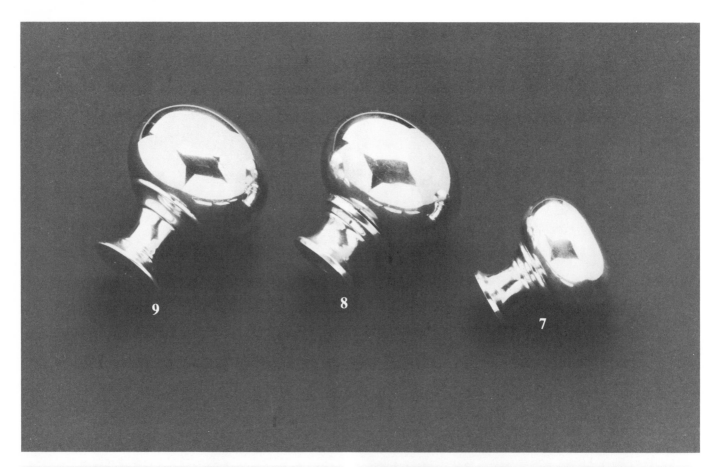

9   8   7

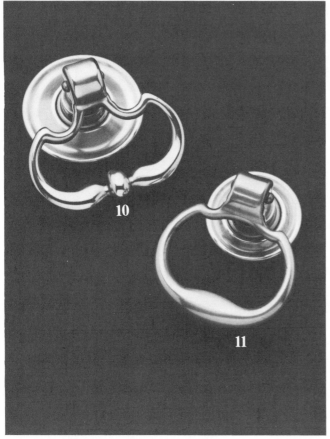

10

11

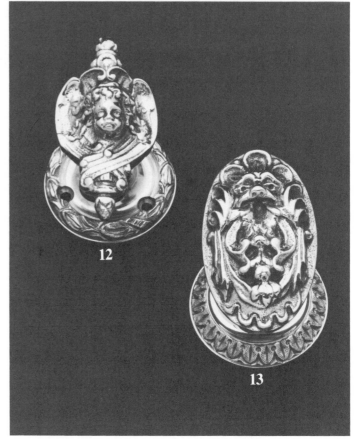

12

13

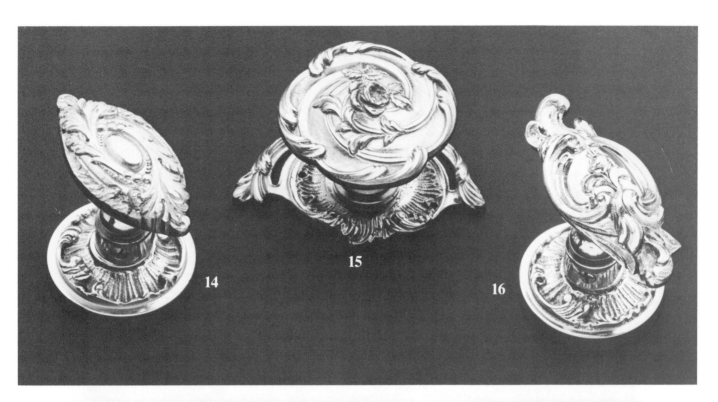

14

15

16

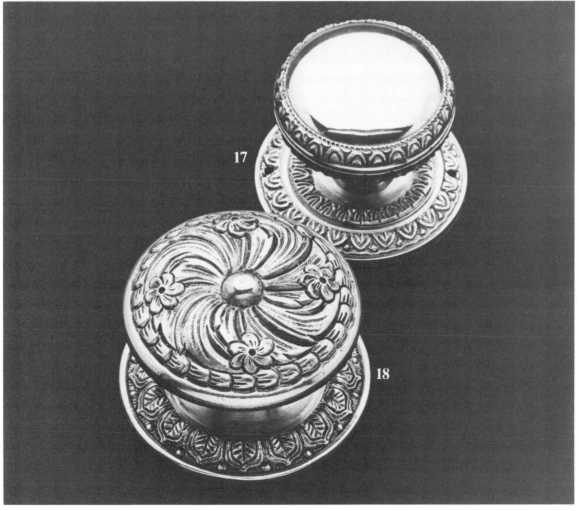

17

18

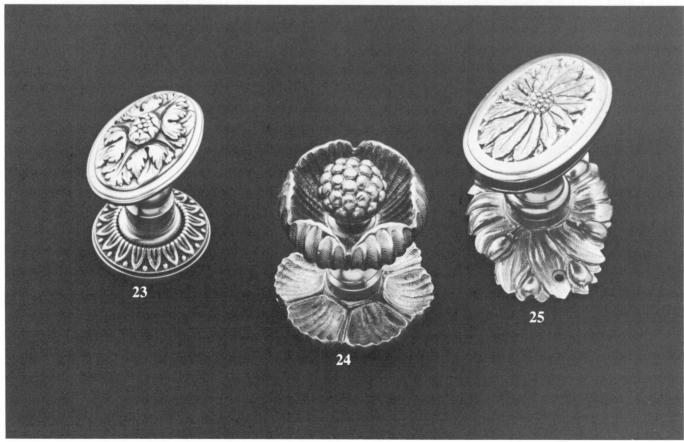

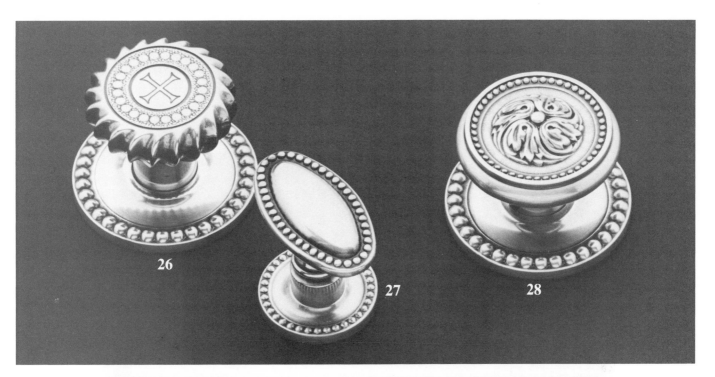

26

27

28

29

30

31

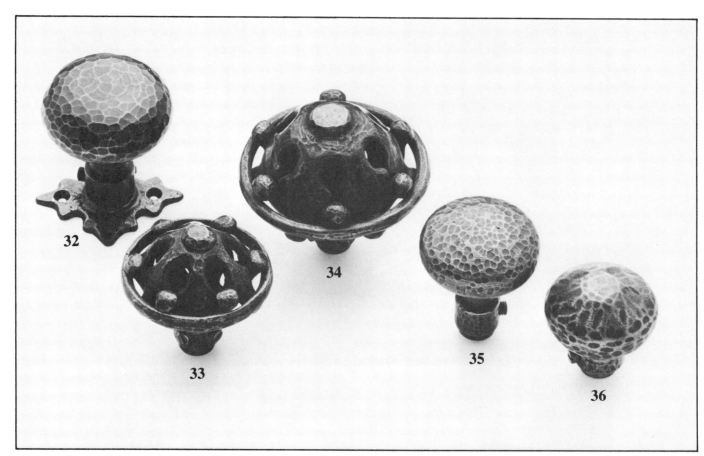

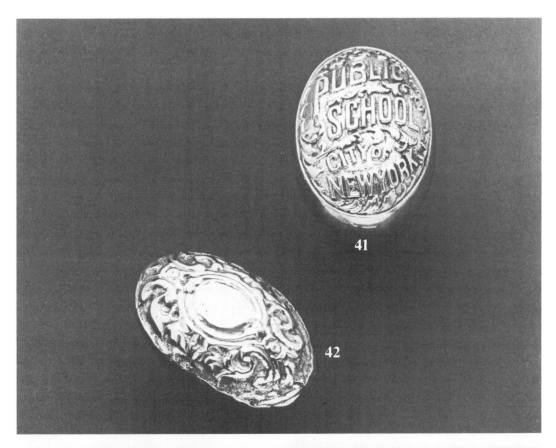

41

42

43

44

45

46

47

48

49

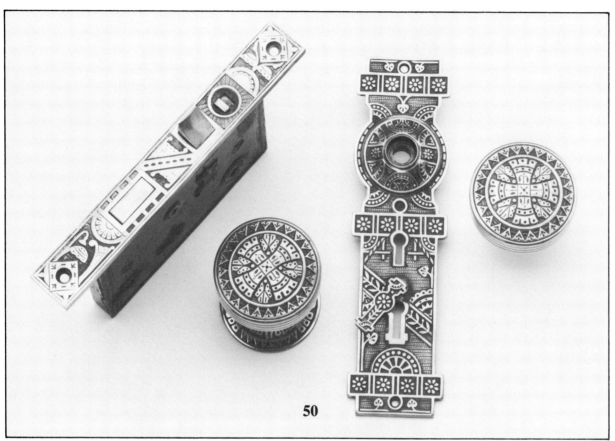

50

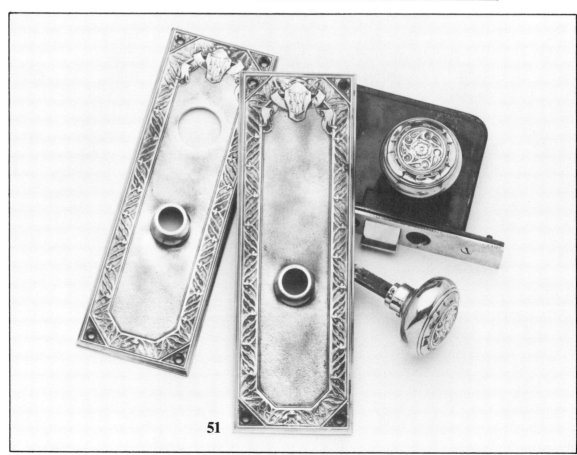

51

52

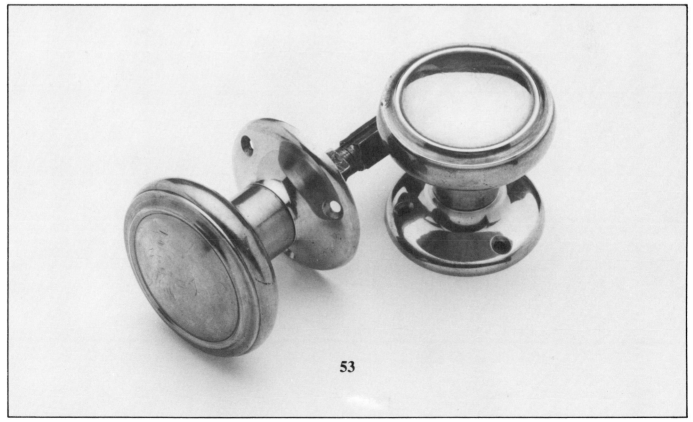

53

54

92

55

56

57

58

59

60

93

61

62

63

64

65

66

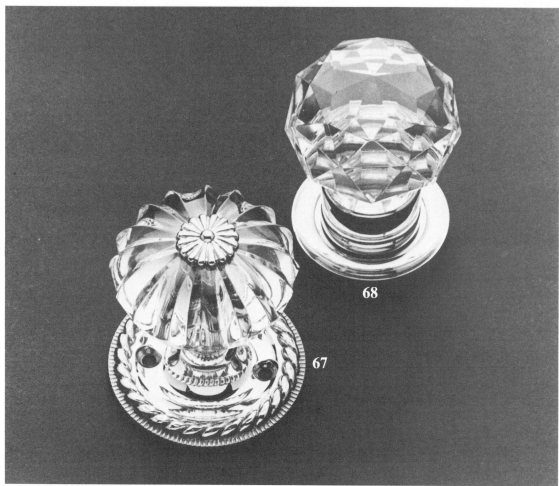

68

67

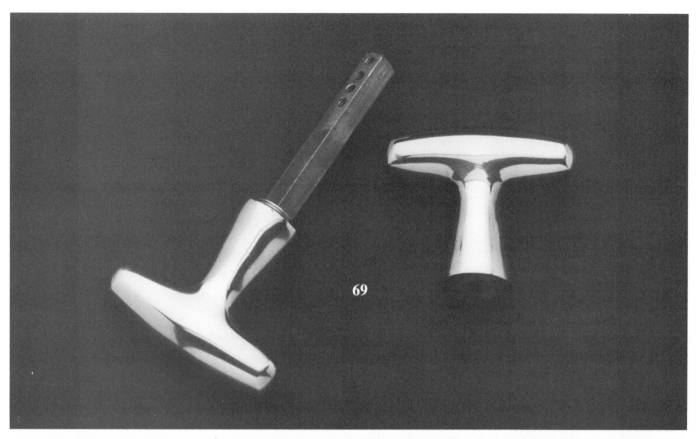

69

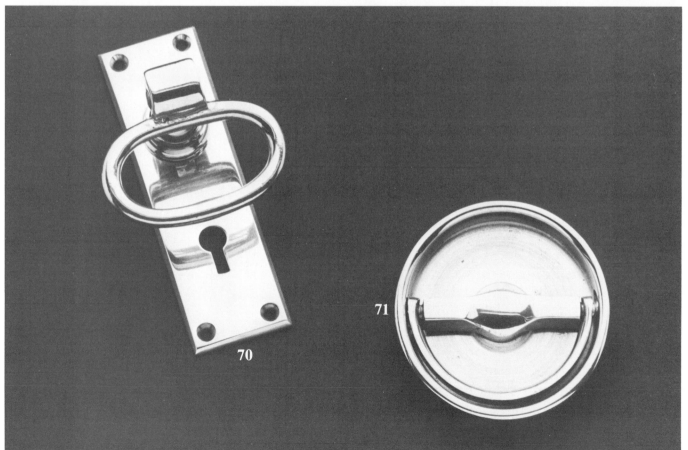

70

71

72

73

74

75

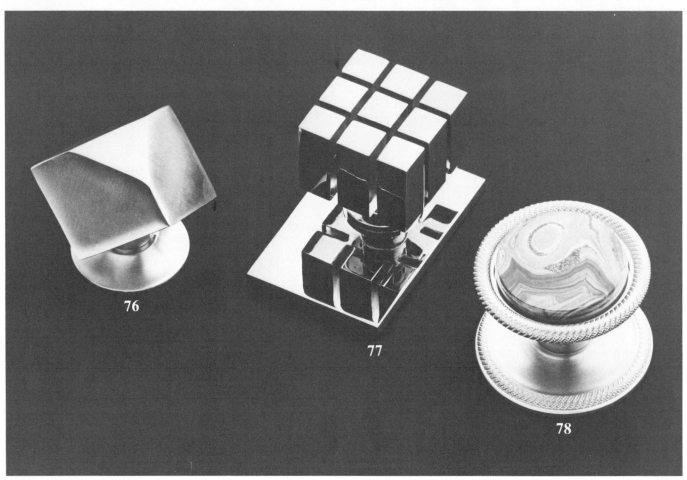

76

77

78

79

80

81

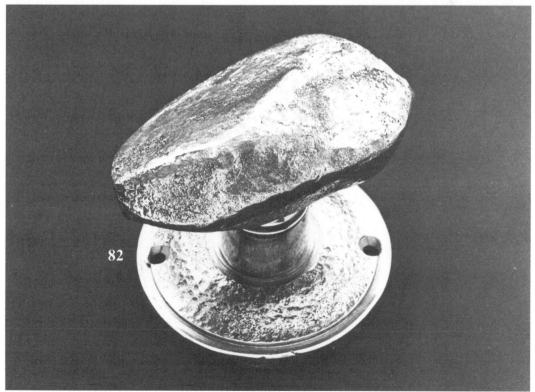

82

83 84 85

86

87

88

89

90

91

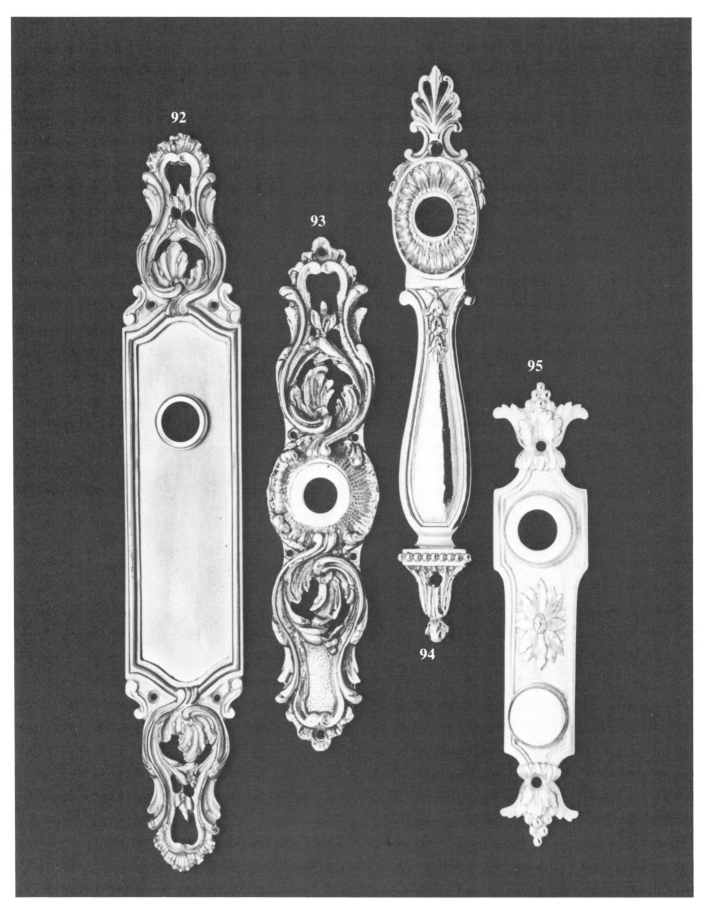

96

97

98

99

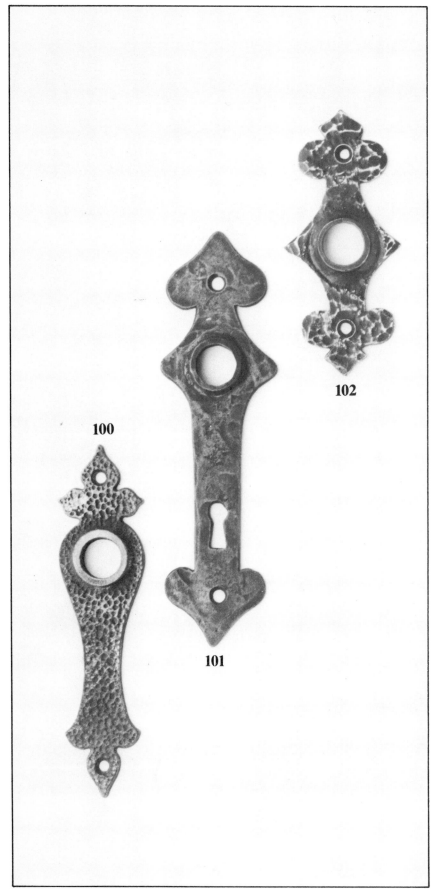

100

101

102

103

104

105

106

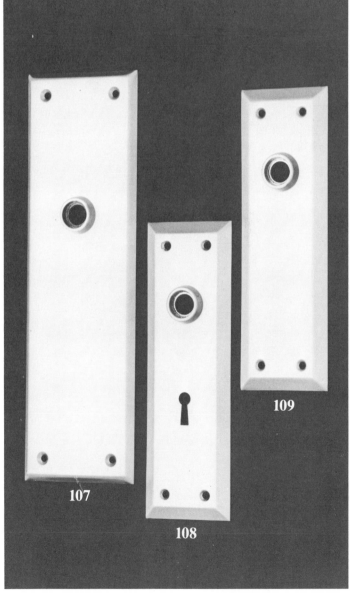

107

108

109

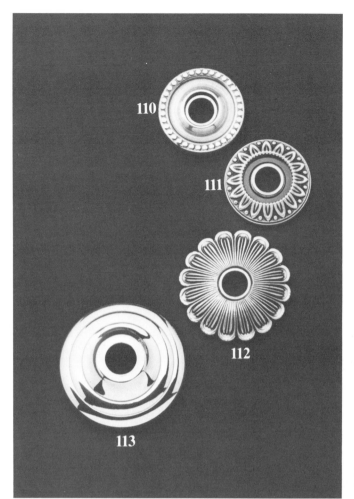

110

111

112

113

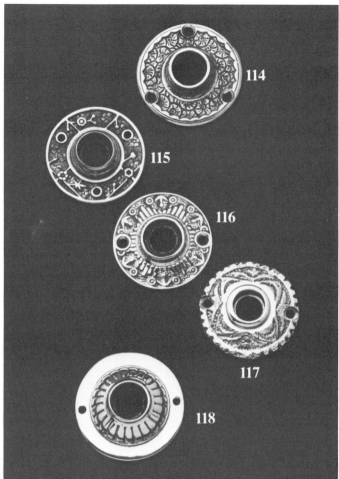

114

115

116

117

118

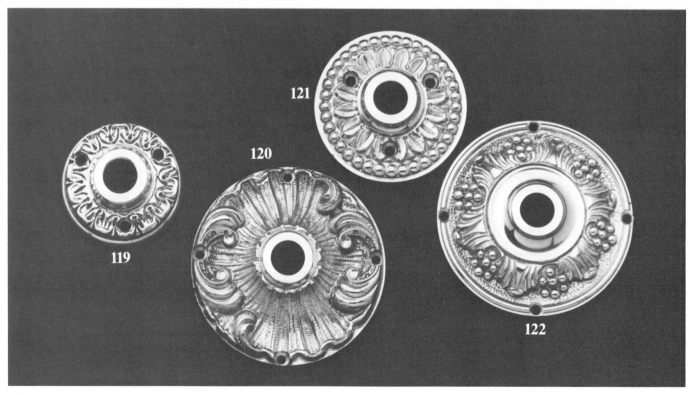

121

120

119

122

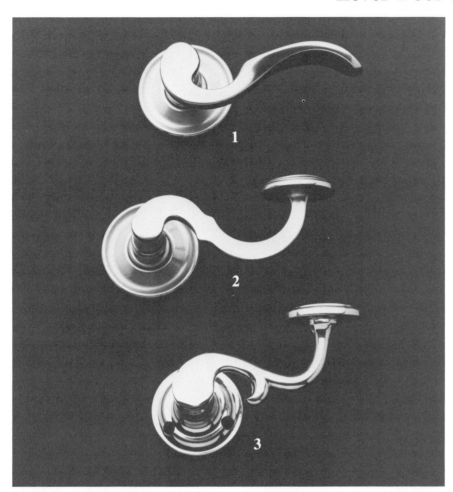

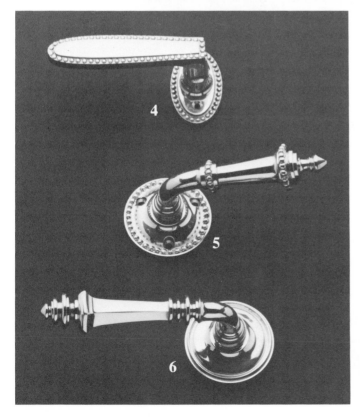

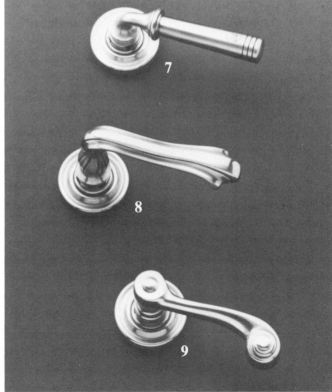

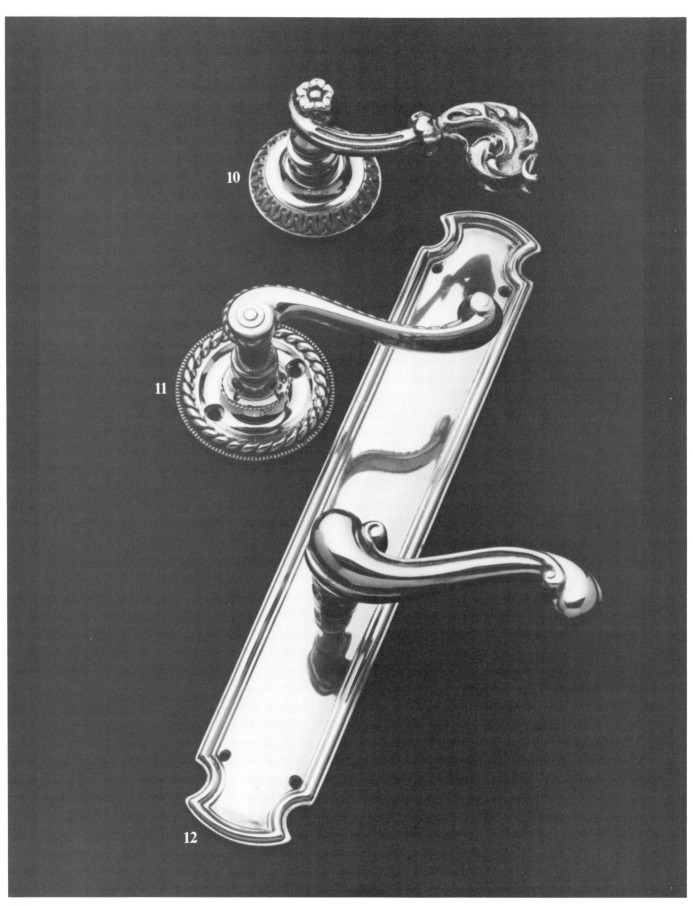

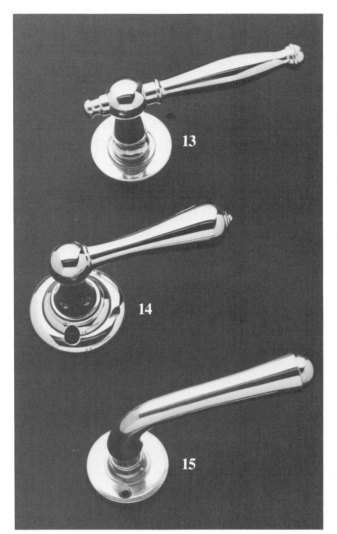

13

14

15

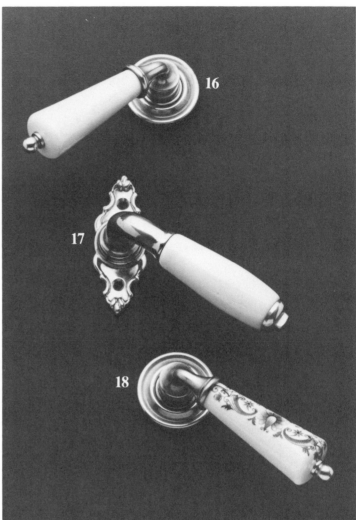

16

17

18

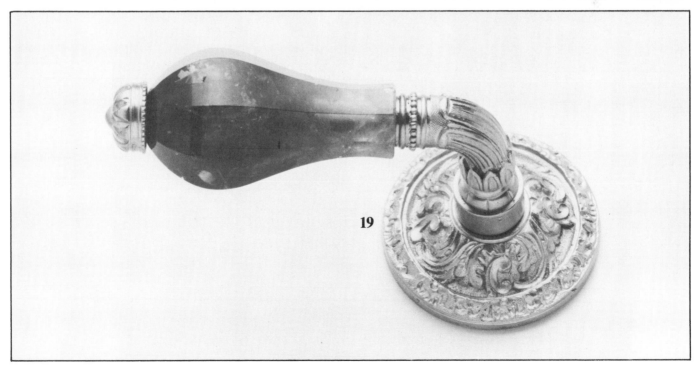

19

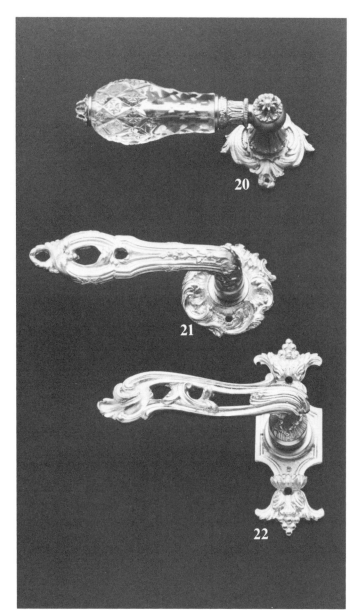

20

21

22

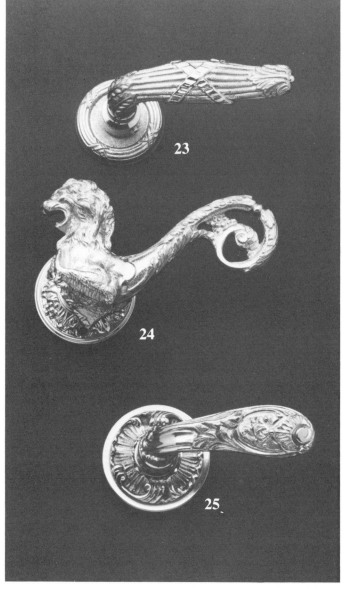

23

24

25

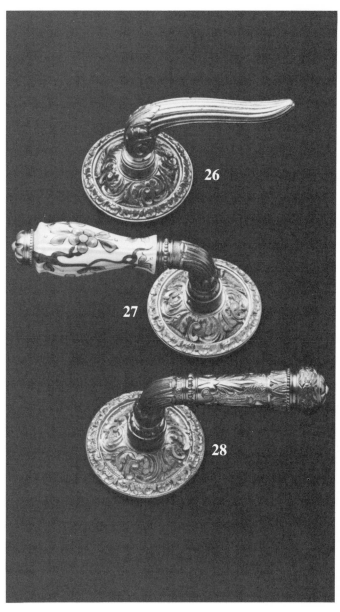

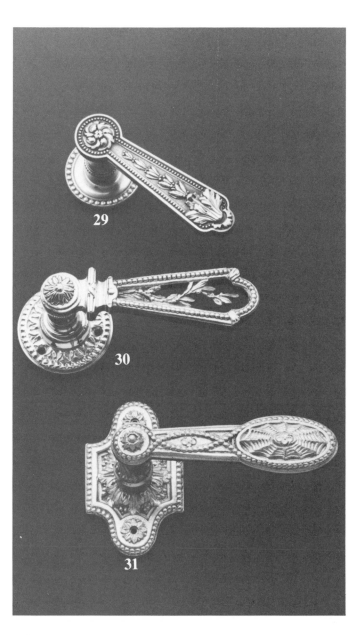

32

33

34

35

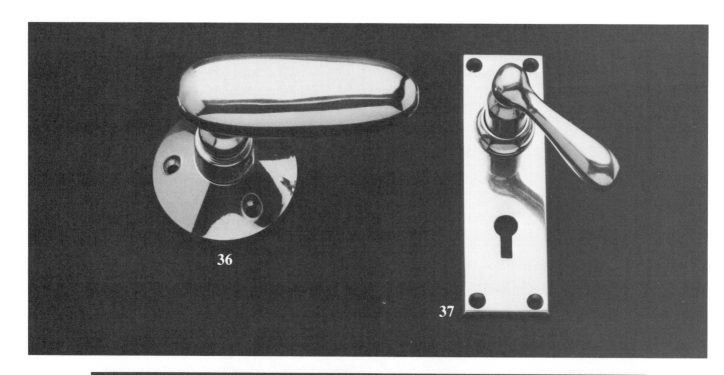

36

37

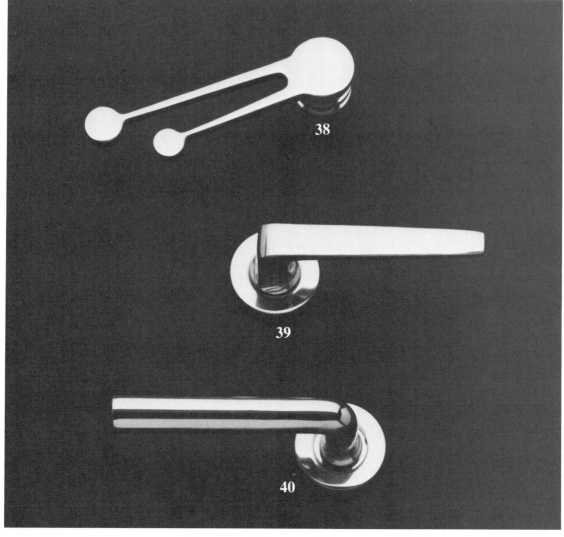

38

39

40

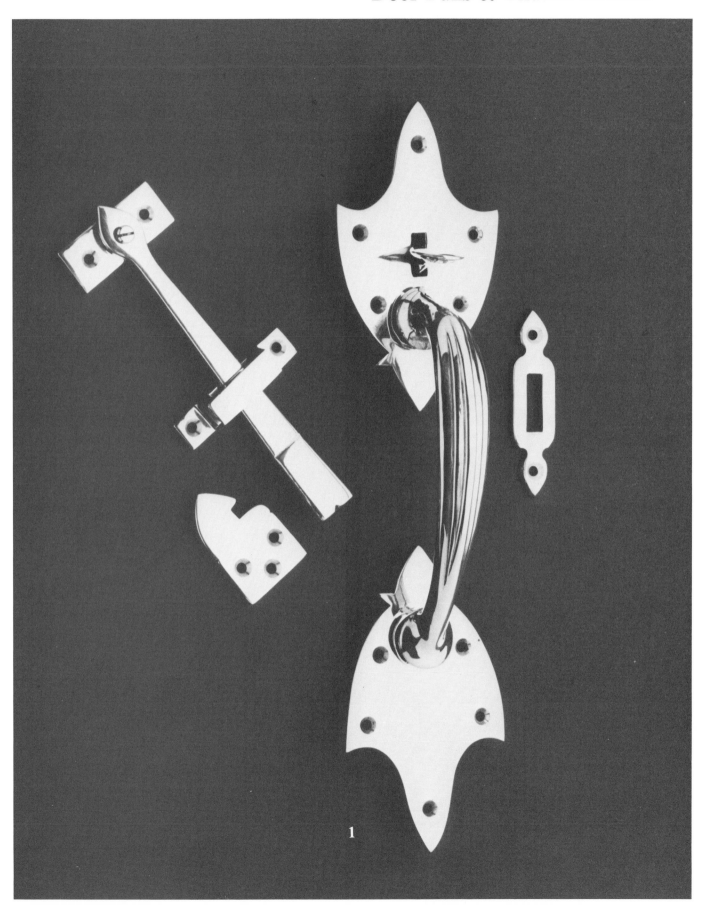

1

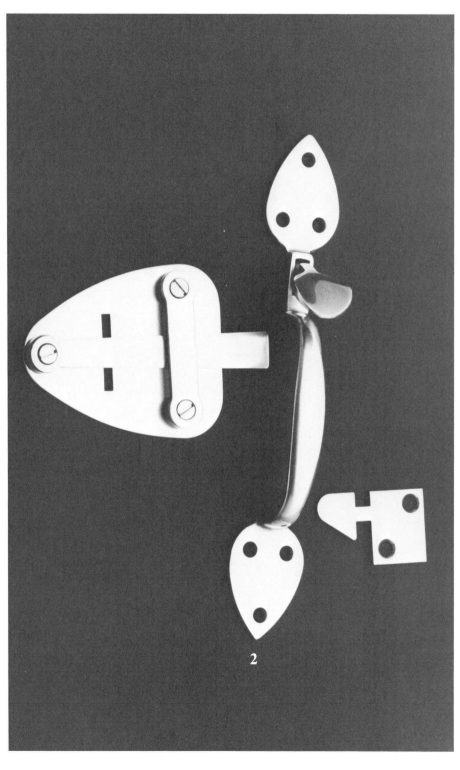

2

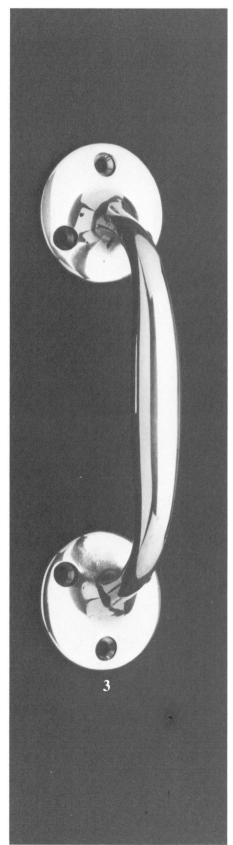

3

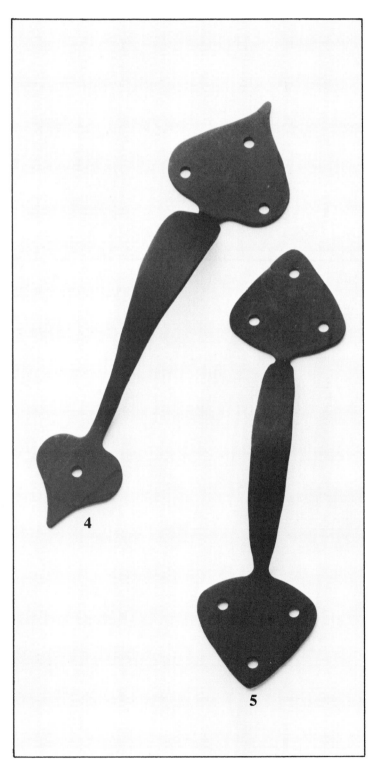

4

5

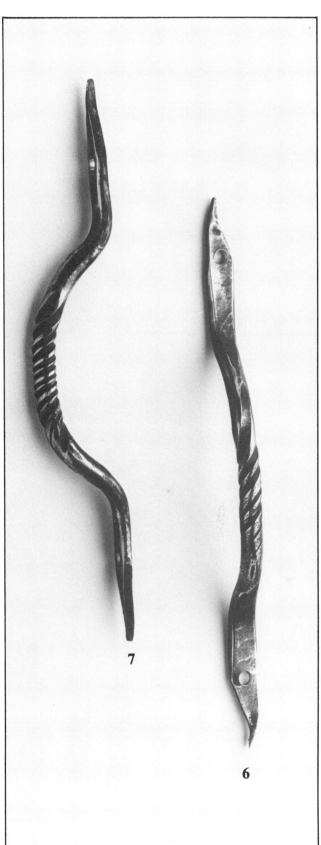

7

6

117

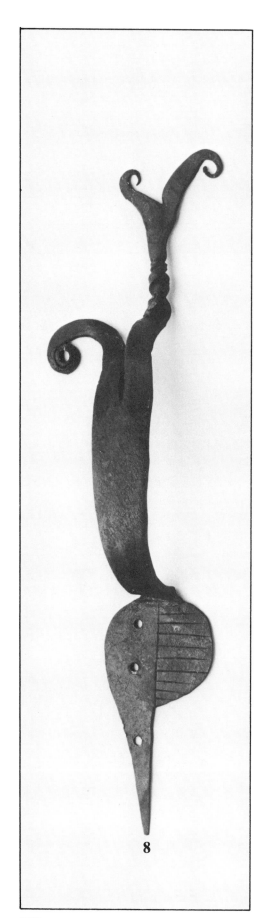

8

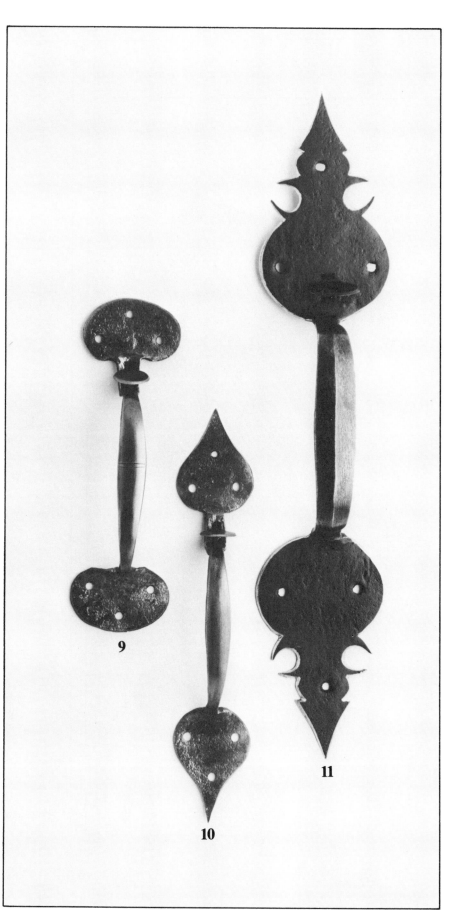

9

10

11

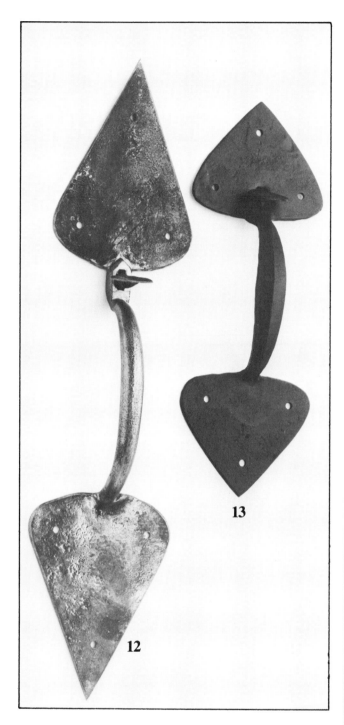

13

12

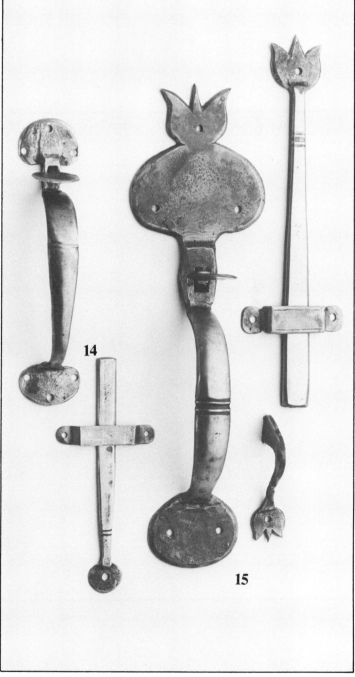

14

15

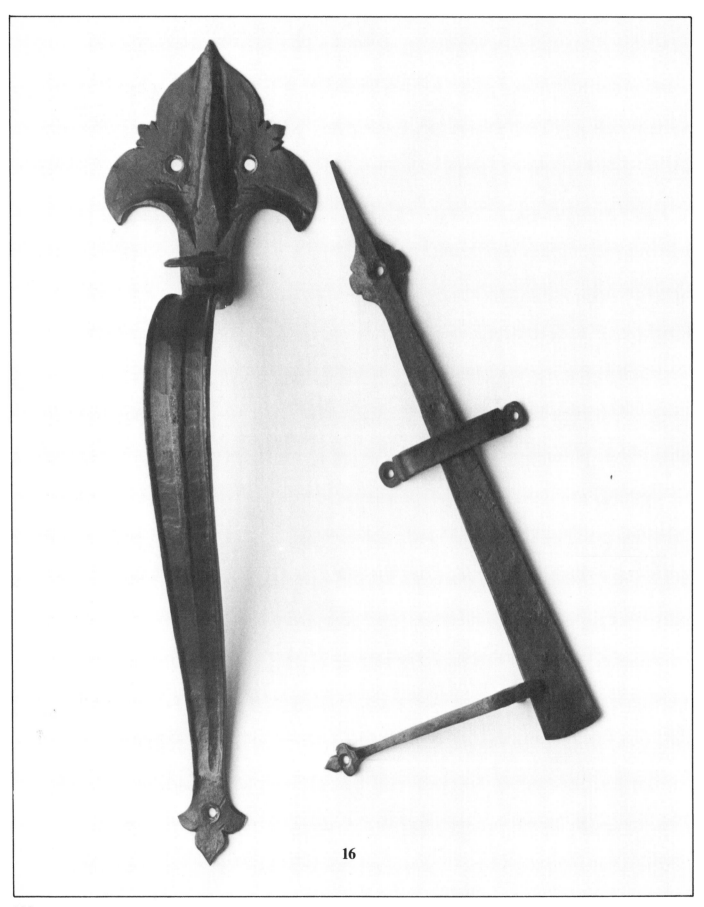

16

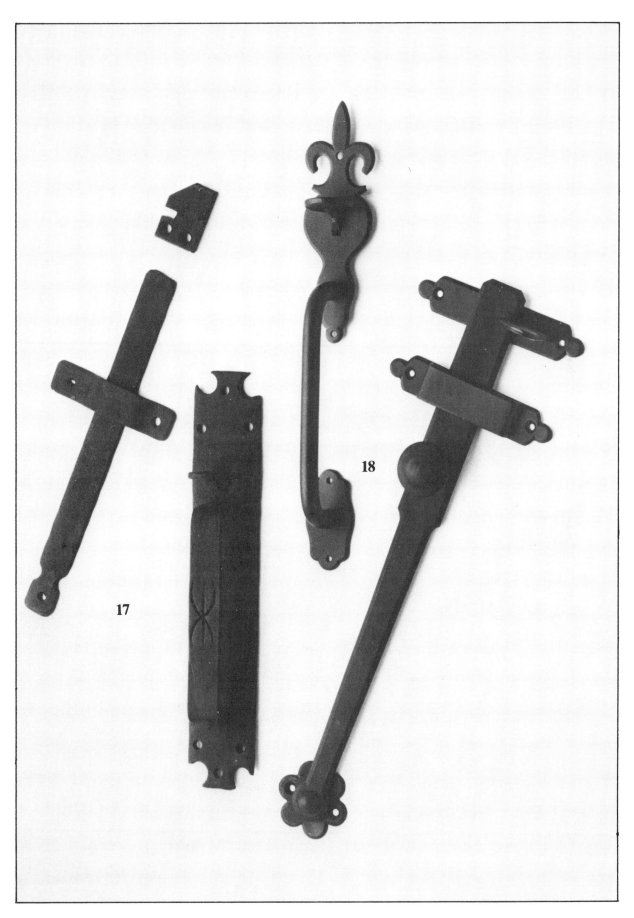

17

18

19

20

122

21

22

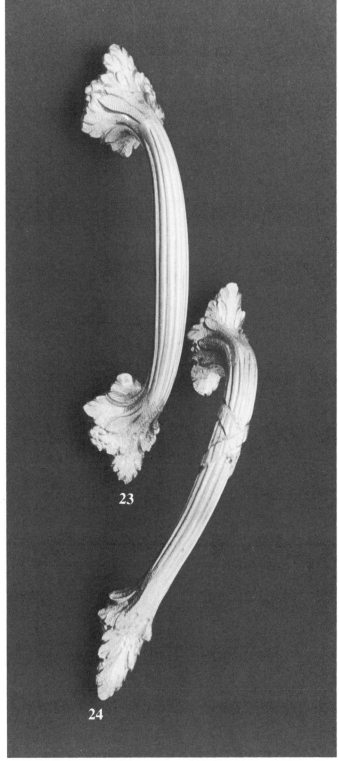

23

24

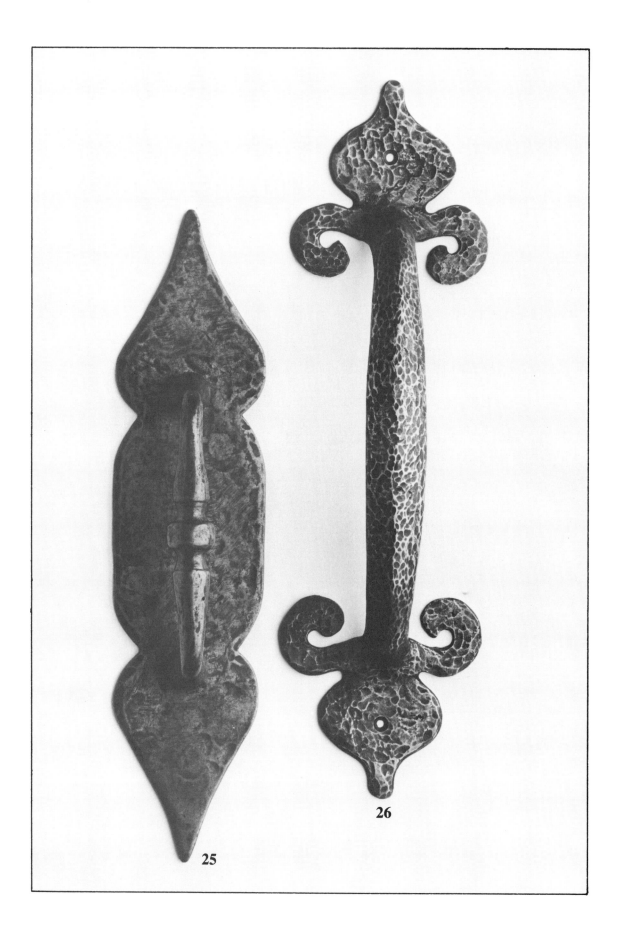

25

26

124

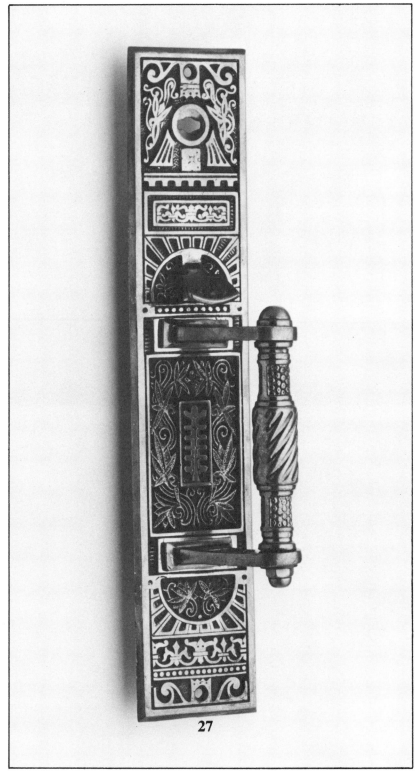

27

28

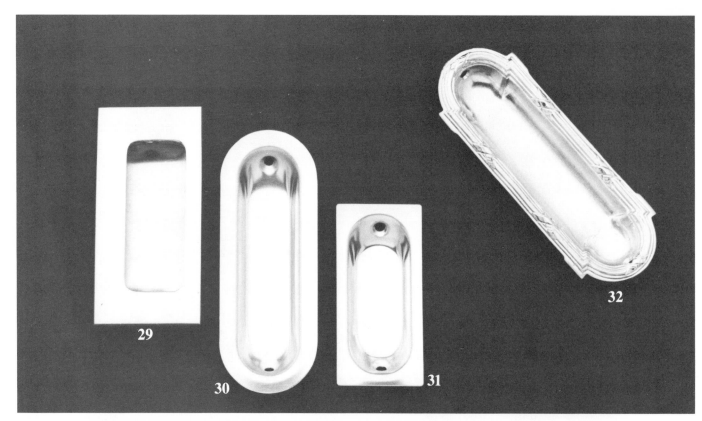

29

30

31

32

33

34

35

36

37

Sources & Specifications

Door Knobs, Plates & Roses

1 Door knob and rose (Colonial)
Baldwin
Solid, hot-forged brass
Knob diameter: 2″, rose diameter: 1¾″

2 Door knob and rose (Georgian)
Kraft Hardware
Solid brass
Knob diameter: 3½″, rose diameter: 3½″

3 Door knob and rose
Quincy
Wrought brass
Knob diameter: 2¼″, rose diameter: 3″

4 Door knob and rose
Baldwin
Solid, hot-forged brass
Knob: 2½″ × 1½″, rose diameter: 1¾″

5 Door knob and rose (Colonial)
Baldwin
Solid, hot-forged brass
Knob: 2⅜″ × 1⁷⁄₁₆″, rose diameter: 1¾″

6 Door knob and rose (Colonial)
Baldwin
Solid, hot-forged brass
Knob diameter: 2″, rose diameter: 1¾″

7–9 Door knobs
Ball and Ball
Solid brass
Diameters: 1½″, 2″, and 2″

10 Drop ring and rose (Colonial)
Baldwin
Solid, hot-forged brass
Ring length: 2¹¹⁄₁₆″, rose diameter: 2¼″

11 Drop ring and rose (Colonial)
Baldwin
Solid, hot-forged brass
Ring length: 2¹¹⁄₁₆″, rose diameter: 1¾″

12 Door knob and rose
H. Pfanstiel
Solid brass
Knob: 3″ × 1¾″, rose diameter: 2⅛″

13 Door knob and rose
H. Pfanstiel
Solid brass
Knob: 3″ × 2″, rose diameter: 3⅛″

14 Door knob and rose
H. Pfanstiel
Solid brass
Knob: 3¼″ × 1½″, rose diameter: 2⅛″

15 Door knob and rose
Sherle Wagner International
Solid brass
Knob diameter: 2¾″, rose: 3¾″ × 2½″

16 Door knob and rose
H. Pfanstiel
Solid brass
Knob: 3¾″ × 1½″, rose diameter: 2⅛″

17 Door knob and rose
Impex Associates
Stamped brass, hollow
Knob diameter: 2½″, rose diameter: 3″

18 Door knob and rose
Impex Associates
Stamped brass, hollow
Knob diameter: 3¼″, rose diameter: 3⅜″

19 Door knob and rose
Sherle Wagner International
Solid brass
Knob diameter: 2½″, rose diameter: 2¼″

20 Door knob and rose
H. Pfanstiel
Solid brass
Knob diameter: 2⅛″, rose diameter: 2⅛″

21 Door knob and rose
The Broadway Collection
Solid brass
Knob diameter: 2¹⁄₁₆″, rose diameter: 2½″

22 Door knob and rose
H. Pfanstiel
Solid brass
Knob diameter: 2¼″, rose diameter: 2⅛″

23 Door knob and rose (Louis XVI)
Baldwin
Solid, hot-forged brass
Knob: 2⁵⁄₁₆″ × 1⁷⁄₁₆″, rose diameter: 1¾″

24 Door knob and rose
Sherle Wagner International
Solid brass
Knob diameter: 2¼″, rose diameter: 2¼″

25 Door knob and rose
Sherle Wagner International
Solid brass
Knob: 2¾″ × 1¾″, rose: 3½″ × 2″

26 Door knob and rose
Baldwin
Solid, hot-forged brass
Knob diameter: 2¼″, rose diameter: 2¾″

27 Door knob and rose
Baldwin
Solid, hot-forged brass
Knob: 2⁹⁄₁₆″ × 1¹³⁄₃₂″, rose diameter: 1¾″

28 Door knob and rose
Baldwin
Solid, hot-forged brass
Knob diameter: 2¼″, rose diameter: 2¾″

29 Door knob and rose
Omnia Industries
Die-cast brass
Knob diameter: 2⅜″, rose diameter: 2″

30 Door knob and rose
Omnia Industries
Die-cast brass
Knob diameter: 2¼″, rose diameter: 2″

31 Door knob and rose
H. Pfanstiel
Solid brass
Knob diameter: 2⅛″, rose diameter: 2⅛″

32 Door knob and rose (Gothic)
Erco
Hammered cast bronze
Knob diameter: 2¼″, rose diameter: 3″

33, 34 Door knobs (Gothic)
Erco
Hammered cast bronze
Knob diameters: 2½″ and 3¼″

35 Door knob (Gothic)
Erco
Hammered cast bronze
Diameter: 2¼″

36 Door knob (Gothic)
Erco
Hammered cast bronze
Diameter: 2″

37 Door knob (Victorian)
Ritter & Son
Lost-wax cast bronze
Diameter: 2½″

38 Door knob (Victorian)
Ritter & Son
Lost-wax cast bronze
Diameter: 2″

39 Door knob (Victorian)
Ritter & Son
Lost-wax cast bronze
Diameter: 2¼″

40 Door knob (Victorian)
Ritter & Son
Lost-wax cast bronze
Diameter: 2⅛″

41 Antique school door knob
Urban Archeology
Cast brass
Length: 2½″, width: 1⅝″

42 Door knob (Victorian)
The Renovator's Supply
Cast brass
Length: 2½″, width: 1½″

43 Door knob (Victorian)
The Renovator's Supply
Cast brass
Diameter: 2″

44 Door knob (Victorian)
The Renovator's Supply
Cast brass
Diameter: 2¼″

45 Door knob (Victorian)
The Renovator's Supply
Cast brass
Diameter: 2¼″

46 Door knob (Victorian)
The Renovator's Supply
Cast brass
Diameter: 2¼″

47 Door knob (Victorian)
The Renovator's Supply
Cast brass
Diameter: 2″

48 Door knob and plate (Victorian)
Restoration Hardware
Cast brass
Knob diameter: 2¼″, plate: 2½″ × 8½″

49 Antique knob set, plates and mortise lock (Victorian)
By-Gone Days Antiques
Cast brass
Knob diameter: 2⅛″, plate: 5¼″ × 1¾″
lock scalp: 5¼″ × 1″, backset: 2⅜″

50 Antique knob set with plate, rose and mortise lock (Victorian)
By-Gone Days Antiques
Cast brass
Knob diameter: 2½″, plate: 8½″ × 2¼″,
rose diameter: 2½″, lock scalp: 8″ × 1⅛″,
backset: 3⅛″

51 Original Woolworth Building knob set, plates and mortise lock
Urban Archeology
Cast bronze
Knob diameter: 2⅛″, plate: 9½″ × 3″,
lock scalp: 7¼″ × 1⅛″, backset: 2¾″

52 Original Biltmore Hotel knob set, roses and mortise lock
Urban Archeology
Cast brass
Knob diameter: 2⅛″, rose diameter: 2¼″,
lock scalp: 6″ × 1″, backset: 2¾″

53 Antique knob set (early 20th century)
Bob Pryor Associates
Cast bronze
Knob diameter: 2⅛″, rose diameter: 2″

54 Delft door knob and gold-plated rose
Sherle Wagner International
Delft china, hand painted, and gold-plated brass
Knob diameter: 2¾″, rose diameter: 2⅜″

55 Door knob and rose
Plexacraft Metals
Porcelain knob, brass rose and shank
Knob diameter: 1¾″, rose diameter: 2″

56 Door knob and rose
Plexacraft Metals
Porcelain knob and rose, brass shank
Knob diameter: 2¼″, rose diameter: 2⅝″

57 Door knob and rose
Baldwin
White nylon-coated knob, brass rose
Knob diameter: 2¼″, rose diameter: 2¼″

58 Door knob and rose
Baldwin
Limoges porcelain knob, brass rose
Knob diameter: 2¼″, rose diameter: 2¼″

59 Door knob and rose
The Renovator's Supply
Porcelain knob, brass rose
Knob diameter: 2¼″, rose diameter: 2½″

60 Door knob and rose
Baldwin
Rosewood knob, brass rose
Knob diameter: 2″, rose diameter: 2¼″

61 Door knob and rose
Baldwin
Limoges porcelain knob with applied design, forged brass rose
Knob diameter: 2¼″, rose diameter: 2¼″

62 Door knob and rose
Baldwin
Limoges porcelain knob with applied design, forged brass rose
Knob diameter: 2¼″, rose diameter: 2¼″

63 Door knob and rose
Omnia Industries
Porcelain knob with applied design, solid brass rose
Knob diameter: 2½″, rose diameter: 2¾″

64 Door knob and rose
Omnia Industries
Porcelain knob and rose, applied design
Knob diameter: 2⅜″, rose diameter: 2¾″

65 Door knob and rose
Ball and Ball
Glass knob, brass rose
Knob diameter: 2″, rose diameter: 2¼″

66 Door knob set
Restoration Hardware
Glass knob, brass shank, steel spindle
Diameter: 2″

67 Door knob and rose
The Broadway Collection
Lead crystal knob, brass rose
Knob diameter: 2¼″, rose diameter: 2½″

68 Door knob and rose
Period Furniture Hardware
Cut crystal knob, brass rose
Knob diameter: 2″, rose diameter: 2¼″

69 Door knob set
The Merit Brass Collection
Cast brass
Length: 2⅞″, projection: 2¼″

70 Drop ring and plate
The Merit Brass Collection
Cast brass
Plate: 4″ × 1⅜″

71 Drop "D" ring knob
The Merit Brass Collection
Cast brass
Diameter: 2½″

72 Door knob and rose
Omnia Industries
Solid brass
Knob diameter: 2″, rose diameter: 3⅛″

73 Door knob and rose
Baldwin
Solid, hot-forged brass
Knob diameter: 2″, rose diameter: 1¾″

74 Door knob and rose
Baldwin
Solid, hot-forged brass
Knob diameter: 2¼″, rose diameter: 1¾″

75 Door knob and rose
Baldwin
Solid, hot-forged brass
Knob diameter: 2″, rose diameter: 2⅛″

76 Door knob and rose
Sherle Wagner International
Brushed chrome
Knob diameter: 3″, rose diameter: 1¾″

77 Door knob and rose
Sherle Wagner International
Polished chrome
Overall knob size: 1⅞″ × 1⅞″ × 1¼″,
rose: 3½″ × 2⅜″

78 Door knob and rose
Sherle Wagner International
Brushed chrome and malachite
Knob diameter: 2⅝″, rose diameter: 2⅝″

79 Door knob and rose
Kraft Hardware
Lucite knob, mirrored rose
Knob diameter: 2½″, rose diameter: 3″

80 Door knob and rose
Kraft Hardware
Lucite knob, mirrored rose
Knob diameter: 2″, rose diameter: 3″

81 Door knob and rose
Baldwin
Clear acrylic knob, brass rose
Knob diameter: 2″, rose diameter: 2¼″

82 Door knob and rose
Kraft Hardware
Cast brass
Knob length: 2¾″, rose diameter: 2¼″

83–85 Schlage cylinder lock and knob sets
Courtesy of **Simon's Hardware**

86 Door knob and rose
Quincy
Wrought brass
Knob diameter: 2¼″, rose diameter: 3″

87 Door knob
Baldwin
Wrought brass
Diameter: 2″

88 Door knob and rose
Quincy
Wrought brass
Knob diameter: 2″, rose diameter: 2¼″

89 Door knob and plate
Quincy
Wrought brass
Knob diameter: 2¼″, plate: 2″ × 10″

90 Door knob and plate
The Merit Brass Collection
Cast brass
Plate: 4″ × 1⅜″

91 Door knob and plate
Quincy
Wrought brass
Knob diameter: 2¼″, plate: 7″

92 Door knob plate
Sherle Wagner International
Solid brass
Length: 12″, width: 2″

93 Door knob plate
H. Pfanstiel
Solid brass
Length: 8″, width: 2″

94 Door knob plate
Sherle Wagner International
Solid brass
Length: 9″, width: 1½″

95 Door knob plate
Sherle Wagner International
Solid brass
Length: 7¼″, width: 1½″

96 Door knob plate (Victorian)
The Renovator's Supply
Cast brass
Length: 7¾″, width: 2¾″

97 Door knob plate (Victorian)
The Renovator's Supply
Cast brass
Length: 6⅝″, width: 1¾″

98 Door knob plate (Victorian)
The Renovator's Supply
Cast brass
Length: 5⅞″, width: 1¾″

99 Door knob plate (Victorian)
The Renovator's Supply
Cast brass
Length: 7³⁄₈″, width: 2⁵⁄₁₆″

100 Door knob plate
Erco
Hammered cast bronze
Length: 5½″, width: 1⅜″

101 Door knob plate
Erco
Hammered cast bronze
Length: 6½″, width: 2″

102 Door knob plate
Erco
Hammered cast bronze
Length: 4¼″, width: 1⅞″

103 Door knob plate (Victorian)
Ritter & Son
Lost-wax cast bronze
Length: 8½″, width: 2¾″

104 Door knob plate (Victorian)
Ritter & Son
Lost-wax cast bronze
Length: 4⅞″, width: 1½″

105 Door knob plate (Victorian)
Ritter & Son
Lost-wax cast bronze
Length: 8″, width: 1¾″

106 Door knob plate (Victorian)
The Renovator's Supply
Cast brass
Length: 5¼″, width: 1⅝″

107 Door knob plate
Baldwin
Wrought brass
Length: 10″, width: 3″

108 Door knob plate
Baldwin
Wrought brass
Length: 7¼″, width: 2¼″

109 Door knob plate
Baldwin
Wrought brass
Length: 7¼″, width: 2¼″

110 Door knob rose
Baldwin
Solid, hot-forged brass
Diameter: 1¾″

111 Door knob rose
Baldwin
Solid, hot-forged brass
Diameter: 1¾″

112 Door knob rose
Baldwin
Solid, hot-forged brass
Diameter: 2¼″

113 Door knob rose
The Broadway Collection
Solid brass
Diameter: 2½″

114 Door knob rose (Victorian)
Ritter & Son
Lost-wax cast bronze
Diameter: 2³⁄₁₆″

115 Door knob rose (Victorian)
Ritter & Son
Lost-wax cast bronze
Diameter: 2″

116 Door knob rose (Victorian)
Ritter & Son
Lost-wax cast bronze
Diameter: 2″

117 Door knob rose (Victorian)
The Renovator's Supply
Cast brass
Diameter: 2″

118 Door knob rose (Victorian)
Ritter & Son
Lost-wax cast bronze
Diameter: 2¼″

119 Door knob rose
H. Pfanstiel
Cast brass
Diameter: 2″

120 Door knob rose
H. Pfanstiel
Cast brass
Diameter: 3¼″

121 Door knob rose
H. Pfanstiel
Cast brass
Diameter: 2½″

122 Door knob rose
H. Pfanstiel
Cast brass
Diameter: 3¼″

Lever Door Handles

1 Lever door handle and rose
Baldwin
Solid, hot-forged brass
Lever length: 4″, rose diameter: 2¼″

2 Lever door handle and rose
Baldwin
Solid, hot-forged brass
Lever length: 4″, rose diameter: 2¼″

3 Lever door handle and rose
H. Pfanstiel
Solid brass
Lever length: 4″, rose diameter: 2⅛″

4 Lever door handle and rose
Omnia Industries
Solid brass
Lever length: 3⅝″, rose: 2³/₁₆″ × 1⅜″

5 Lever door handle and rose
H. Pfanstiel
Solid brass
Lever length: 4¼″, rose diameter: 2⅛″

6 Lever door handle and rose
H. Pfanstiel
Solid brass
Lever length: 4½″, rose diameter: 2⅛″

7 Lever door handle and rose
Baldwin
Solid, hot-forged brass
Lever length: 3½″, rose diameter: 1¾″

8 Lever door handle and rose
Baldwin
Solid, hot-forged brass
Lever length: 3⅝″, rose diameter: 1¾″

9 Lever door handle and rose
Baldwin
Solid, hot-forged brass
Lever length: 3⅜″, rose diameter: 1¾″

10 Lever door handle and rose
H. Pfanstiel
Solid brass
Lever length: 4″, rose diameter: 2⅛″

11 Lever door handle and rose
The Broadway Collection
Solid brass
Lever length: 4⅛″, rose diameter: 2½″

12 Lever door handle and backplate
The Broadway Collection
Solid brass
Lever length: 4¹⁵/₁₆″, backplate: 1¹⁵/₁₆″ × 11¼″

13 Lever door handle and rose
Omnia Industries
Solid brass
Lever length: 3¾″, rose diameter: 1¾″

14 Lever door handle and rose
The Broadway Collection
Solid brass
Lever length: 3¼″, rose diameter: 2″

15 Lever door handle and rose
Omnia Industries
Solid brass
Lever length: 3¾″, rose diameter: 1⅝″

16 Lever door handle and rose
Baldwin
Limoges porcelain and solid, hot-forged brass
Lever length: 4″, rose diameter: 1¾″

17 Lever door handle and rose
Omnia Industries
Porcelain and solid brass
Lever length: 4½″, rose diameter: 3⅜″

18 Lever door handle and rose
Baldwin
Limoges porcelain, applied design, and forged brass
Lever length: 4″, rose diameter: 1¾″

19 Lever door handle and rose
Sherle Wagner International
Amethyst and gold-plated brass
Lever length: 4½″, rose diameter: 2¾″

20 Lever door handle and rose
Sherle Wagner International
Cut crystal and solid brass
Lever length: 4¾″, rose: 2½″ × 2¼″

21 Lever door handle and rose
Sherle Wagner International
Solid brass with brushed chrome finish
Lever length: 4¾″, rose diameter: 2¼″

22 Lever door handle and rose
Sherle Wagner International
Solid brass with brushed chrome finish
Lever length: 4½″, rose: 4½″ × 1½″

23 Lever door handle and rose
Sherle Wagner International
Solid brass
Lever length: 3¾″, rose diameter: 1⅞″

24 Lever door handle and rose
H. Pfanstiel
Solid brass
Lever length: 4½″, rose diameter: 2⅛″

25 Lever door handle and rose
H. Pfanstiel
Solid brass
Lever length: 3¼″, rose diameter: 2⅛″

26 Lever door handle and rose
Sherle Wagner International
Antique gold-plated brass
Lever length: 4″, rose diameter: 2¾″

27 Lever door handle and rose
Sherle Wagner International
Porcelain, hand painted, and solid brass
Lever length: 4½″, rose diameter: 2¾″

28 Lever door handle and rose
Sherle Wagner International
Solid brass
Lever length: 4¼″, rose diameter: 2¾″

29 Lever door handle and rose
Baldwin
Solid, hot-forged brass
Lever length: 3⅝″, rose diameter: 1¾″

30 Lever door handle and rose
H. Pfanstiel
Solid brass
Lever length: 4½″, rose diameter: 2⅛″

31 Lever door handle
Sherle Wagner International
Solid brass
Lever length: 4½″, rose: 3⅜″ × 2″

32 Lever door handle and rose
Erco
Hammered cast bronze
Lever length: 3¾″, rose: 2⅝″ × 2¼″

33 Lever door handle and rose
Erco
Hammered cast bronze
Lever length: 3½″, rose diameter: 3⅛″

34 Lever door handle and rose
Erco
Hammered cast bronze
Lever length: 4¼″, rose: 2½″ × 2¼″

35 Antique dummy lever door handle and backplate
Urban Archeology
Cast brass
Lever length: 4½″, backplate: 13″ × 5¼″

36 Lever door handle and rose
H. Pfanstiel
Solid brass
Lever length: 3¼″, rose diameter: 2⅛″

37 Lever door handle and backplate
The Merit Brass Collection
Cast brass
Lever length: 2⅝″, backplate: 4″ × 1⅜″

38 Lever door handle
Sherle Wagner International
Polished chrome
Length: 5¼″

39 Lever door handle and rose
Omnia Industries
Solid brass
Lever length: 3⅞″, rose diameter: 1¾″

40 Lever door handle and rose
Omnia Industries
Solid brass
Lever length: 4¼″, rose diameter: 1¾″

Door Pulls & Thumb Latches

1 Thumb latch door pull set
Period Furniture Hardware
Solid brass
Pull overall length and width: 12½″ × 3½″, projection: 2½″
projection: 2½″

2 Thumb latch door pull (Early American)
Baldwin
Solid, hot-forged brass
Pull overall length: 8½″, projection: 1⅜″

3 Door pull
The Merit Brass Collection
Cast brass
Overall length: 8″

4 Heart door pull (Colonial)
Acorn
Steel, black finish
Overall length: 8½″

5 Spade door pull (Colonial)
Acorn
Steel, black finish
Overall length: 7½″

6 Door pull
Barry Berman, Valley Forgeworks, Ltd.
Hand-forged brass
Overall length: 9″

7 Door pull
Barry Berman, Valley Forgeworks, Ltd.
Hand-forged copper
Overall length: 9″

8 Door pull
Craig Kaviar, Kaviar Forge
Hand-forged iron
Overall length and width: 12¼″ × 3½″

9 Bean thumb latch door pull (Colonial)
Mark E. Rocheford, Hammerworks
Hand-forged iron
Overall length and width: 7½″ × 2¼″

10 Onion thumb latch door pull (Colonial)
Mark E. Rocheford, Hammerworks
Hand-forged iron
Overall length and width: 9¼″ × 1¾″

11 Pineapple thumb latch door pull
Mark E. Rocheford, Hammerworks
Hand-forged iron
Overall length and width: 15″ × 3″

12 Spade thumb latch door pull (Colonial)
Mark E. Rocheford, Hammerworks
Hand-forged iron
Overall length and width: 17½″ × 4″

13 Arrow thumb latch door pull (Colonial)
Mark E. Rocheford, Hammerworks
Hand-forged iron
Overall length and width: 11″ × 4″

14 Bean thumb latch door pull set (Colonial)
Lance Cloutier, The Ram's Head Forge
Hand-forged iron
Pull overall length and width: 7″ × 1½″

15 Pineapple thumb latch door pull set
Lance Cloutier, The Ram's Head Forge
Hand-forged iron
Pull overall length and width: 12″ × 3¾″

16 Thumb latch door pull set
Mark E. Bokenkamp, Bokenkamp's Forge
Hand-forged iron
Pull overall length and width: 13″ × 3½″

17 Norfolk thumb latch door pull set
Robert H. Klar, Salmon Falls Forge
Hand-forged iron
Pull overall length and width: 9″ × 1½″

18 Thumb latch door pull set
Baldwin
Forged iron
Pull overall length: 10″, projection: 1⅞″

19 Thumb latch door pull (Gothic)
Erco
Hammered cast bronze
Overall length and width: 13¾″ × 4¾″, projection: 2⅛″

20 Thumb latch door pull (Gothic)
Erco
Hammered cast bronze
Overall length and width: 17″ × 3½″, projection: 2″

21 Door pull
Erco
Hammered cast bronze
Boring: 5½″

22 Ram's Head door pull
Ronald H. Kass, Ronald H. Kass Forge
Hand-forged iron
Overall length: 7″

23 Door pull
Sherle Wagner International
Cast brass
Overall length: 4¾″

24 Door pull
Sherle Wagner International
Cast brass
Overall length: 5″

25 Door pull (Gothic)
Erco
Hammered cast bronze
Overall length and width: 12⅞″ × 3″

26 Door pull (Gothic)
Erco
Hammered cast bronze
Overall length and width: 14¼″ × 4″

27 Antique offset door pull thumb latch (Victorian)
Urban Archeology
Cast bronze
Overall length and width: 13″ × 2½″, projection: 2½″

28 Antique cup escutcheon door pulls
By-Gone Days Antiques
Solid brass
Overall length and width: 15″ × 3¼″

29 Flush door pull
The Merit Brass Collection
Cast brass
Overall length and width: 3½″ × 1¾″, mortise depth: ½″

30 Flush door pull
Stanley Hardware
Stamped brass
Overall length and width: 4″ × 1½″, mortise depth: ½″

31 Flush door pull
Stanley Hardware
Stamped brass
Overall length and width: 2¾″ × 1¹⁵⁄₁₆″, mortise depth: ¹¹⁄₃₂″

32 Flush door pull
Sherle Wagner International
Solid brass
Overall length and width: 4⅜″ × 1½″

33–35 Mirror door edge pull
Kraft Hardware
Chrome
Lengths: 2″, 4″, and 6″

36 Door pull
Kraft Hardware
Nylon
Boring: 10½″, diameter: 1⅜″

37 Offset door pull
Kraft Hardware
Nylon
Boring: 10½″, diameter: 1⅜″

4

Latches & Catches

THE distinction between a latch and a catch is not always clear. Webster defines a catch as "a device (as a rod, bar, or hook) for temporarily holding immovable an otherwise moving or movable mechanism: as (1) a *latch* [our italics] especially on a door, window, or trunk," and "a device that holds something in place by entering a notch or cavity; specifically: the *catch* that holds a door or gate when closed even if not bolted." Defining one word by using the other does nothing to alleviate the confusion.

There is some agreement, however, with respect to two groups of latches and catches. Any device that does its securing by means of a horizontal bar that pivots down to bridge the gap between a door and a jamb or between two doors to engage a keeper on the other side—as does a simple H latch or the business end of a thumblatch—is a latch. And a roller, ball, magnetic, or friction catch—any holding device, in other words, that doesn't employ any sort of bolt, bar, rod, or hook—is always a catch. Everything else, it seems, could be decided with a coin toss.

Some Latch & Catch Terms

Ball Catch.   A catch whose strike holds a communicating projection or finger by means of the pressure exerted by one or two spring-loaded balls.

Cupboard Turn.   A simple latch of metal or wood consisting of a knob connected to a rod that communicates on the other side of a cupboard door with a rotating finger which, when turned down on the inside, secures the door.

Dutch Door Quadrant.   A quadrant-shaped latch fastened to the bottom leaf of a Dutch door that pivots around the point where the quadrant's radii converge to engage a strike attached to the upper door leaf so as to fasten the two doors.

Friction Catch.   A catch whose strike holds a communicating projection or finger by means of the pressure applied by the spreading apart of its flexible sides.

Magnetic Catch.   A catch with a magnetic strike that holds a communicating plate made of a material that is attracted by a magnet.

Magnetic Push Catch.   A magnetic catch with an inward and outward moving strike that retracts and projects by means of springs on successive applications of pressure.

Roller Catch.   A catch whose strike holds a communicating projection or finger by means of pressure applied by one or two spring-loaded rollers.

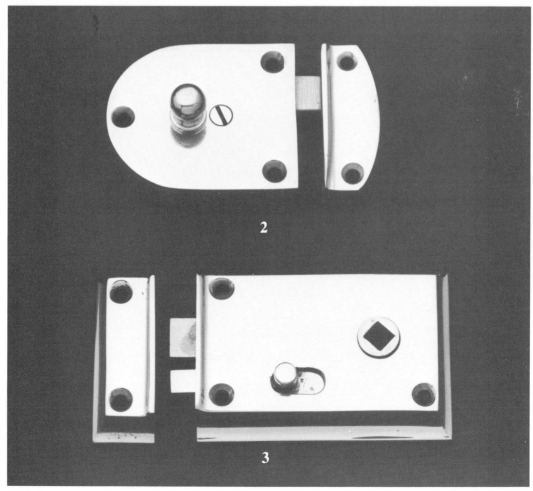

1

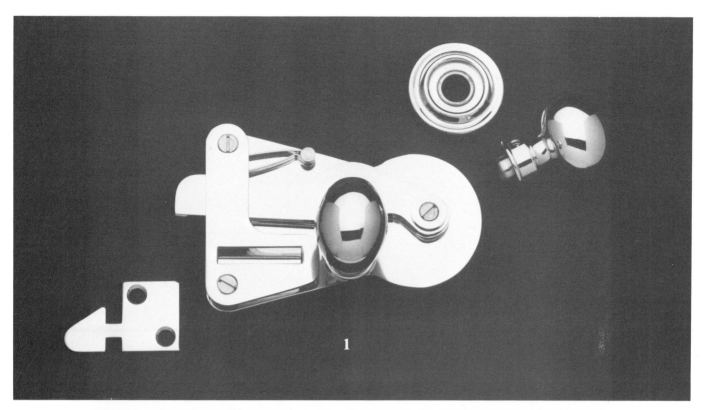

2

3

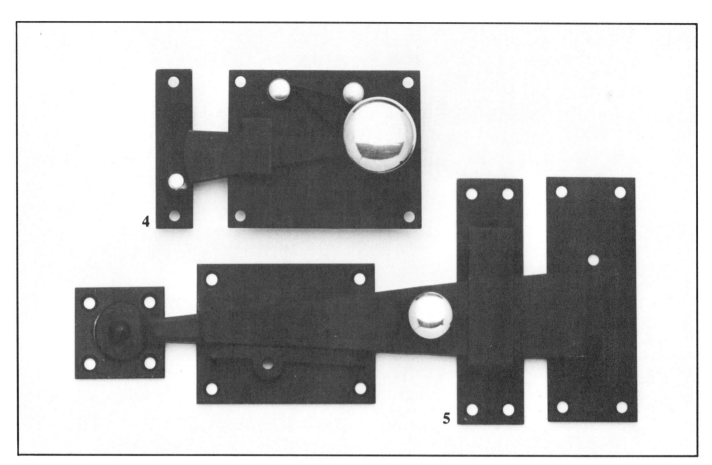

4

5

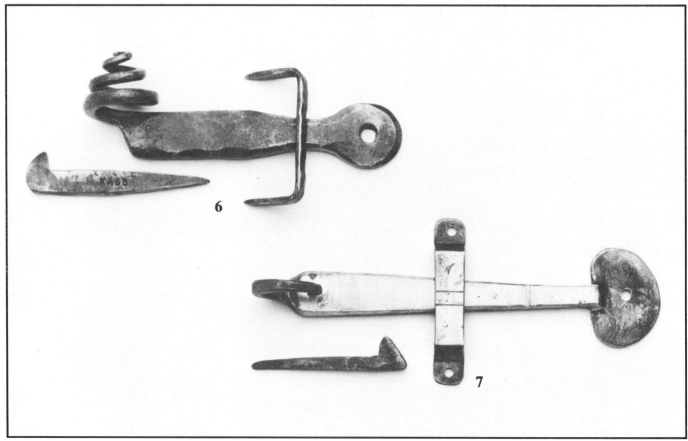

6

7

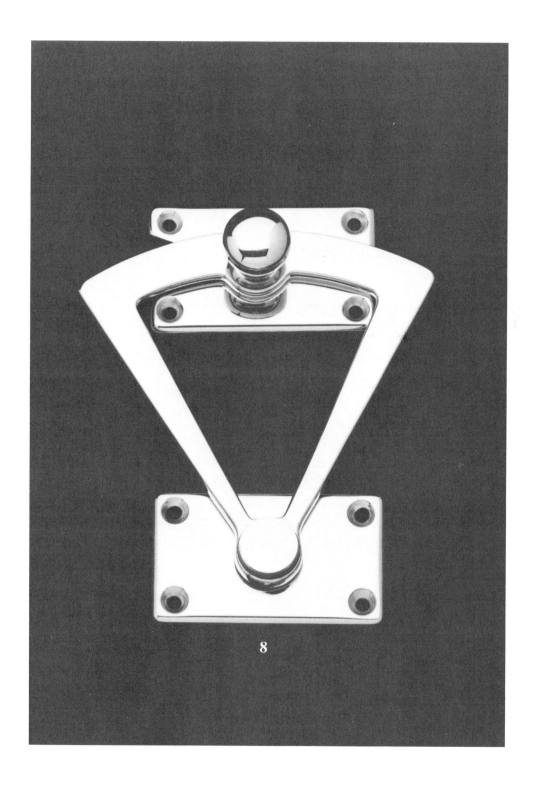

8

Cabinet & Cupboard Latches & Catches

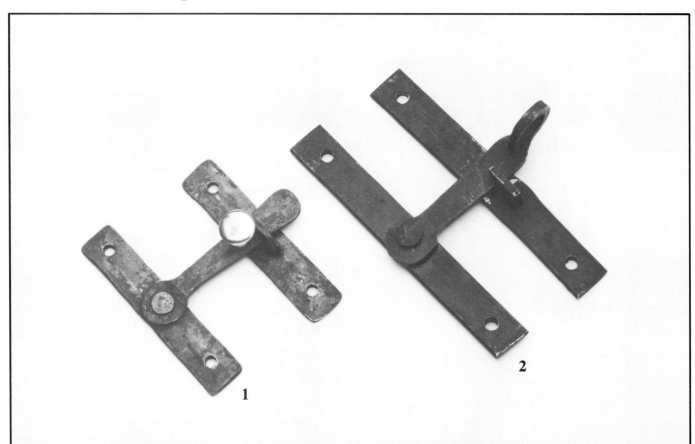

1

2

3

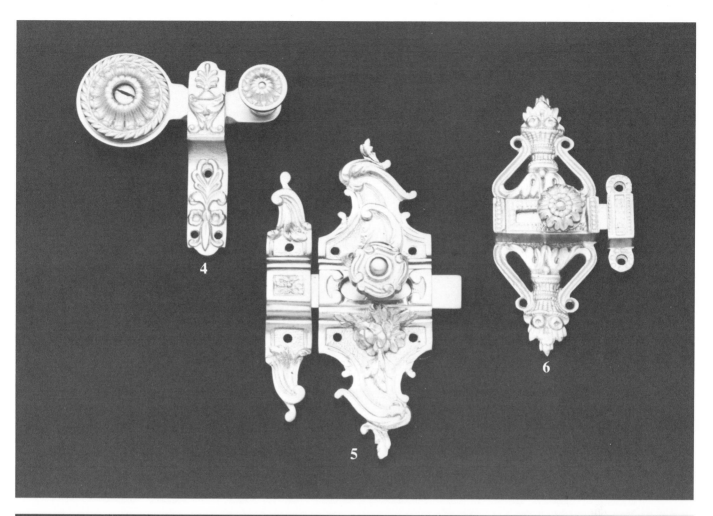

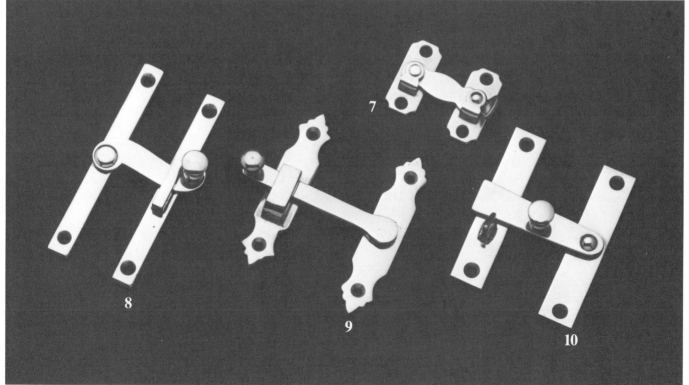

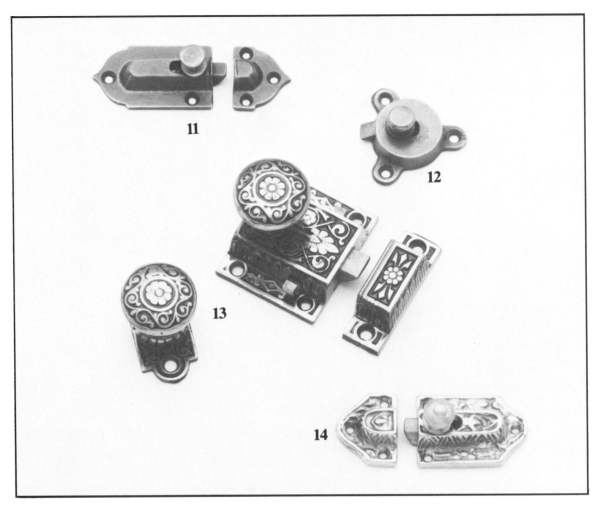

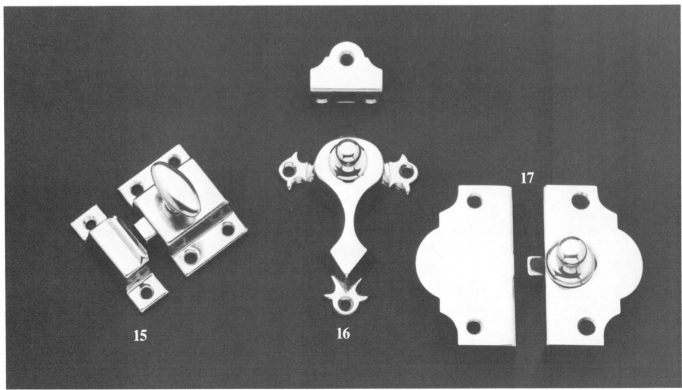

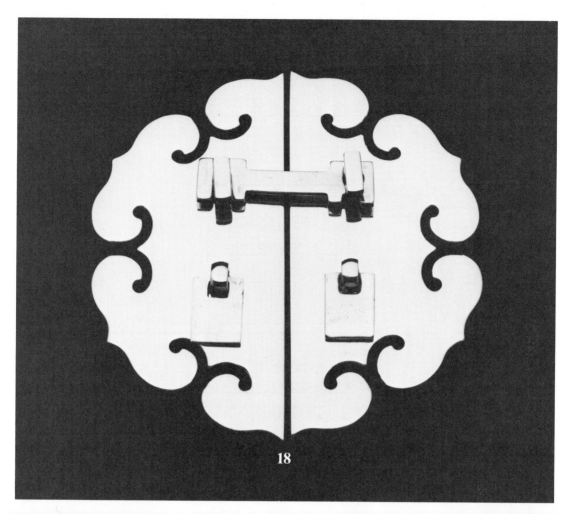

18

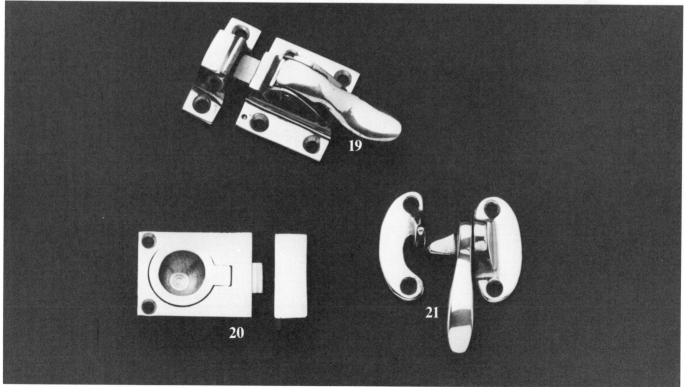

19

20

21

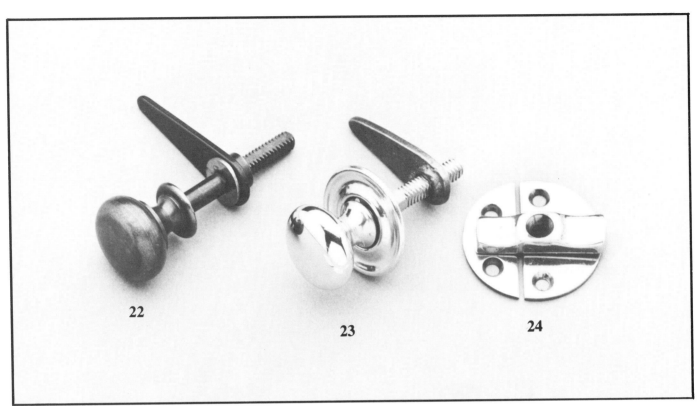

22   23   24

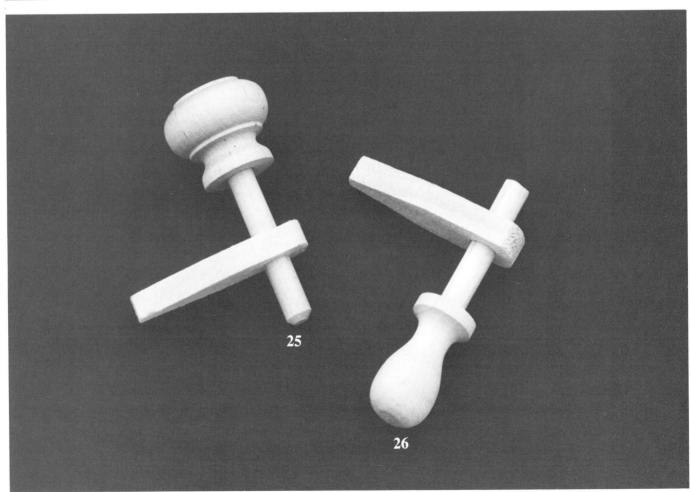

25   26

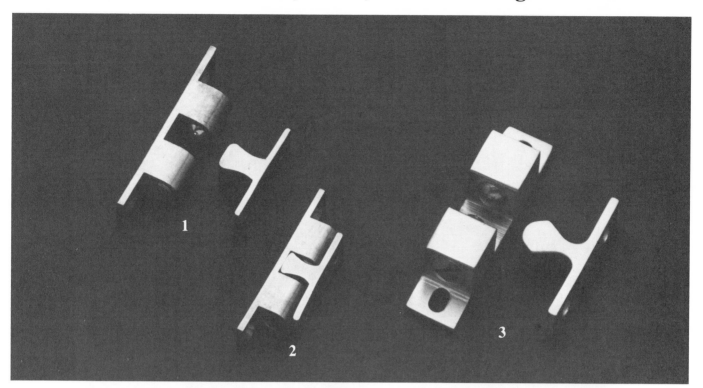

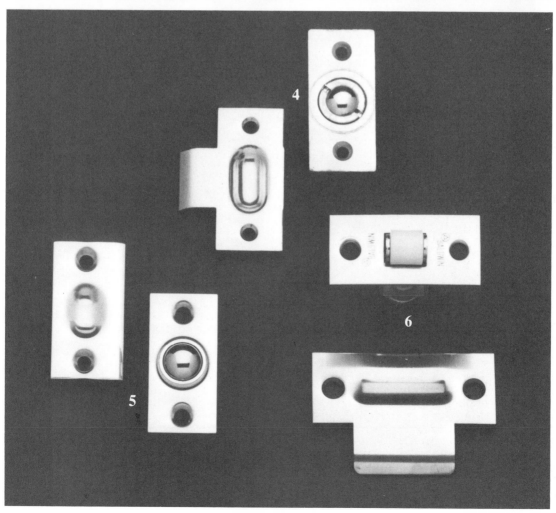

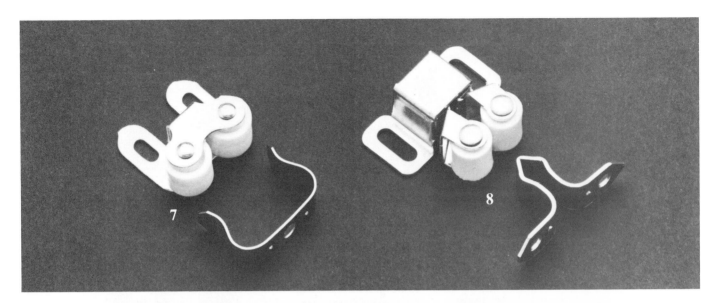

7

8

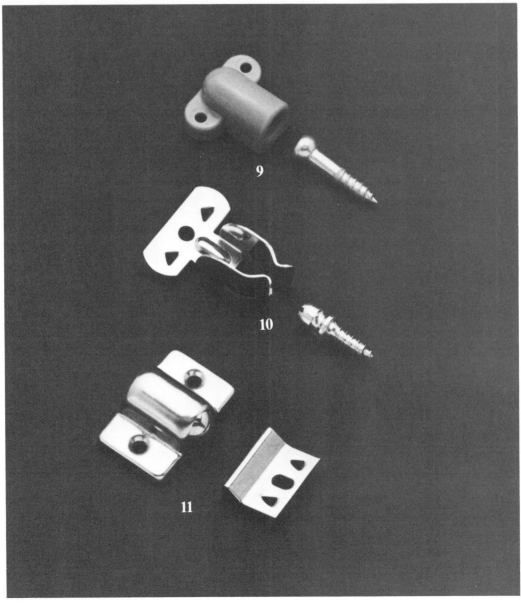

9

10

11

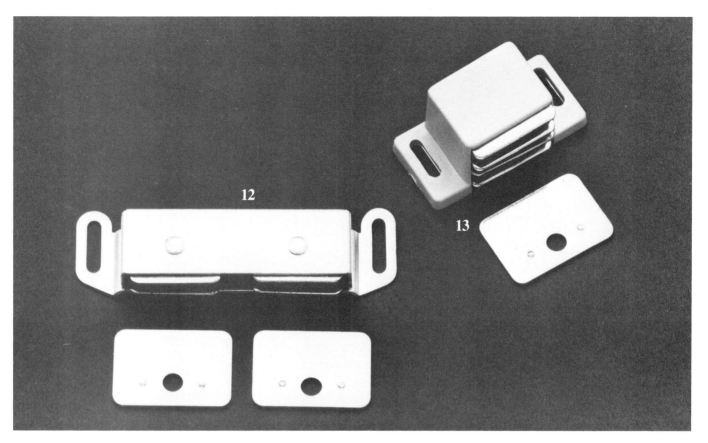

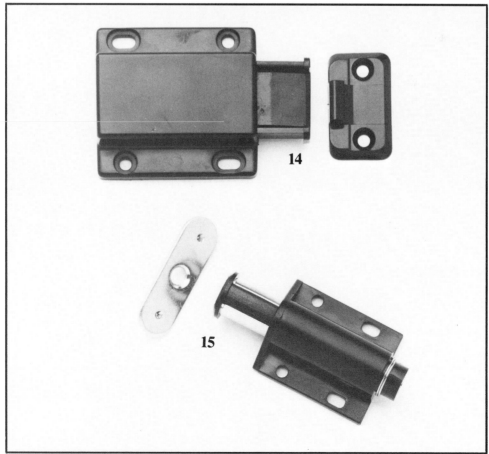

Sources & Specifications

Door Latches & Catches

1 Passage door latch and trim
Baldwin
Solid, hot-forged brass
Overall latch length and width: 4¾″ × 3¼″,
backset: 2½″

2 Rim door latch
The Merit Brass Collection
Cast brass
Overall length and width: 2½″ × 2⅛″

3 Rim door latch
The Merit Brass Collection
Cast brass
Overall length and width: 3½″ × 2⅜″,
backset: 2½″

4 Cupboard latch
Ball and Ball
Forged iron and brass
Overall length and width: 3½″ × 2½″,
knob diameter: 1¼″

5 Door latch
**Peter A. Renzetti, The Arden Forge
Company**
Hand-forged iron
Overall length and width: 9½″ × 4″, knob
diameter: ¾″

6 Pig-tail door latch
Ronald H. Kass, Ronald H. Kass Forge
Hand-forged iron
Overall length: 2½″

7 Bean door latch
Lance Cloutier, The Ram's Head Forge
Hand-forged iron
Overall length: 6½″

8 Dutch door quadrant
Baldwin
Solid, hot-forged brass
Overall length and width: 4¾″ × 4″, base:
2½″ × 1½″

Cabinet & Cupboard Latches & Catches

1 H bar latch
**Steve Kayne, Steve Kayne Hand Forged
Hardware**
Hand-forged iron and brass
Plate: 3⅛″, bar: 3″

2 H bar latch
Richard C. Swenson, Swenson's Forge
Hand-forged iron
Plate: 4½″, bar: 3⅜″

3 Double wardrobe latch
Bob Patrick, Big Anvil Forge
Hand-forged iron
Overall length and width: 6½″ × 5½″

4 Cabinet latch
Sherle Wagner International
Gold-plated brass
Overall length and width: 3″ × 3″

5 Cabinet latch
Sherle Wagner International
Gold-plated brass
Overall length and width: 5″ × 2½″

6 Cabinet latch
Sherle Wagner International
Gold-plated brass
Overall length and width: 4″ × 2″

7 H bar latch
Stanley Hardware
Steel, brass finish
Plate: 1½″, bar: 1¾″

8 H bar latch
Period Furniture Hardware
Cast brass
Plate: 4″, bar: 2⅛″

9 H bar latch
Kraft Hardware
Solid brass
Plate: 3¼″, bar: 3¼″

10 H bar latch
Paxton
Solid brass
Plate: 3″, bar: 2⅝″

11 Spring cabinet latch
Horton Brasses
Cast brass
Overall: 3⅛″ × 1¼″

12 Tip table catch
Horton Brasses
Solid brass
Diameter: 1¼″

13 Antique passage door catch
(Victorian)
Urban Archeology
Cast bronze
Catch overall: 3″ × 2¼″, knob diameters:
1¼″

14 Spring cabinet latch (Victorian)
The Renovator's Supply
Cast brass
Overall: 3¼″ × 1½″

15 Cupboard catch
Stanley Hardware
Steel, brass finish
Overall: 1¾″ × 1¾″

16 Tilt table catch
Ball and Ball
Solid brass
Overall: 2⅞″ × 2¼″

17 Cabinet catch
Ball and Ball
Solid brass
Overall: 3″ × 2½″

18 Cabinet latch (Oriental)
Period Furniture Hardware
Solid brass
Diameter: 6″

19 Offset cupboard catch
The Merit Brass Collection
Cast brass
Case and strike overall: 1⅞″ × 1½″, strike
offset: ⅜″

20 Ring pull catch
The Merit Brass Collection
Cast brass
Case overall: 2″ × 1¼″, mortise depth:
¹¹⁄₁₆″

21 Cabinet catch
The Merit Brass Collection
Cast brass
Overall length: 2½″

22 Cupboard turn
Horton Brasses
Solid brass, antique finish
Knob diameter: 1″

23 Cupboard and backplate
Ball and Ball
Solid brass, polished bright finish
Knob diameter: 1″, backplate diameter:
1¼″

24 Turnbutton and backplate
The Merit Brass Collection
Cast brass turn, wrought backplate
Backplate diameter: 1½″

25 Cupboard turn
Horton Brasses
Wood
Knob diameter: 1½″, shank diameter: ⅜″

26 Cupboard turn
Horton Brasses
Wood
Knob diameter: ⅞″, shank diameter: ⅞″

Ball, Roller, Friction, & Magnetic Catches

1, 2 Double ball catches
Selby Furniture Hardware
Solid brass
Strike lengths and widths: 1¹/₁₆″ × ⅜″
and 1¹¹/₁₆″ × ⁵/₁₆″
(Tension is adjustable and operation is head-on or sideways.)

3 Double ball catch
Glynn-Johnson
Extruded bronze
Strike length and width: 2³/₁₆″ × ½″
(Tension is adjustable and operation is head-on or sideways.)

4 Ball catch
Jaybee
Solid brass, steel ball
Strike length and width: 2⅛″ × 1¹/₁₆″
(Tension is adjustable.)

5 Ball catch
Baldwin
Solid brass, steel ball
Strike length and width: 2⅛″ × 1¹/₁₆″
(Tension is adjustable.)

6 Roller catch
Baldwin
Solid brass, nylon roller
Strike length and width: 2¾″ × 1⅛″

7 Double roller catch
Jaybee
Stamped steel and plastic
Catch overall: ⁷/₁₆″ × 1″ × 1¹/₁₆″

8 Double roller catch
Jaybee
Stamped steel and plastic
Catch overall: ⁹/₁₆″ × 1³/₁₆″ × 1¼″

9 Friction catch
Home Hardware
Plastic strike, steel screw
Strike length: 1″

10 Friction catch
Jaybee
Steel
Catch length and width: 1¼″ × 1″

11 Ball-bearing friction catch
Selby Furniture Hardware
Nickel-plated steel
Catch length and width: 1⅛″ × ¾″

12 Double-door magnetic catch
Jaybee
Aluminum case
Catch overall: 1³/₃₂″ × ²⁹/₃₂″ × 3⁷/₁₆″

13 Double magnetic catch
Jaybee
Plastic case
Catch overall: ²⁹/₃₂″ × ¹⁵/₁₆″ × 2″

14 Magnetic push latch
Selby Furniture Hardware
Black polypropylene
Case length and width: 1¾″ × 1⅝″

15 Magnetic push latch
Selby Furniture Hardware
Black polypropylene
Case length: 1¼″

5

Hooks, Bolts & Hasps

IF you haven't taken a close look at what's available these days in the way of hooks, bolts, and hasps and such, you may be surprised. This seemingly mundane decorative hardware family is fairly brimming with beautifully designed and exceptionally well-made devices that could add far more than you might think to your interior's appearance and provide a welcome extra measure of security in the process.

If you think, for instance, that all door hooks on the market today are of the flimsy hardware store variety, you obviously aren't aware of the more substantial beauties being forged and cast in gleaming brass by several of the best decorative hardware manufacturers, and you certainly haven't seen what's being handsomely shaped on the anvils of a whole new breed of blacksmiths. Even the hardworking yet unimaginative hasp is transformed under their hammers into an object worthy of admiration.

Easily the noblest members of this underappreciated group are the bolts—surface bolts, slide bolts, flush bolts, chain bolts, barrel bolts, and the like—and the selection here can be astounding. These heftier door fasteners harken back to the days when castle doors were sealed against intruders with mammoth metal shafts. Tiny inch-long cabinet bolts may conjure up a picture less grand, but such is not the case for the cremone bolt, the undisputed king of bolts and perhaps the most magnificent single piece of decorative hardware, measuring, as it almost always does, end-to-end a good seven feet.

Some Hook, Bolt & Hasp Terms

Barrel Bolt. A cylindrical bolt mounted on a plate having a raised case that contains the bolt and guides it into a recess in a jamb or some other suitable cylindrical socket.

Bolt. Any bar moved through guides into a recess or strike to secure a door and prevent its opening.

Cabin Door Hook. A heavy door hook and staple with backplates for attaching and generally used in nautical installations.

Cane Bolt. A heavy bolt attached at the bottom of a door and dropped into a floor strike to secure the door.

Chain Bolt. A spring-loaded bolt applied at the top of a door and retracted downward against the resistance of its spring by pulling on a chain.

Chain Door Fastener. A strong chain attached at one end to a plate at the edge of a door and carrying on its other end a grooved waferlike fastener that slips into a slot in a keeper attached to the jamb, the chain being just long enough to permit a slight opening of the door.

Cremone Bolt. A long surface-applied bolt used for securing French doors, the top and bottom bolts moving apart to engage strikes at the top and bottom of the door frame and coming together again in response to the rotating of a knob or lever located in between.

Flush Bolt. Any bolt mortised in to be flush with the face or edge of a door.

Hasp. A hinged strap with a slot near its free end so that it may be thrown over a staple and be secured there by means of a hook or padlock.

Slide Bolt. Any bolt having as a feature a sliding bolt or bar.

Strike. Any metal fastening on a door frame into which a bolt is projected to secure a door.

Box Strike. A strike that provides a complete housing to enclose a thrown bolt.

Mortise Strike. A strike mortised into the edge of a door jamb and surrounding a deeper recess in the frame.

Surface Strike. A strike projecting out just beyond the face of a door jamb.

Universal Strike. A strike that may be mounted back on a jamb to act as a standard mortise strike or farther forward to serve as a surface strike.

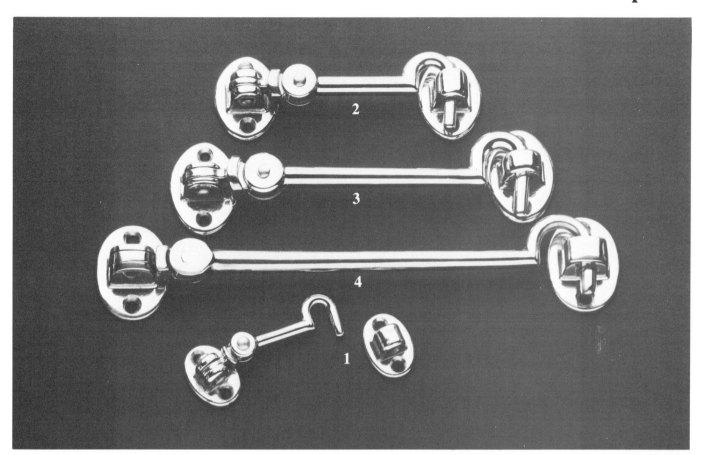

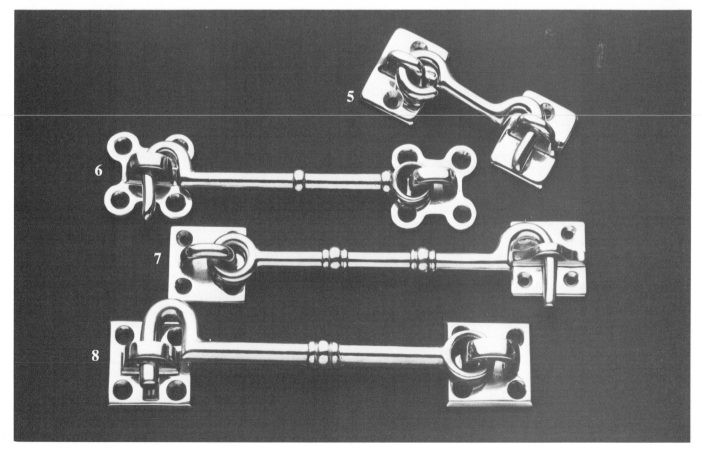

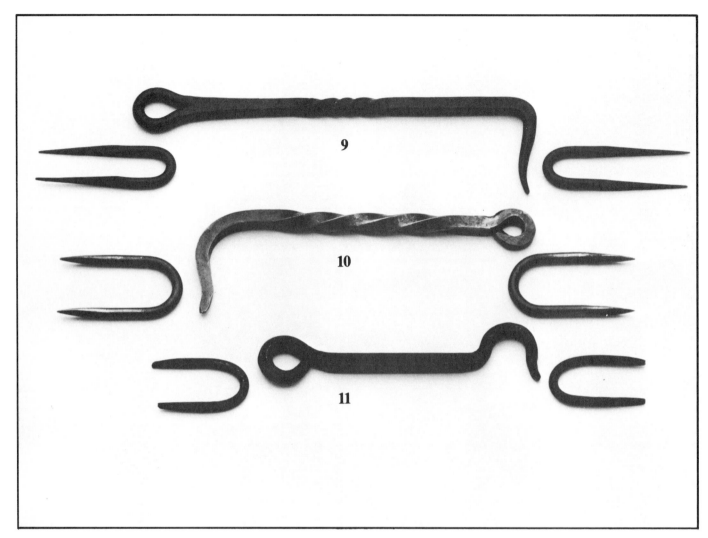

9

10

11

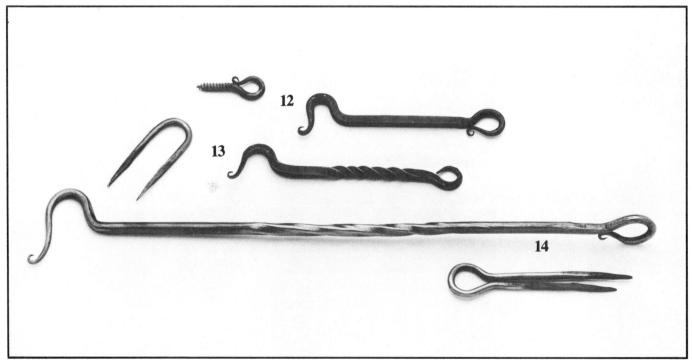

12

13

14

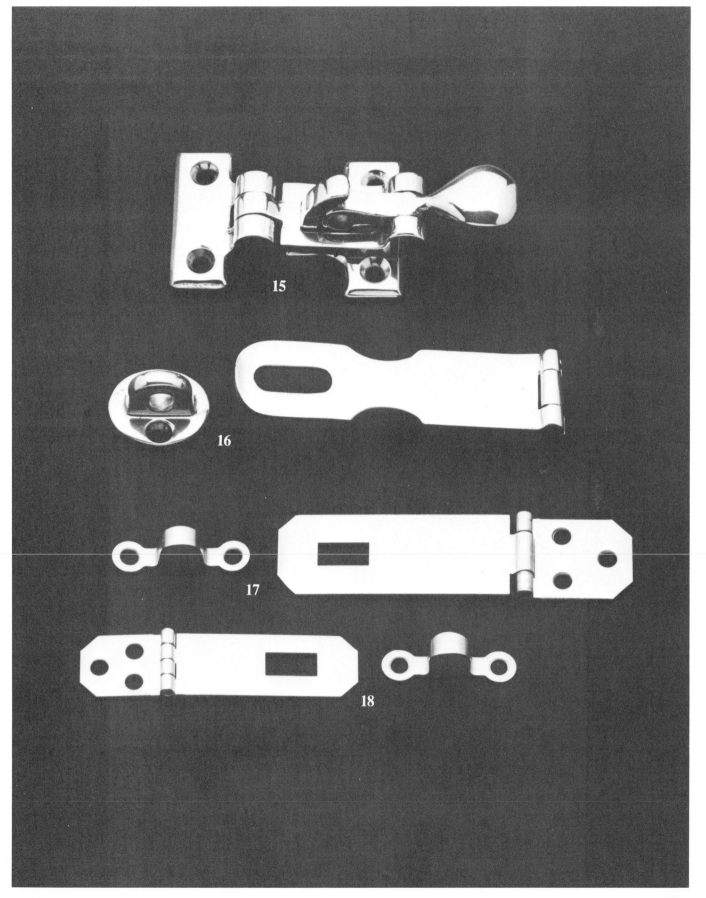

15

16

17

18

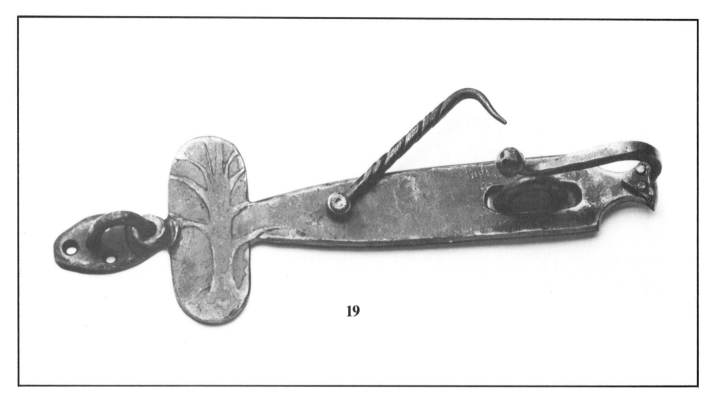

19

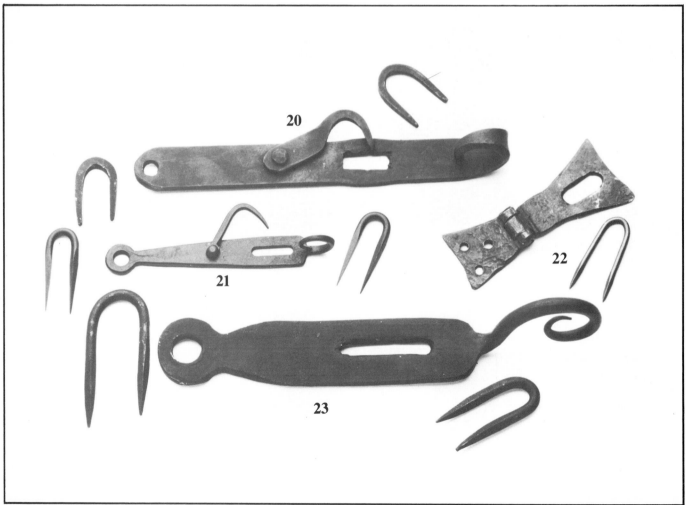

20

21

22

23

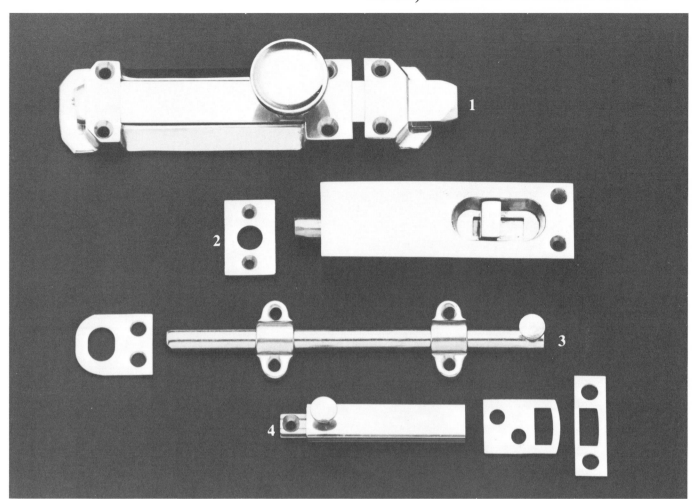

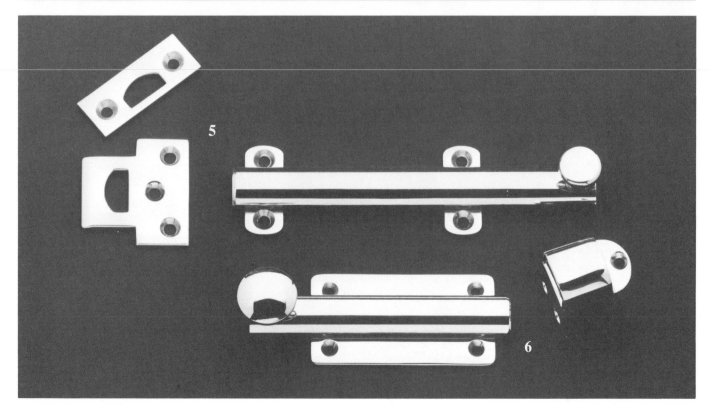

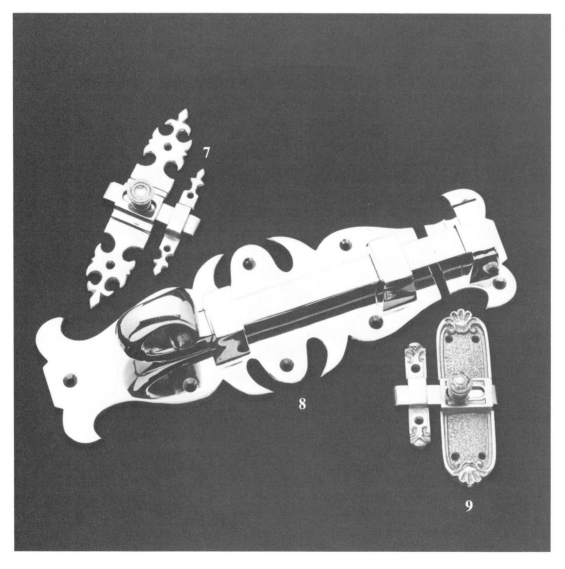

7

8

9

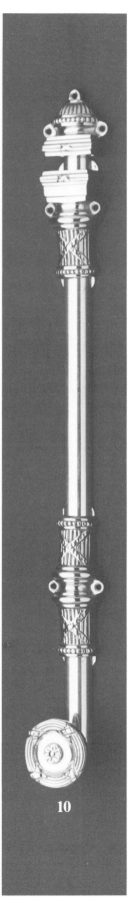

10

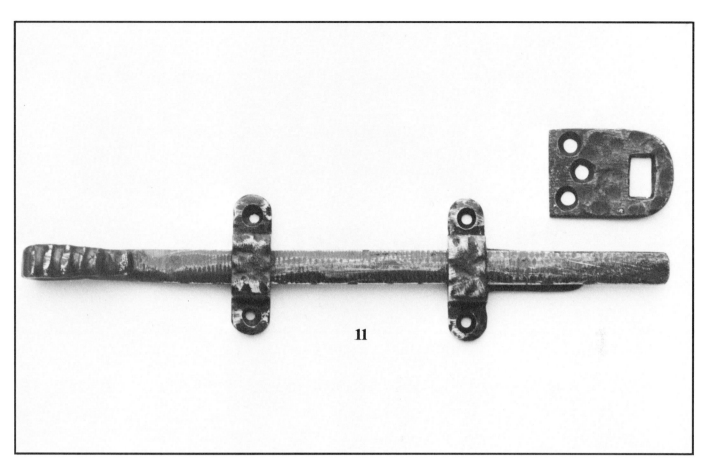

11

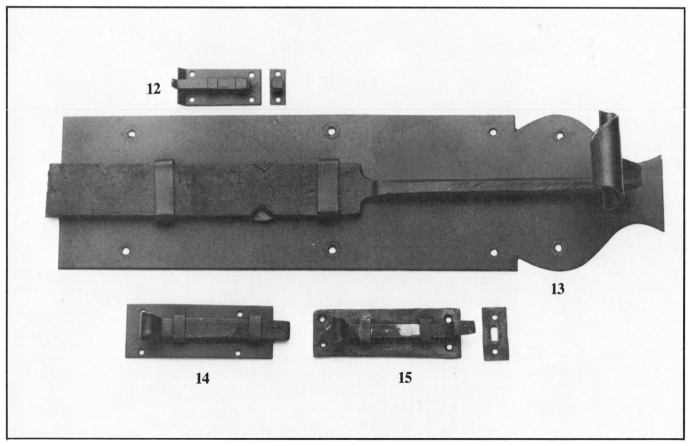

12

13

14

15

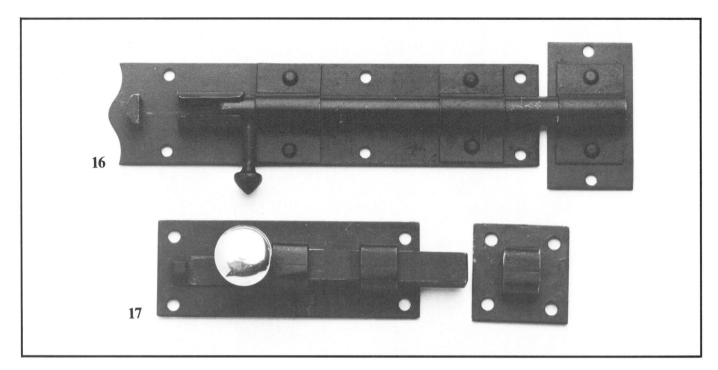

16

17

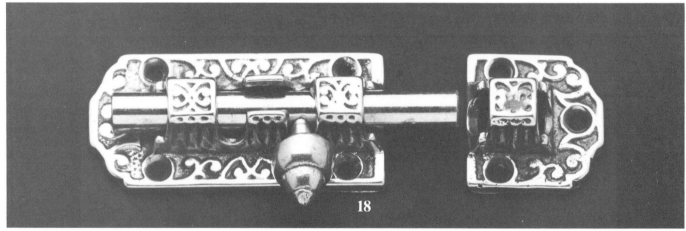

18

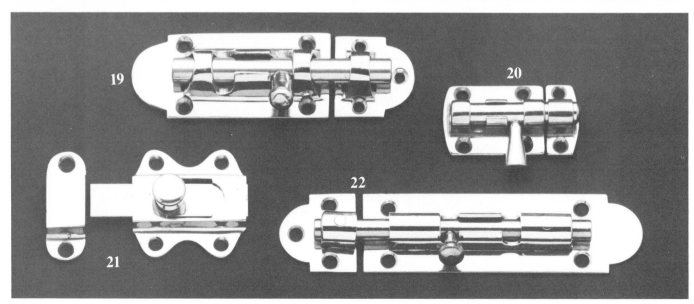

19

20

21

22

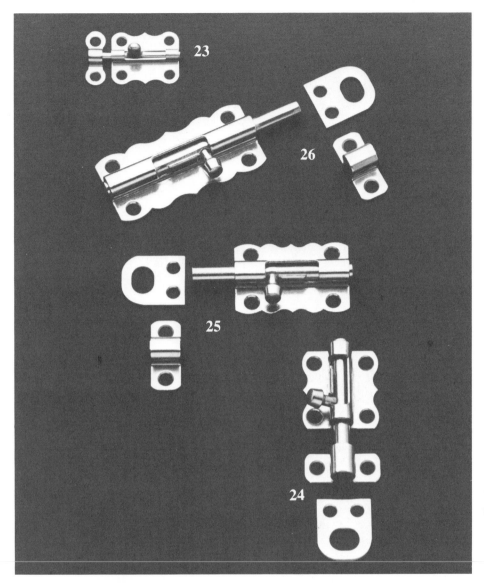

23

26

25

24

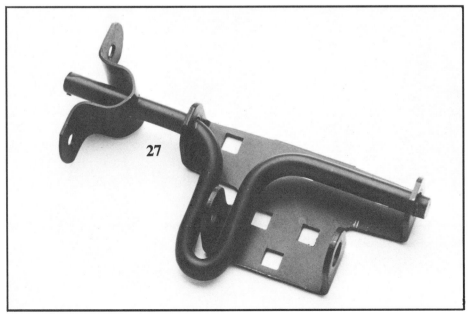

27

159

28

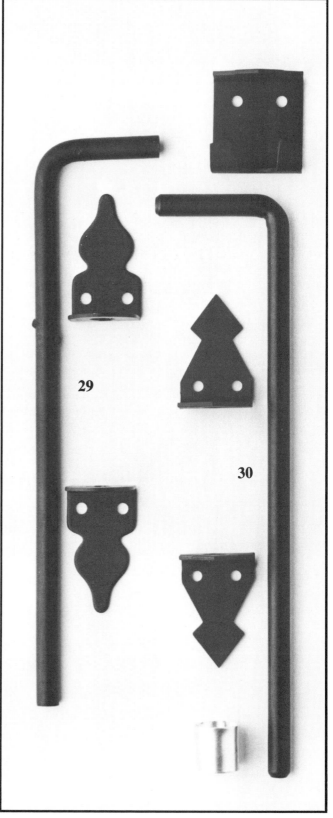

29

30

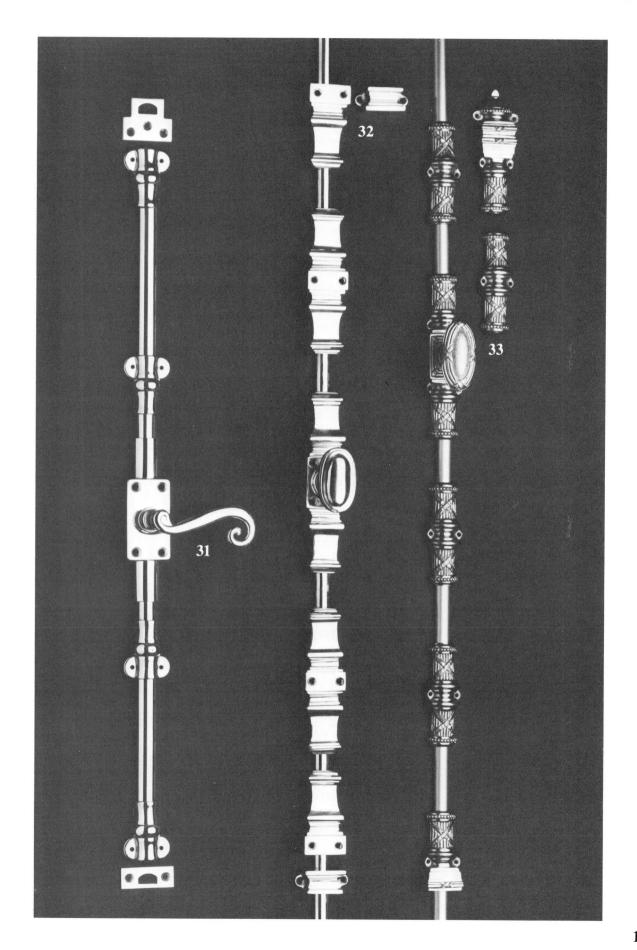

32

31

33

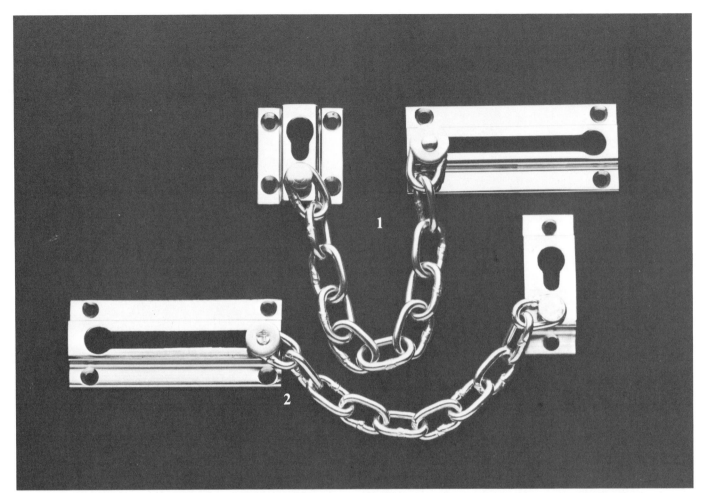

1

2

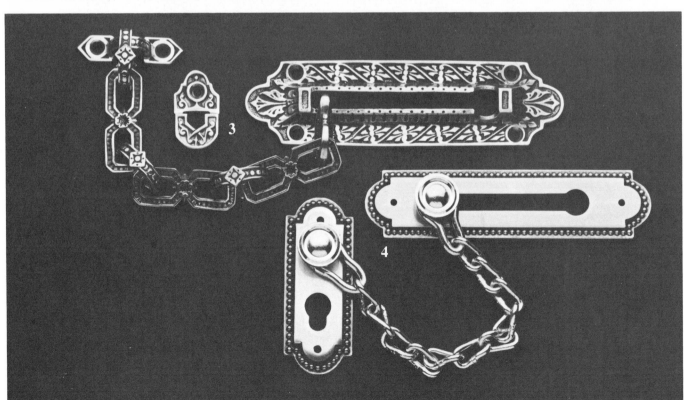

3

4

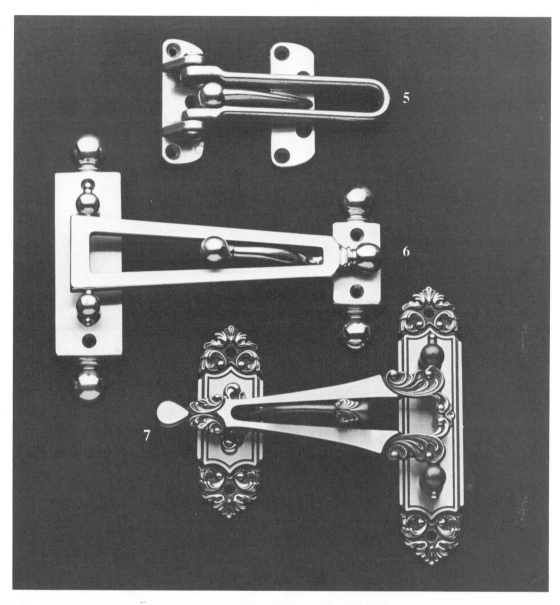

5

6

7

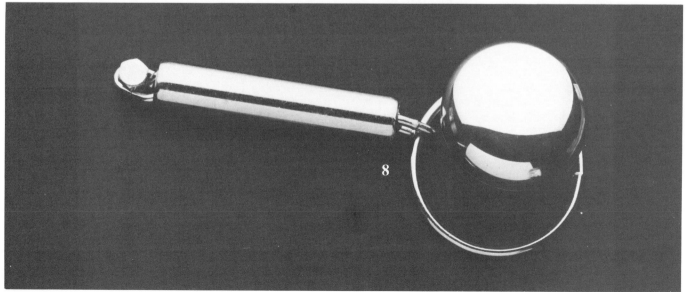

8

Sources & Specifications

Door & Cabinet Hooks & Hasps

1–4 Cabin door hooks
Baldwin
Solid, hot-forged brass
Hook lengths: 2½″, 4″, 6″, and 8″

5 Cabin door hook
Baldwin
Solid, hot-forged brass
Hook length: 2½″

6 Cabin door hook
The Merit Brass Collection
Cast brass
Hook length: 5″

7 Cabin door hook
Garrett Wade
Solid, hot-forged brass
Hook length: 6″
(Discontinued Baldwin hook available in limited supply through Garrett Wade.)

8 Cabin door hook
The Merit Brass Collection
Cast brass
Hook length: 6″

9 Door hook and staples
Peter A. Renzetti, The Arden Forge Company
Hand-forged iron
Hook length: 7″

10 Door hook and staples
Ronald H. Kass, Ronald H. Kass Forge
Hand-forged iron
Hook length: 5¾″

11 Door hook and staples
Richard C. Swenson, Swenson's Forge
Hand-forged iron
Hook length: 4½″

12 Door hook and screw eye
Steve Kayne, Steve Kayne Hand Forged Hardware
Hand-forged iron
Hook length: 6¼″

13 Door hook and staple
Steve Kayne, Steve Kayne Hand Forged Hardware
Hand-forged iron
Hook length: 5½″

14 Shutter or casement window hook
Steve Kayne, Steve Kayne Hand Forged Hardware
Hand-forged iron
Hook length: 16″

15 Hasp
The Merit Brass Collection
Cast brass
Overall length and width: 3⅞″ × 1¾″

16 Hasp
The Merit Brass Collection
Cast brass
Overall length and width: 3½″ × 1″

17 Hasp
Stanley Hardware
Solid brass
Overall length and width, closed: 3″ × 1″

18 Hasp
Stanley Hardware
Solid brass
Overall length and width, closed: 2¾″ × ¾″

19 Hook hasp
Lance Cloutier, The Ram's Head Forge
Hand-forged iron
Overall length and width: 13½″ × 4½″

20 Rattail hook/hasp and staples
Richard C. Swenson, Swenson's Forge
Hand-forged iron
Overall length: 8½″

21 Rattail hook/hasp and staples
Peter A. Renzetti, The Arden Forge Company
Hand-forged iron
Overall length: 5″

22 Butterfly hasp and staple
Steve Kayne, Steve Kayne Hand Forged Hardware
Hand-forged iron
Overall length, closed: 2¾″

23 Rattail hasp and staples
Robert H. Klar, Salmon Falls Forge
Hand-forged iron
Overall length: 10″

Slide, Cane & Cremone Bolts

1 Surface bolt
Omnia Industries
Solid brass
Overall length: 5¾″
(Surface strike shown.)

2 Flush cupboard bolt
The Merit Brass Collection
Cast brass
Overall length: 3″
(Mortise strike shown.)

3 Surface bolt
Stanley Hardware
Steel, brass finish
Overall length: 6″
(Universal strike shown.)

4 Surface bolt
Stanley Hardware
Solid brass
Overall length: 2½″
(Universal strike and mortise strike shown.)

5 Surface bolt
Baldwin
Extruded brass
Overall length: 6″
(Universal strike and mortise strike shown.)

6 Dutch door bolt
Baldwin
Extruded brass
Overall length: 5⅝″
(Box strike shown.)

7 Surface cabinet bolt
H. Pfanstiel
Solid brass
Overall length and width: 5½″ × 2¼″
(Surface strike shown.)

8 Surface door bolt
Period Furniture Hardware
Cast brass
Overall length and width: 11″ × 3½″
(Box strike shown.)

9 Surface cabinet bolt
H. Pfanstiel
Solid brass
Overall length and width: 4″ × 2¼″
(Surface strike shown.)

10 Surface door bolt
H. Pfanstiel
Solid brass
Overall length and width: 17″
(Box strike shown.)

11 Surface door bolt
Erco
Hammered cast bronze
Overall length: 9″
(Universal strike shown.)

12 Mini slide bolt
Peter A. Renzetti, The Arden Forge Company
Hand-forged iron
Overall length: 2½″
(Surface strike shown.)

13 Surface slide bolt
Mark E. Rocheford, Hammerworks
Hand-forged iron
Overall length and width: 14½″ × 3½″

14 Spring slide bolt
Peter A. Renzetti, The Arden Forge Company
Hand-forged iron
Overall length: 3½″

15 Offset slide bolt
Craig Kaviar, Kaviar Forge
Hand-forged iron
Overall length: 3½″
(Mortise strike shown.)

16 Barrel bolt
Peter A. Renzetti, The Arden Forge Company
Hand-forged iron
Overall: 9″
(Surface strike shown.)

17 Surface bolt
Ball and Ball
Iron and brass
Plate length and width: 4½″ × 1¾″, knob diameter: 1″
(Surface strike shown.)

18 Barrel bolt (Victorian)
The Renovator's Supply
Cast brass
Overall length: 4½″
(Surface strike shown.)

19 Barrel bolt
The Merit Brass Collection
Cast brass
Overall length: 4¼″
(Surface strike shown.)

20 Barrel bolt
Omnia Industries
Solid brass
Overall length: 2″
(Surface strike shown.)

21 Cupboard bolt
The Merit Brass Collection
Cast brass
Overall length: 2⅛″
(Surface strike shown.)

22 Barrel bolt
Baldwin
Wrought brass
Overall length: 5½″
(Surface strike shown.)

23 Mini barrel bolt
Stanley Hardware
Solid brass
Plate length: 1⅜″
(Surface strike shown.)

24–26 Barrel bolts
Stanley Hardware
Steel, brass plated
Plate lengths: 1^{25}/₃₂″, 2⁵/₃₂″, and 3¹/₃₂″
(Universal strikes and surface strikes shown.)

27 Slide gate bolt
PTI-Dolco/Simpson Hardware
Steel, zinc plated and black lacquer painted
Overall length: 6″
(Two-way surface strike shown.)

28 Antique chain bolt (Victorian)
By-Gone Days Antiques
Cast iron
Overall length: 10″, chain length: 24″

29 Cane bolt
PTI-Dolco/Simpson Hardware
Steel, zinc plated and black lacquer painted
Bolt: 12″

30 Cane bolt
Arrowsmith Industries
Steel, zinc plated and black enamel painted
Bolt: 12″

31 Cremone bolt
Baldwin
Forged, wrought and extruded brass
Overall length: 7′, lever length: 4″
(Universal strike and mortise strike shown.)

32 Cremone bolt
Kraft Hardware
Cast and extruded brass
Overall length: 7′
(Surface strikes shown.)

33 Cremone bolt
Kraft Hardware
Cast and extruded brass
Overall length: 7′
(Box strike shown.)

Chain Door Fasteners & Door Guards

1 Chain door fastener
Baldwin
Extruded brass
Door plate length: 3½″

2 Chain door fastener
Quincy
Solid brass
Door plate length: 3⅜″

3 Chain door fastener (Victorian)
Ritter & Son
Lost-wax cast bronze
Door plate length: 5¾″

4 Chain door fastener
Impex Associates
Solid brass
Door plate length: 5⅛″

5 Door guard
VSI Hardware
Cast Zamac, brass plated
Overall length: 3¾″

6 European security latch
Valli and Colombo (USA)
Solid brass
Overall length: 5″

7 European security latch
Valli and Colombo (USA)
Solid brass
Overall length: 5⅛″

8 Chain door guard
Brookstone
Steel, gold-like finish
Ring diameter: approximately 3″

165

6

Locks

Mortise door locks are hardly what you would call decorative; what you do see of them and possibly admire (knobs and plates and such) is only their trim. The only visible part of the lock itself is its face (the portion flush with the edge of the door) and that is visible only when the door is open.

For those who prefer seeing all of a lock, there are surface locks. Such locks—also called rim locks and box locks—attach directly to the surface of the door with no mortising whatsoever. A narrow hole is drilled through for a spindle to communicate with a knob on the opposite side; that is the only wood removing that is required.

Mortise locks and surface locks are generally handed. You will need a right-hand lock for a right-hand door, a left-hand lock for a left-hand door, a right-hand reverse bevel lock for a right-hand reverse door and a left-hand reverse bevel lock for a left-hand reverse door. (For clarification of handings see pages 5–9.)

Furniture locks are also frequently mortised—mostly into doors and drawers—but often in a way that hides only one half. Like other mortised-in locks, these can be fitted with trim: just a simple or decorative escutcheon to protect the wood around the keyhole from the key with a most satisfying classic keyhole-shaped opening.

Some Lock Terms

Backset.   The distance between the face of a lock and the hub, keyhole, or cylinder.

Box Lock.   *See* Surface Lock.

Cabinet Lock.   Any small lock used on cabinets or furniture.

Dead Bolt.   A lock bolt with a square head operated by a key or knob but having no spring.

Drop Escutcheon.   An escutcheon or key plate with a pivoting pendant attached that drops to cover the keyhole.

Face.   The part of a mortise lock that shows at the edge of the door through which the latch bolt or dead bolt projects.

Hub.   The rotating part of a lock through which the spindle passes.

Latch Bolt.   A bevel-headed spring-action bolt retracted by a knob or lever door handle.

Lip.   The part of a strike that projects at an angle beyond the face of the door jamb to receive the beveled latch bolt and conduct it into the strike's recess.

Live Bolt.   *See* Latch Bolt.

Surface Lock.   A door lock applied to the surface of a door with its strike applied to the face of the jamb.

Thumb Turn.   A small knob turned by thumb and finger to retract or throw a dead bolt.

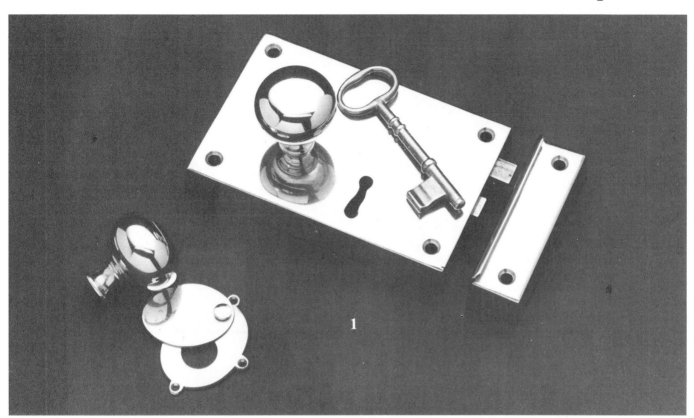

1

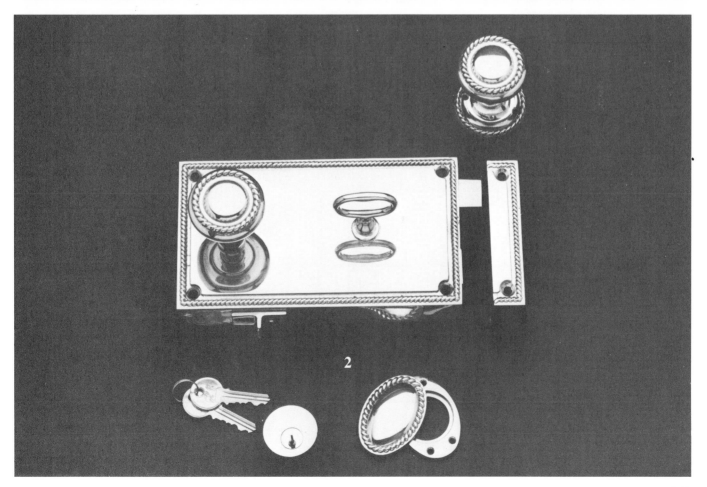

2

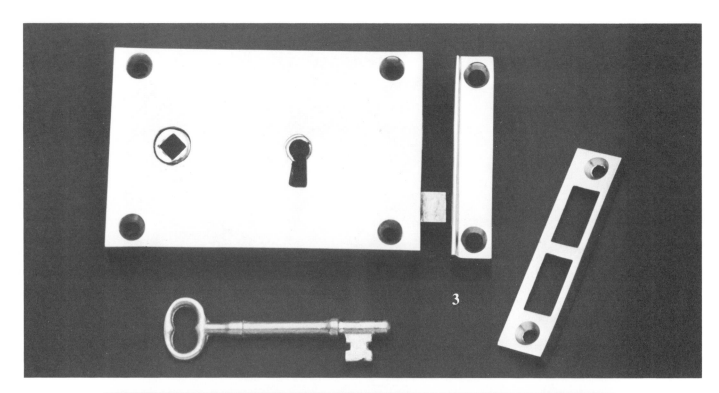

3

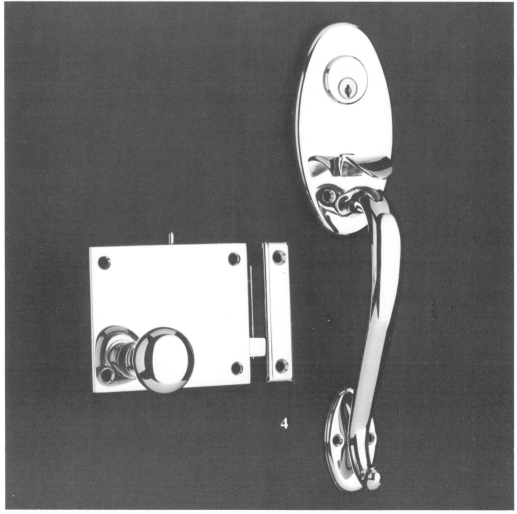

4

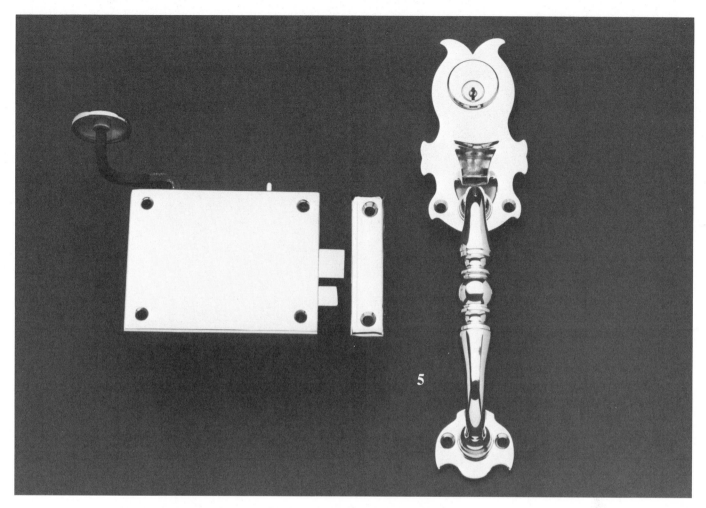

5

6

7

8

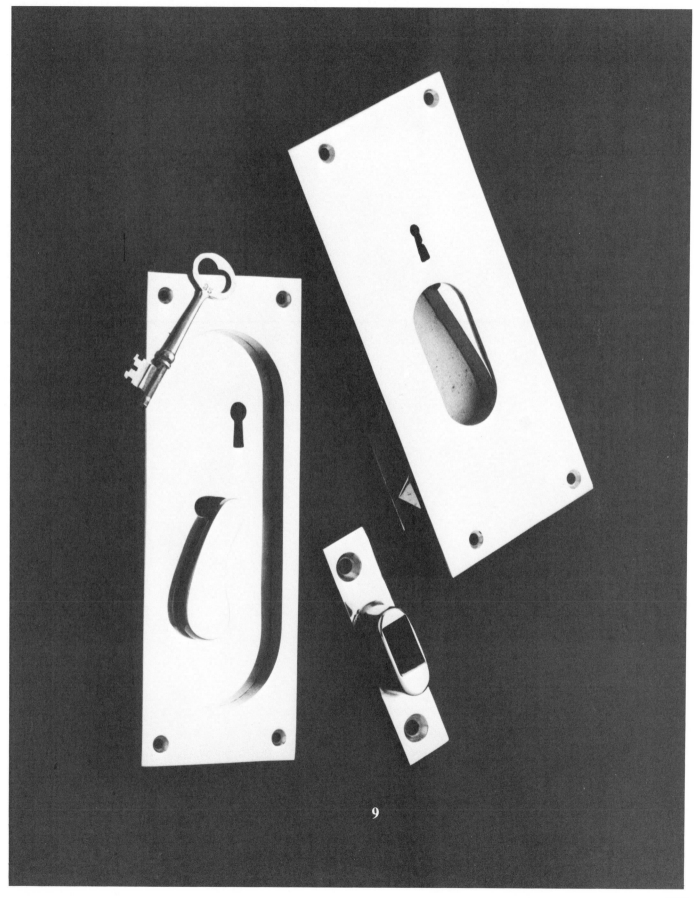

9

10

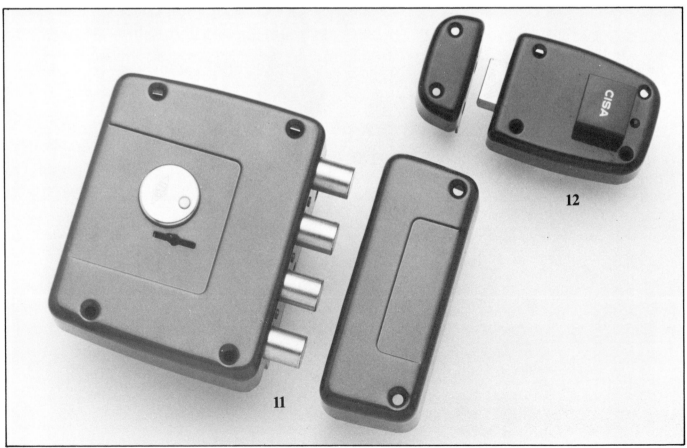

11

12

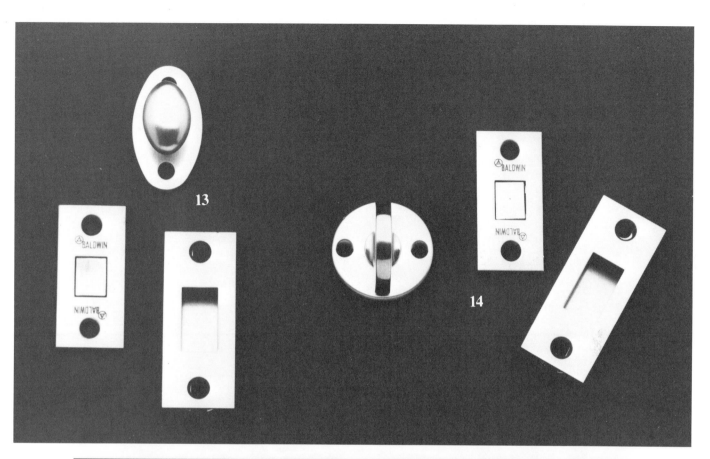

13

14

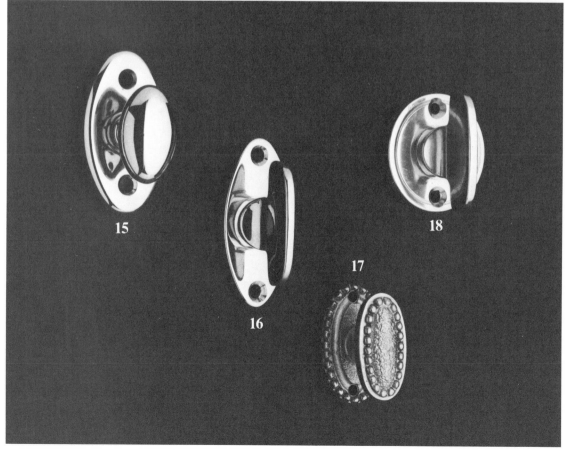

15

16

18

17

Furniture Locks & Escutcheons

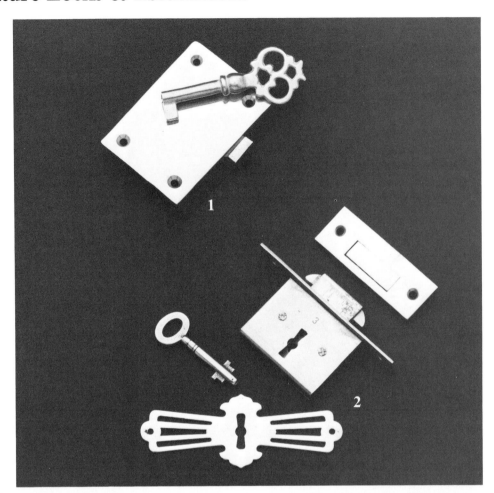

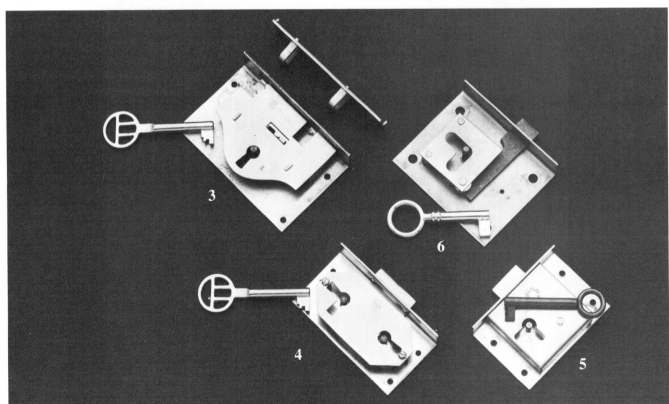

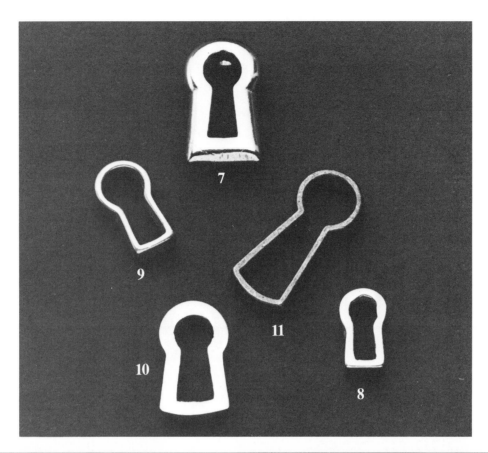

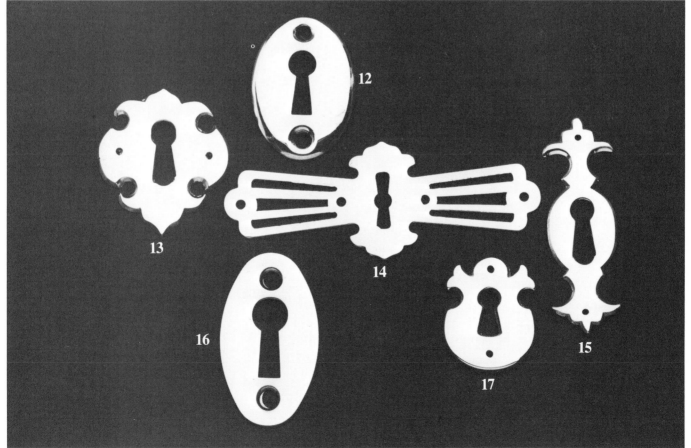

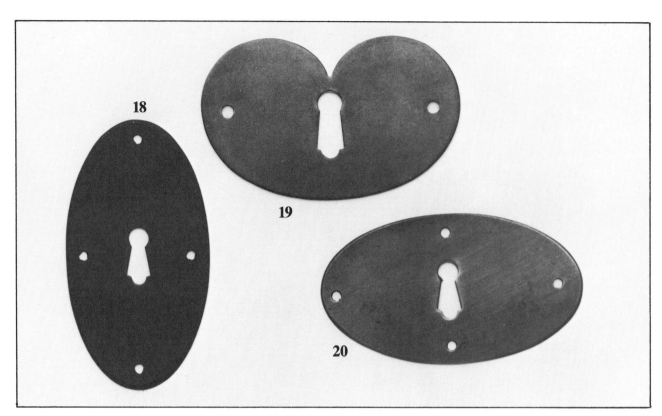

18

19

20

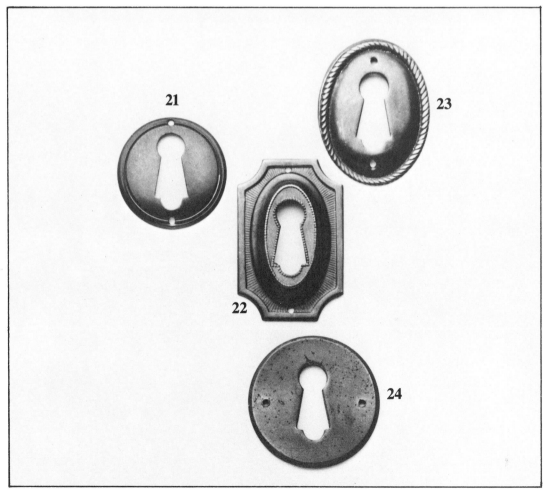

21

23

22

24

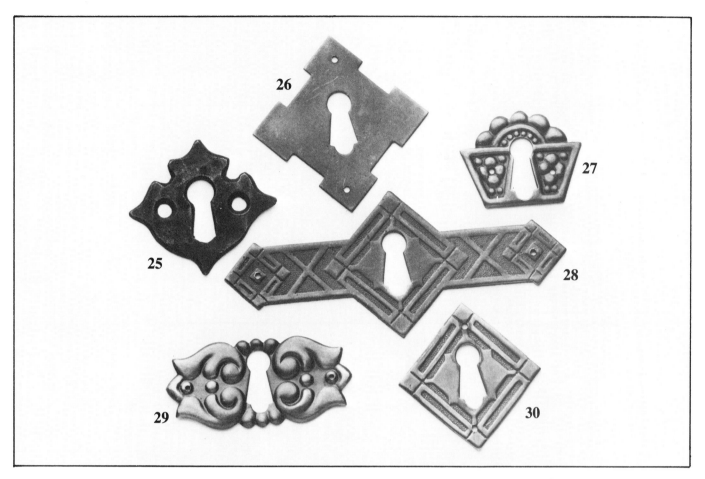

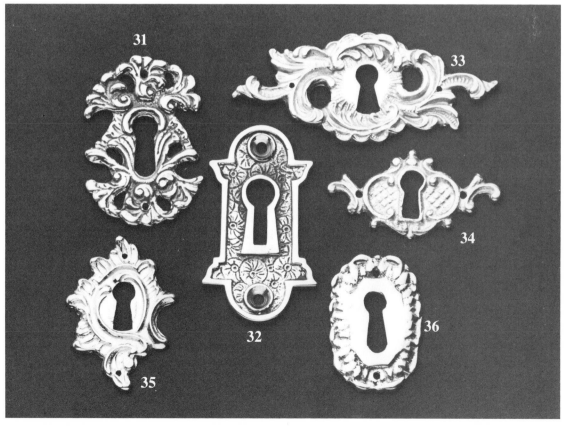

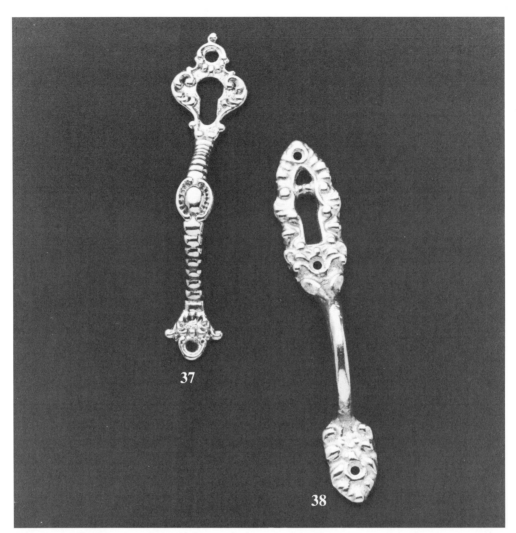

37

38

39

40

41

Sources & Specifications

Surface Door Locks & Turnpieces

1 Rim lock set
Ball and Ball
Solid brass
Case and keeper: 6″ × 4″

2 Rim lock set
The Broadway Collection
Solid brass
Case: 7⅜″ × 4$\frac{5}{16}$″, knob diameter: 1$\frac{15}{16}$″, backset: 5$\frac{15}{16}$″

3 Rim lock
The Merit Brass Collection
Cast brass
Case: 3¼″ × 5″ × $\frac{9}{16}$″, backset: 2″

4 Entrance door rim lock set
Baldwin
Solid, hot-forged brass
Case: 4¾″ ×3¾″ × 1″, backset: 3½″, outside trim, overall length: 12¾″

5 Entrance door rim lock set
Baldwin
Solid, hot-forged brass
Case: 4¾″ × 3¾″ × 1″, backset: 3½″, outside trim, overall length: 12″

6 Iron rim lock set
Ball and Ball
Iron case, brass trim
Case and keeper: 6″ × 4″

7 Iron rim lock set
Ball and Ball
Iron case, brass trim
Case and keeper: 6″ × 4″

8 U.S. Navy surplus surface lock set
Garrett Wade
Cast bronze
Case and keeper: 5¾″ × 5⅛″

9 U.S. Navy surplus sliding door lock
Garrett Wade
Cast bronze
Pull plate length and width: 8″ × 3″, lock case length and width: 7⅞″ × 3½″

10 Security deadbolt
Medeco Security Locks
Special high-tensile-strength alloy, satin bronze finish
Case: 4⅛″ × 4⅛″, backset: 2¾″, throw: 1⅛″

11 Rim lock
Omnia Industries
Painted steel case, nickel-plated steel bolts
Case: 6″ × 5″, throw: 1½″

12 Rim double throw deadbolt
Omnia Industries
Steel case, brass bolt, ABS plastic knob
Case: 3½″ × 2⅝″, maximum throw: ⅞″

13, 14 Mortise bolts and trim
Baldwin
Tubular forged brass
Bolt face: 2¼″, mortise depth: 3¾″, backset: 2¾″, throw: $\frac{9}{16}$″

15–17 Thumbpieces
Simon's Hardware
Chrome, chrome, brass
Backplate lengths: 2″, 2⅛″, and 1½″

18 Thumbpiece
Omnia Industries
Solid brass
Backplate diameter: 1$\frac{9}{16}$″

Furniture Locks & Escutcheons

1 "Governor Winthrop" desk lock
Period Furniture Hardware
Solid brass
Overall: 2¾″ × 1$\frac{15}{16}$″ × ½″

2 Roll top desk lock and escutcheon
Ball and Ball
Steel lock, brass escutcheon
Lock face length: 3¼″, escutcheon: 3¾″ × 1⅜″

3 Half mortise chest lock
Paxton
Steel
Overall: 3⅛″ × 2⅛″ × $\frac{11}{16}$″, selvedge: 3⅛″ × $\frac{11}{16}$″, backset: 1⅜″

4 Half mortise drawer lock
Paxton
Steel and brass
Overall: 2$\frac{3}{16}$″ × 1$\frac{9}{16}$″ × ½″, selvedge: 2$\frac{3}{16}$″ × ½″, backset: $\frac{13}{16}$″

5 Half mortise desk lock
Period Furniture Hardware
Steel and brass
Length and width: 2¼″ × 1⅜″

6 Half mortise drawer lock
Ball and Ball
Iron and brass
Overall: 1½″ × 1¼″ × ½″

7 Insert escutcheon with lipped edge
Paxton
Cast brass
Length: 1″

8–11 Insert escutcheons
Paxton
Cast brass
Lengths: ⅝″, ¾″, ⅞″, and 1⅛″

12 Escutcheon
Quincy
Solid brass
Length: 1$\frac{1}{16}$″

13 Escutcheon
Ball and Ball
Solid brass
Length: 1½″

14 Roll top desk lock escutcheon
Paxton
Solid brass
Length and width: 3¾″ × 1⅜″

15 Escutcheon
Ball and Ball
Solid brass
Length: 2½″

16 Escutcheon
Baldwin
Solid brass
Length: 2″

17 Escutcheon
Paxton
Cast brass
Length: 1$\frac{15}{16}$″

18 Escutcheon
Horton Brasses
Solid brass
Length and width: 3½″ × 2″

19 Escutcheon
Horton Brasses
Solid brass
Length and width: 3½″ × 2¼″

20 Escutcheon
Horton Brasses
Solid brass
Length and width: 3½″ × 2″

21 Escutcheon
Horton Brasses
Solid brass
Length: 1⅛″

22 Escutcheon
Horton Brasses
Solid brass
Length: 1⅝″

23 Escutcheon
Horton Brasses
Solid brass
Length: 1½″

24 Escutcheon
Horton Brasses
Solid brass
Length: 1¼″

25 Escutcheon
Erco
Cast bronze
Length: 1¾″

26 Escutcheon
Horton Brasses
Solid brass
Length: 2⅜″

27 Escutcheon
Horton Brasses
Solid brass
Length: 1½″

28 Escutcheon
Horton Brasses
Solid brass
Length and width: 4¼″ × 1¾″

29 Escutcheon
Horton Brasses
Solid brass
Length: 2¼″

30 Escutcheon
Horton Brasses
Solid brass
Length: 1¾″

31 Escutcheon
Ball and Ball
Solid brass
Length: 2¼″

32 Escutcheon
Ritter & Son
Lost-wax cast bronze
Length: 2½″

33 Escutcheon
The Broadway Collection
Solid brass
Length: 3¼″

34 Escutcheon
Ritter & Son
Solid brass
Length: 2¼″

35 Escutcheon
The Broadway Collection
Solid brass
Length: 2″

36 Escutcheon
Ball and Ball
Solid brass
Length: 1¾″

37 China closet pull escutcheon
(Victorian)
Paxton
Cast brass
Length: 3⅝″

38 China closet pull escutcheon
(Victorian)
Ritter & Son
Cast brass
Length: 4″

39 Drop escutcheon
Sherle Wagner International
Solid brass
Length: 2¼″

40 Antique drop escutcheon
Urban Archeology
Copper
Length: 2¾″

41 Drop escutcheon
Baldwin
Forged brass
Length: 2⁵⁄₁₆″

7

Accessory Door Hardware

PROVIDING it with a pair of hinges and a lock with requisite trim doesn't necessarily satisfy every door's decorative hardware needs, particularly not those of the average front entrance door.

All the accessory door hardware unique to front entrance doors, it should be worth noting, has something to do with some form of communication. Visitors and deliverers, for example, announce their arrival by using a knocker or by ringing the door bell. The postman may deliver the mail through a letter slot. All are front door accessory door hardware.

A kick plate or push plate applied to, respectively, the bottom of a door or along the stile of a door protects the former against the ravages of misdirected feet and the latter from unsightly prints left by too many opening fingers. Another common accessory door hardware item, one that protects a wall from a swinging door and vice versa, is the door bumper, attached to the wall, baseboard, or floor. And to any one of those three places, or even to the door itself, you can install a door holder, to keep an open door securely in place.

Some Accessory Door Hardware Terms

Door Bell.   Now meant to mean any bell device on the outside of an entrance door that depends upon electricity for its operation.

Door Ring.   An entrance door bell device activated by turning a bar or thumb piece located on the outside of an exterior door frame that communicates with a bell located somewhere inside the door frame.

Door Bumper.   Any device, usually equipped with a rubber part or tip, attached to a wall, baseboard, or the floor, meant to stop a door and its knob from coming into contact with the wall.

Door Holder.   Any device used to hold a door in place in an open position.

Door Stop.   Any device used to limit the opening swing of a door.

Kick Plate.   A protective plate applied to the bottom or lower rail of a door.

Push Plate.   A protective plate of metal, plastic, ceramic, or other material attached vertically to the lock stile of a door.

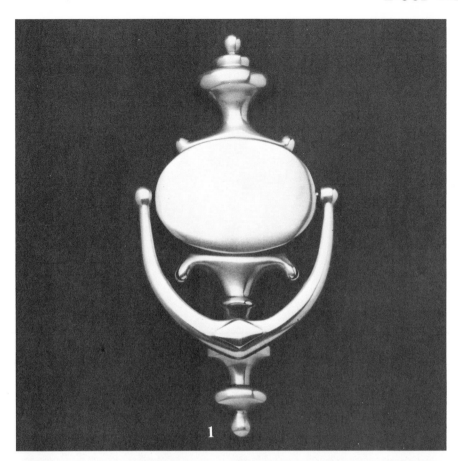

1

2

3

4

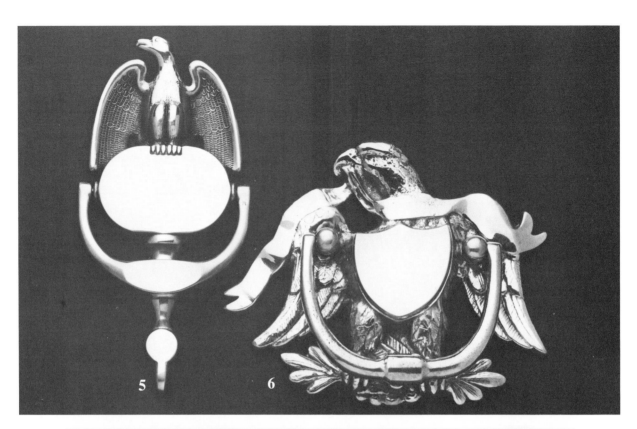

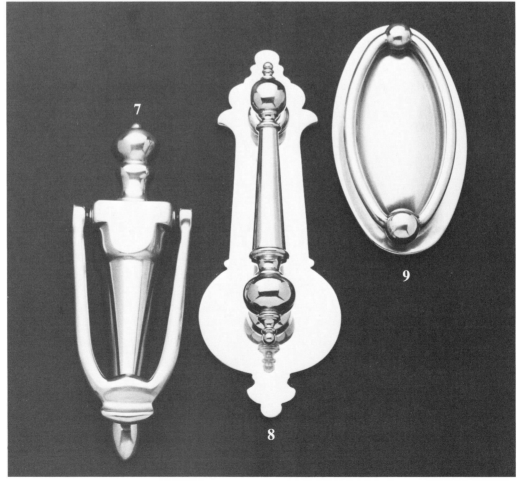

10

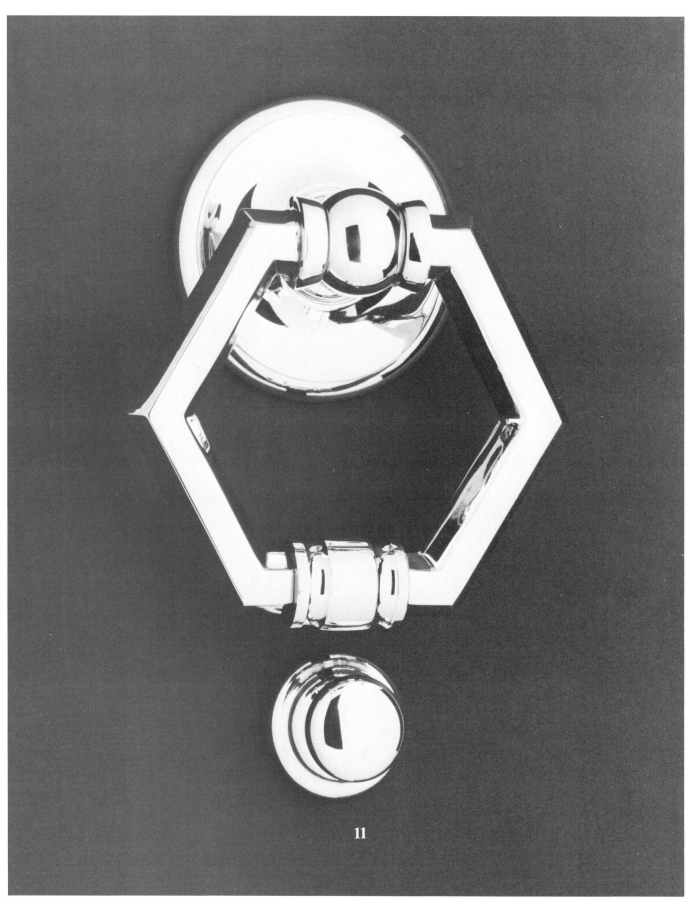

11

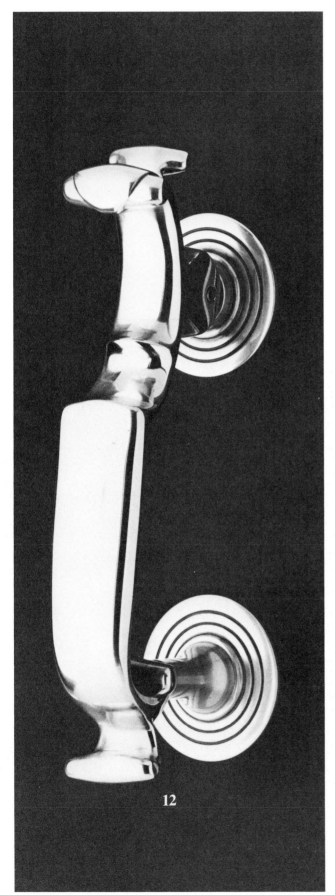

12

13

189

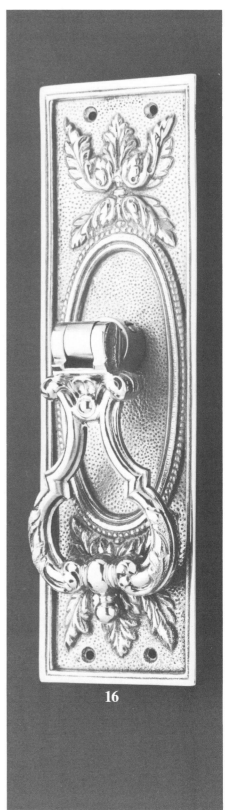

17

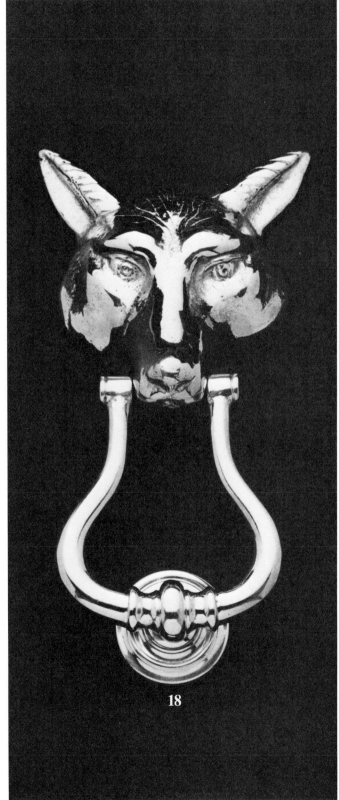

18

19

20

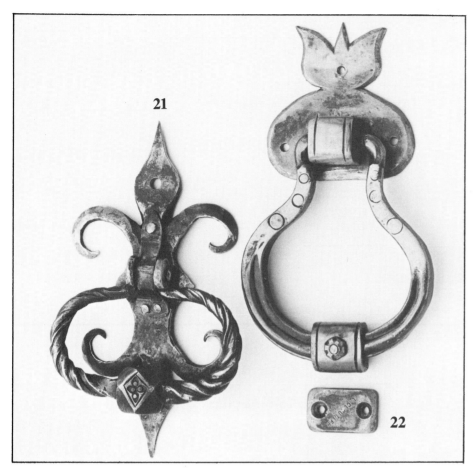

21

22

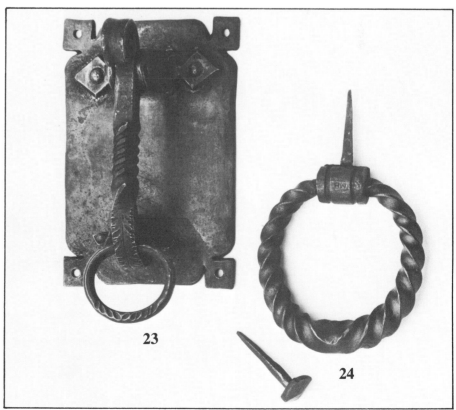

23

24

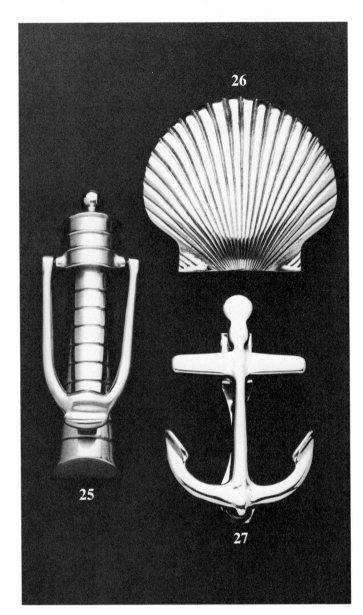

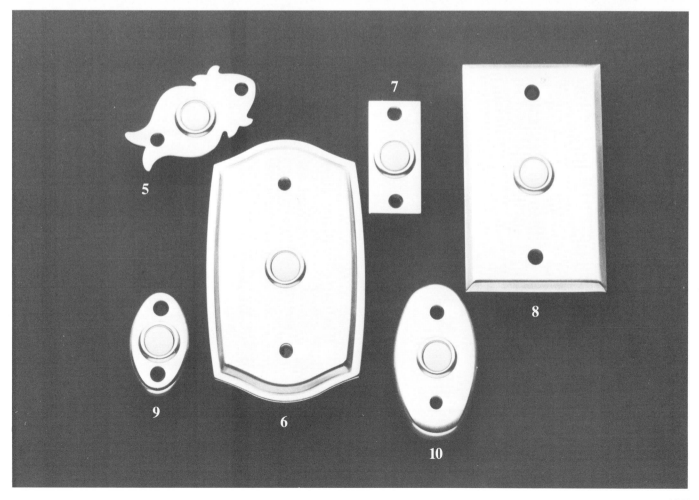

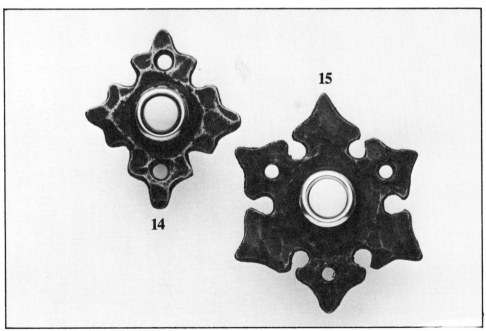

16

17

18

19

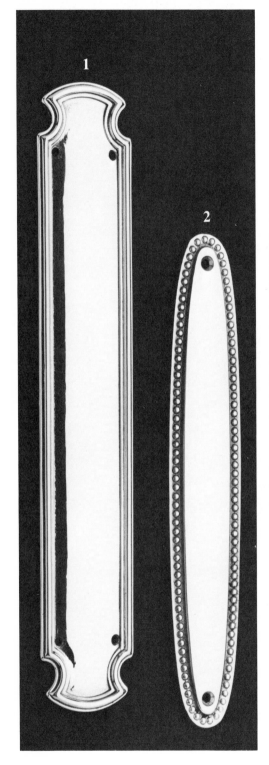

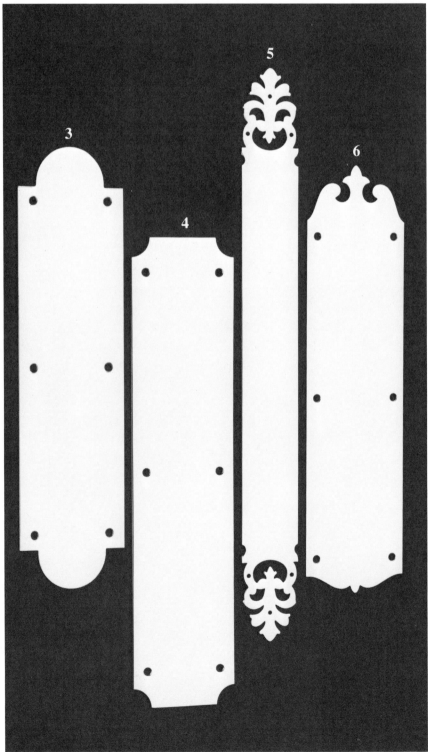

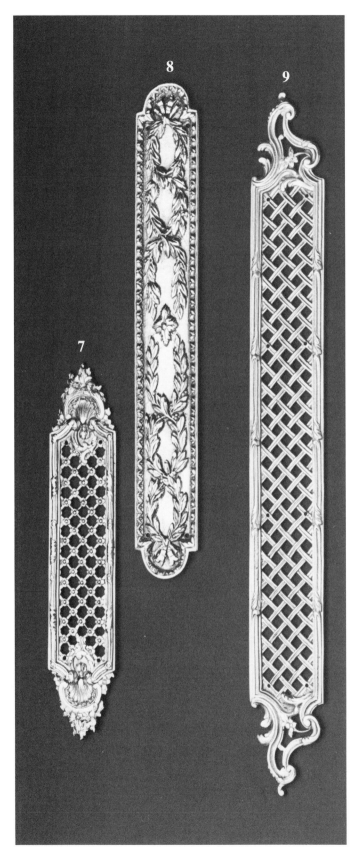

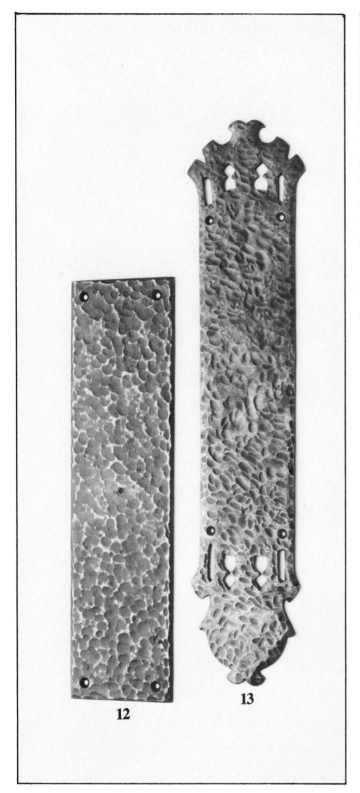

12

13

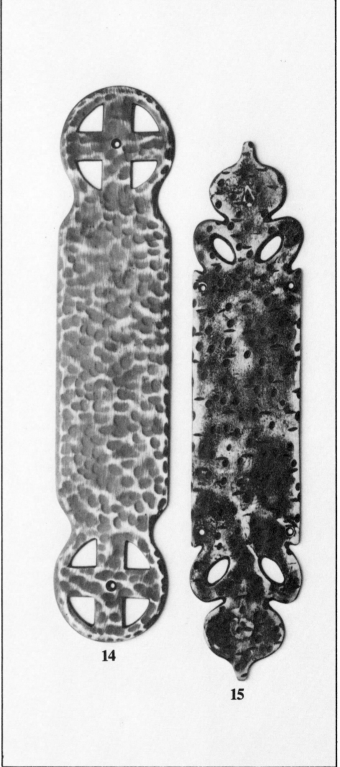

14

15

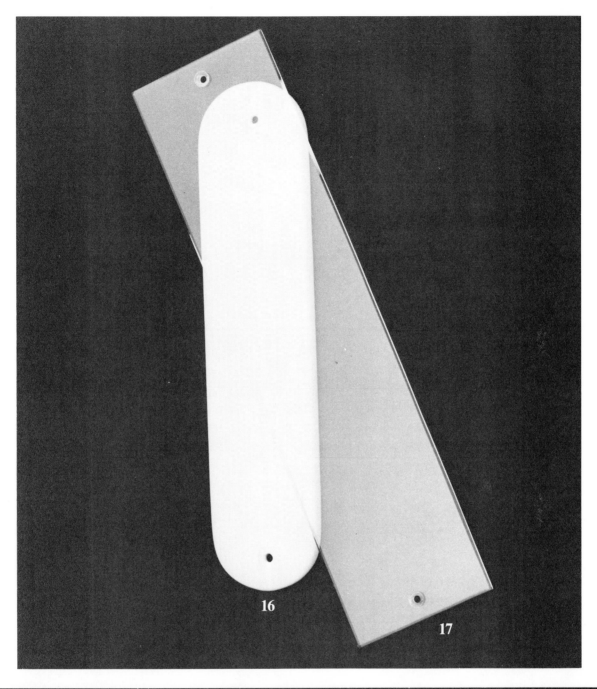

16

17

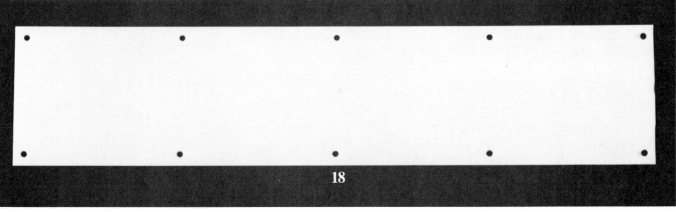

18

Door Bumpers, Stops & Holders

202

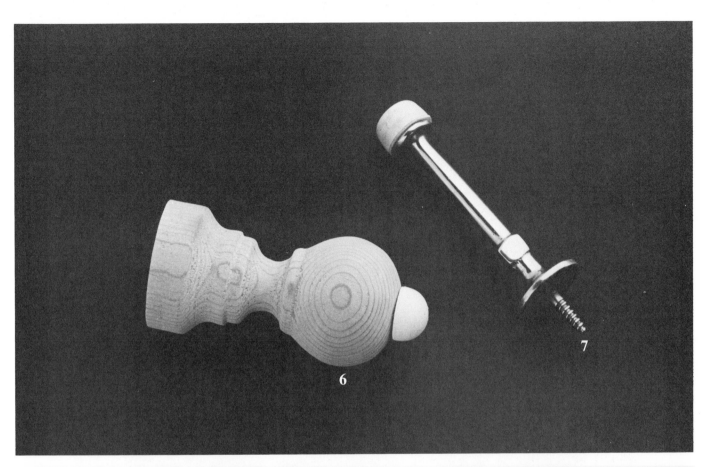

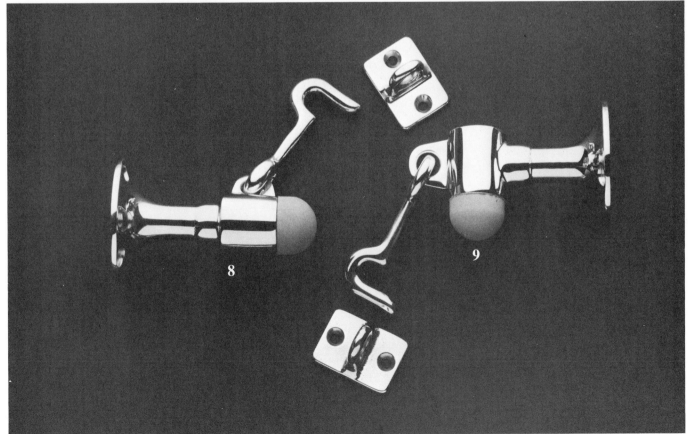

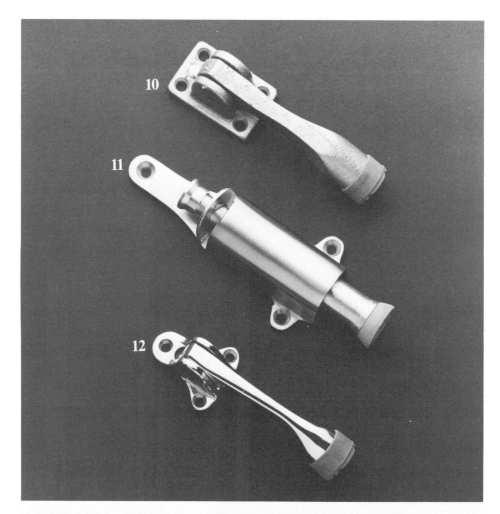

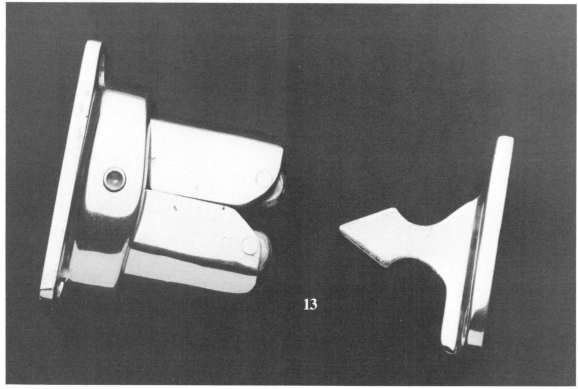

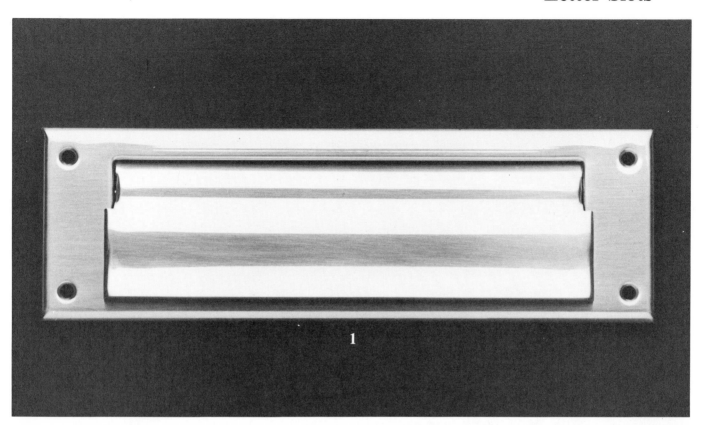

1

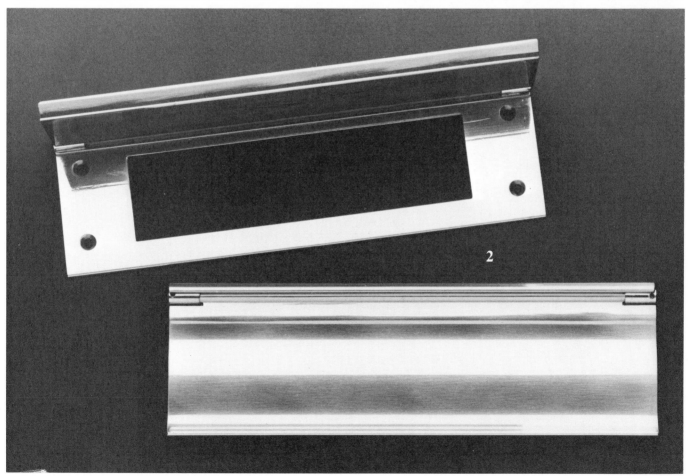

2

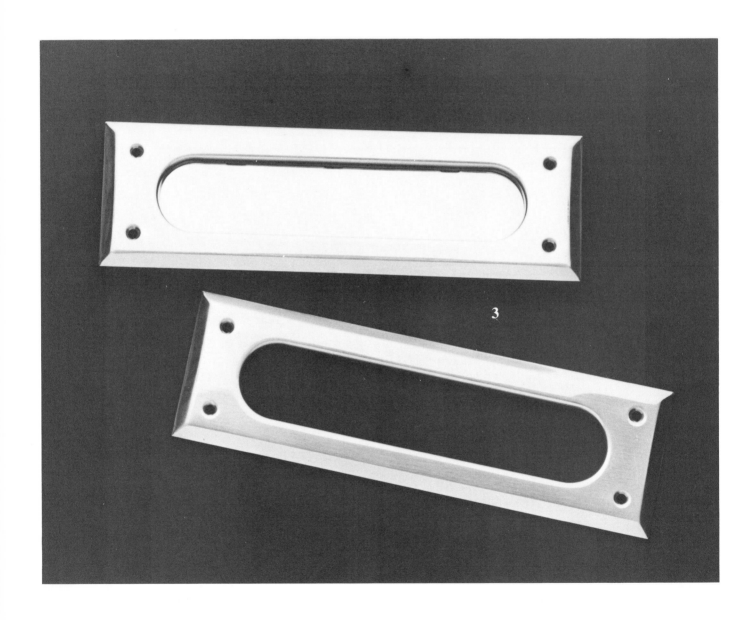

3

206

4

5

Sources & Specifications

Door Knockers

1 Door knocker
Baldwin
Solid, hot-forged brass
Overall: 8½″ × 4⅛″

2 Door knocker
Baldwin
Solid, hot-forged brass
Overall: 4″ × 2¼″

3 Door knocker
Baldwin
Solid, hot-forged brass
Overall: 6½″ × 3½″

4 Door knocker with nameplate
Baldwin
Solid, hot-forged brass
Overall: 4¾″ × 2¼″, card size: 2″ × ⅝″

5 Door knocker
Baldwin
Solid, hot-forged brass
Overall: 8″ × 4″

6 Door knocker
Ball and Ball
Solid, hot-forged brass
Overall: 7½″ × 6¼″

7 Door knocker
Baldwin
Solid, hot-forged brass
Overall: 7½″ × 2½″

8 Door knocker
The Broadway Collection
Solid brass
Overall: 8⅛″ × 3″

9 Door knocker
Baldwin
Solid, hot-forged brass
Overall: 4¾″ × 2¾″

10 Door knocker
Erco
Hammered cast bronze
Overall: 8¾″ × 4¾″

11 Door knocker
Baldwin
Solid, hot-forged brass
Overall: 8¼″ × 7″

12 Door knocker
Baldwin
Solid, hot-forged brass
Overall length: 7¾″

13 Door knocker
Restoration Hardware
Solid brass
Overall length: 7″

14 Door knocker
The Broadway Collection
Solid brass
Overall: 6¾″ × 4¼″

15 Door knocker
Ball and Ball
Solid brass
Overall: 9″ × 6¼″

16 Door knocker
H. Pfanstiel
Solid brass
Overall: 7¾″ × 1¾″

17 Door knocker
Omnia Industries
Solid brass
Overall length: 5¹¹/₁₈″

18 Door knocker
Ball and Ball
Solid brass
Overall: 8½″ × 4½″

19 Door knocker
Erco
Hammered cast bronze
Overall: 12¼″ × 9¼″

20 Door knocker
Erco
Hammered cast bronze
Overall: 6½″ × 3⅝″

21 Door knocker
Bob Patrick, Big Anvil Forge
Hand-forged iron
Overall: 7½″ × 4½″

22 Door knocker
Lance Cloutier, The Ram's Head Forge
Hand-forged iron
Overall: 7¾″ × 4½″

23 Door knocker
Larry B. Wood, The Farm Forge
Hand-forged iron
Overall: 9″ × 4″

24 Door knocker
Mark E. Bokenkamp, Bokenkamp's Forge
Hand-forged iron
Diameter: 4″

25 Door knocker
Baldwin
Solid, hot-forged brass
Overall: 7⁵/₁₆″ × 2½″

26 Door knocker
Custom Decor
Sand-cast brass
Overall: 5″ × 4½″

27 Door knocker
Custom Decor
Sand-cast brass
Overall: 6″ × 4″

28 Door knocker
Terra Sancta Guild
Bronze
Overall length: 6⅝″

29 Door knocker
Terra Sancta Guild
Solid bronze, hand-enameled colors
Overall length: 4⅝″

Door Bell Buttons & Rings

1 Door bell button
Baldwin
Solid brass
Diameter: 1¾″

2 Door bell button
Baldwin
Solid brass
Diameter: 1¾″

3 Door bell button
The Broadway Collection
Solid brass
Diameter: 2¼″

4 Door bell button
The Broadway Collection
Solid brass
Diameter: 2¼″

5 Door bell button
Baldwin
Solid brass
Overall: 2¾″ × 1½″

6 Door bell button
Baldwin
Solid brass
Overall: 5⅛″ × 3¹/₁₆″

7 Door bell button
Baldwin
Solid brass
Overall: 2¼″ × 1″

8 Door bell button
Baldwin
Solid brass
Overall: 4½″ × 2¾″

9 Door bell button
Baldwin
Solid brass
Overall: 2″ × 1⅛″

10 Door bell button
Baldwin
Solid brass
Overall: 3″ × 1^{23}/$_{32}$″

11 Door bell button
Sherle Wagner International
Solid brass
Diameter: 1⅞″

12 Door bell button
Sherle Wagner International
Solid brass
Overall: 7½″ × 2½″

13 Door bell button
Baldwin
Solid brass
Overall: 2″ × 1½″

14 Door bell button
Erco
Hammered cast bronze
Overall: 2⁹/₁₆″ × 2¼″

15 Door bell button
Erco
Hammered cast bronze
Overall: 3⅛″ × 2⅝″

16 Door bell button
Ritter & Son
Lost-wax cast bronze
Diameter: 3″

17 Door bell ring
Restoration Hardware
Solid brass
Bell diameter: 4″

18 Antique door bell ring (dated 1874)
By-Gone Days Antiques
Solid brass
Bell diameter: 4½″, ring plate: 4¾″ × 2¾″

19 Antique door bell ring (dated 1860)
By-Gone Days Antiques
Solid brass
Bell diameter: 4¾″, ring plate: 4½″ × 2¾″

Push & Kick Plates

1 Push plate
The Broadway Collection
Solid brass
Length and width: 11¼″ × 1^{15}/₁₆″

2 Push plate
Omnia Industries
Solid brass
Length and width: 9″ × 1⁹/₁₆″

3 Push plate
Baldwin
Solid, hot-forged brass
Length and width: 12″ × 3½″

4 Push plate
Baldwin
Solid, hot-forged brass
Length and width: 15″ × 3½″

5 Push plate
Baldwin
Solid, hot-forged brass
Length and width: 18½″ × 2″

6 Push plate
Baldwin
Solid, hot-forged brass
Length and width: 12″ × 3½″

7 Push plate
Sherle Wagner International
Solid brass
Length: 16″

8 Push plate
H. Pfanstiel
Solid brass
Length: 15″

9 Push plate
Sherle Wagner International
Solid brass
Length: 21″

10 Push plate
H. Pfanstiel
Solid brass
Length: 9″

11 Push plate
H. Pfanstiel
Solid brass
Length: 11″

12 Push plate
Erco
Hammered cast bronze
Length and width: 13″ × 3½″

13 Push plate
Erco
Hammered cast bronze
Length and width: 17″ × 3¾″

14 Push plate
Erco
Hammered cast bronze
Length and width: 17″ × 3⅝″

15 Push plate
Erco
Hammered cast bronze
Length and width: 16⅜″ × 3⅜″

16 Push plate
Plexacraft Metals
Porcelain
Length and width: 9″ × 2¼″

17 Push plate
Plexacraft Metals
Plexiglas
Length and width: 12″ × 3″

18 Kick plate
Baldwin
Solid brass
Length and width: 28″ × 6″

Door Bumpers, Stops & Holders

1 Wall-mounted door bumper
Baldwin
Solid brass and rubber
Diameter: 1¾″

2 Wall-mounted door bumper
Baldwin
Solid brass and rubber
Diameter: 1″

3 Floor-mounted bumper
Baldwin
Solid brass and rubber
Diameter: 2″

4 Floor-mounted bumper
Baldwin
Forged brass and rubber
Height: 2¹/₁₆″

5 Floor-mounted bumper
Glynn-Johnson
Cast brass and rubber
Height: 2⅞″

6 Wall-mounted door stop
Restoration Hardware
Hand-turned redwood and rubber
Projection: 3″

7 Wall-mounted door stop
The Merit Brass Collection
Cast brass and rubber
Projection: 3″

8 Wall-mounted door stop and holder
Baldwin
Forged brass and rubber
Projection: 3½″

9 Floor-mounted door stop and holder
Baldwin
Forged brass and rubber
Height: 3½″

10 Lever door holder
Baldwin
Cast iron and rubber
Length of arm: 4″

11 Plunger door holder
Glynn-Johnson
Nonferrous metal, plated steel, and rubber
Overall: 6¼″ × 1⅞₁₆″ × 1⅞₁₆″

12 Lever door holder
Baldwin
Forged brass and rubber
Length of arm: 4″

13 Heavy-duty door holder
The Merit Brass Collection
Cast brass
Base: 3″ × 2¼″, keeper: 3⅜″ × 2″

Letter Slots

1 Letter slot
Baldwin
Heavy gauge wrought brass
Overall length and width: 10″ × 3″

2 Letter slot
Baldwin
Solid brass
Overall length and width: 10″ × 3″

3 Letter slot
Baldwin
Wrought brass
Overall length and width: 10″ × 3″

4 Letter slot
Erco
Hammered cast bronze
Overall length and width: 13″ × 3″

5 Antique letter slot
Urban Archeology
Cast bronze
Overall length and width: 7¾″ × 2¾″

8

Hinges

T HE largest of all the decorative hardware families comprises a truly amazing assortment of hinges.

For every type of swinging door (and there are many) there is a perfect hinge (and there are literally hundreds), and for every different hinge there is a reason.

No decorative hardware group so comfortably bridges the gap between architectural hardware and cabinet hardware. On the architectural side are the hardworking butt

door hinges, with their thick leaves securely mortised into both door edge and frame. (For how to mortise a butt hinge to hang a door in a frame, see pages 11–13.) Rising door butts, loose pin butts, tight pin butts, lift-off butts, and spring butts are just a few of the different types.

A small sampling of cabinet hinges includes such beauties from the blacksmith's forge as the aptly named butterfly hinge, the H and H/L hinges (which, as the "Holy Lord" hinge in Colonial days, presumably kept many a witch and even Satan himself at bay), burly strap hinges, and delicate rattails.

Some hinges, like most locks, are handed. To understand how they are and why this is, see pages 5–6. To learn to tell when a particular door should take a right-hand hinge or a left-hand hinge, see page 8.

Some Hinge Terms

Ball Bearing Hinge.   A butt door hinge with ball bearings between the knuckle to reduce wear.

Butterfly Hinge.   A surface-mounted cabinet hinge that has the appearance of a butterfly when opened out flat.

Butt Hinge, or **Butt.**   A hinge mortised into the edge of a door and the edge of the jamb against which the edge of the door will butt when closed.

Concealed Hinge.   A hinge so constructed that no parts are visible when the door is closed.

Continuous Hinge, or **Piano Hinge.**   A hinge that extends the full length of the two surfaces to which its leaves are joined.

Double-Acting Hinge.   Any hinge that permits a door to swing both ways.

Double-Acting Spring Hinge.   A double-acting hinge equipped with a spring to bring the door back in line with the frame.

Fast Pin Hinge.   A hinge whose pin is not removable.

Flap Hinge.   A surface-mounted hinge related to the strap hinge and having elongated leaves extending in both directions.

Gravity Door Hinge.   *See* Rising Butt Hinge.

H Hinge.   A surface-mounted hinge that when applied resembles the letter H.

H/L Hinge.   A surface-mounted hinge that when applied resembles the letters H and L combined.

Hinge Plate.   An ornamental band applied to the surface of a door next to a butt hinge's protruding knuckle to give the effect of a strap hinge.

Invisible Hinge.   *See* Concealed Hinge.

Knuckles.   The joining parts of a hinge through which the pin passes.

Leaf.   The part of a hinge extending out from either side of a knuckle joint.

Lift-off Hinge.   A two-knuckle hinge with the bottom supporting knuckle providing an upright pin over which the supported leaf's knuckle fits.

Loose Pin Hinge.   A hinge whose pin can be removed to facilitate removing a door from its frame.

Offset Hinge.   A hinge with one leaf offset forward or backward to account for an insetting or projecting door.

Pin.   The long rod that passes through a hinge's knuckles to keep the two halves of the hinge joined together.

Rattail Hinge.   A lift-off cabinet hinge with the supporting pin extending below the knuckle to fasten to the cabinet case.

Rising Butt Hinge.   A hinge with a knuckle so designed as to cause an opening door to be lifted slightly and then close by its own weight.

Spring Hinge.   A surface-mounted or butt hinge equipped with one or more springs acting to return the door to the closed position.

Strap Hinge.   A surface-mounted hinge with particularly long flaps.

Tight Pin Hinge.   *See* Fast Pin Hinge.

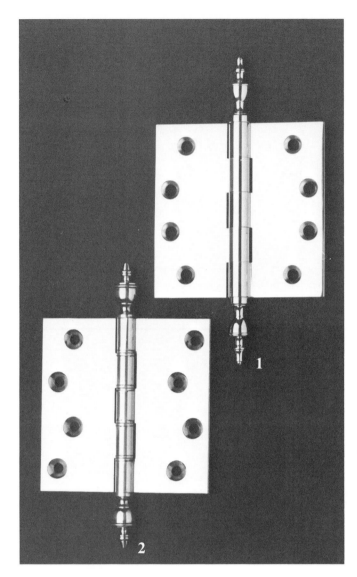

1

2

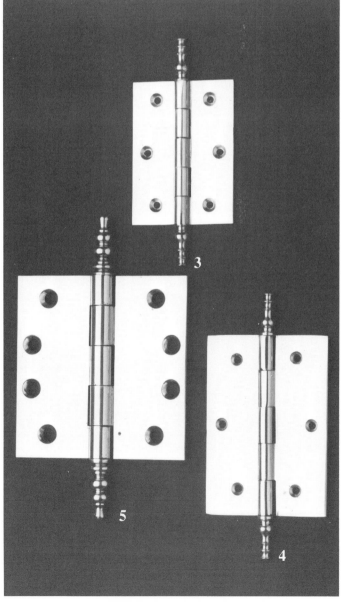

3

5

4

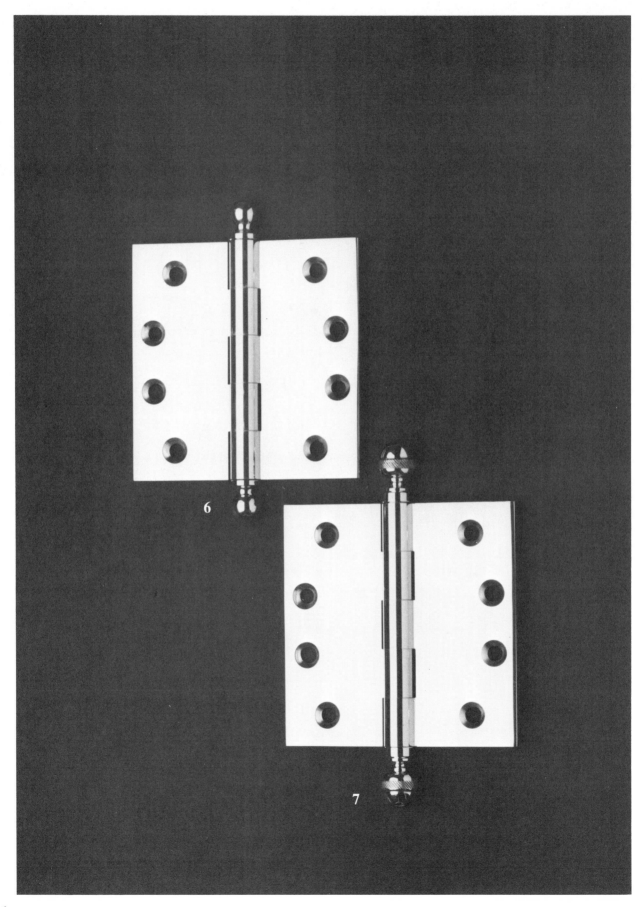

6

7

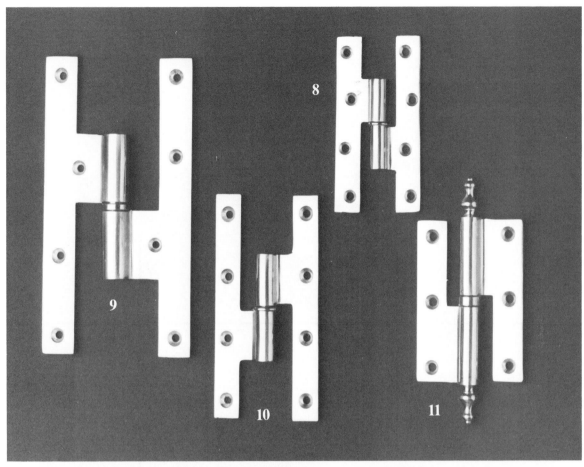

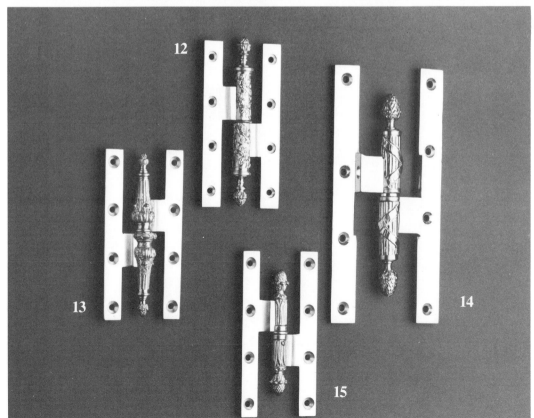

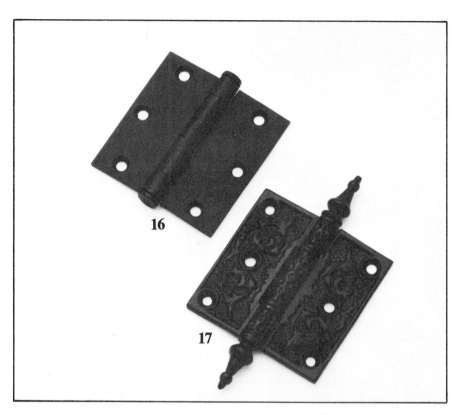

16

17

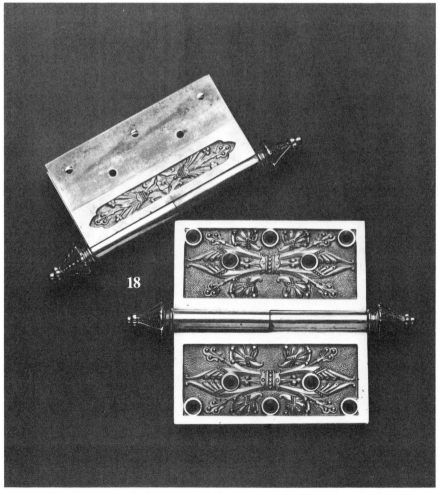

18

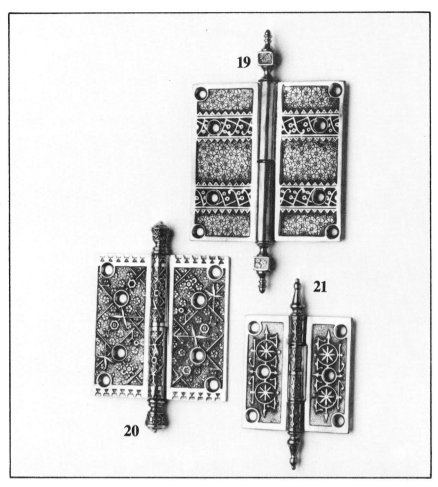

19

21

20

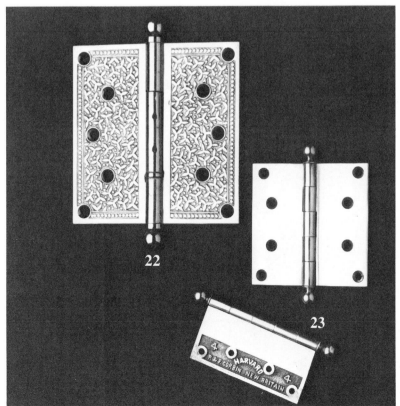

22

23

217

24

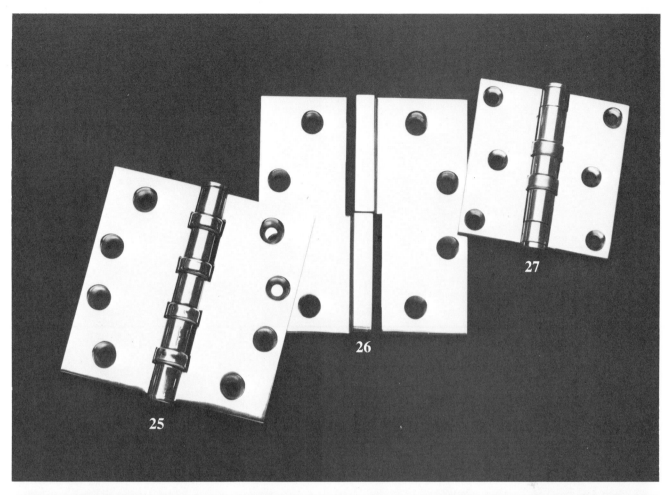

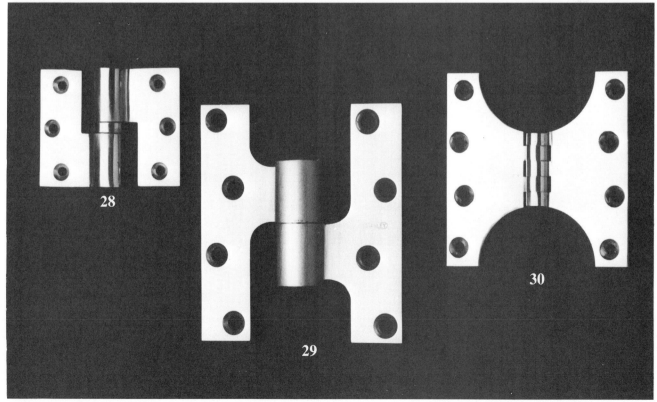

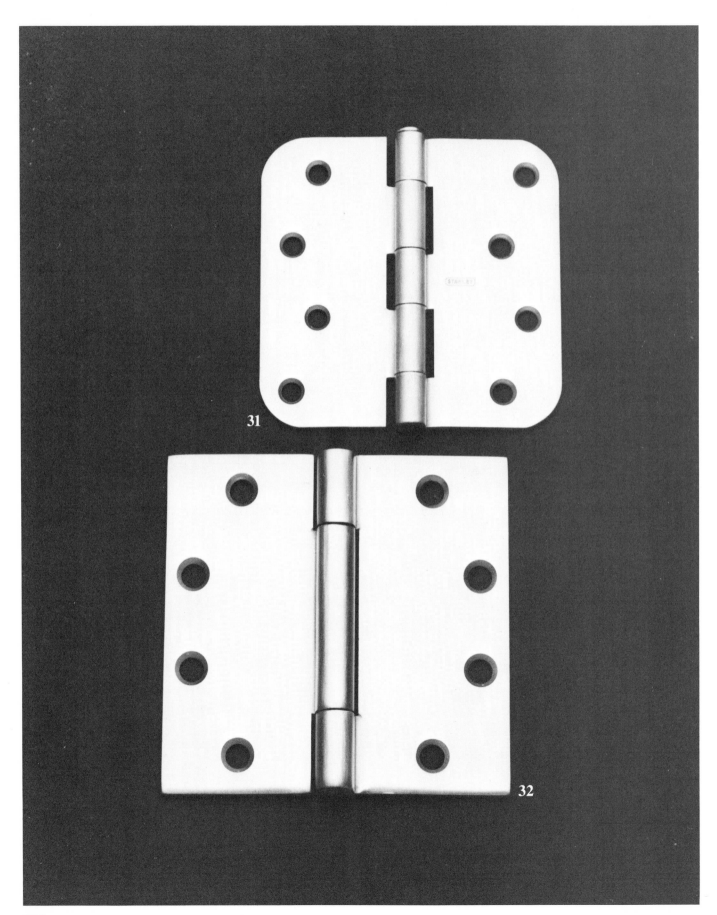

31

32

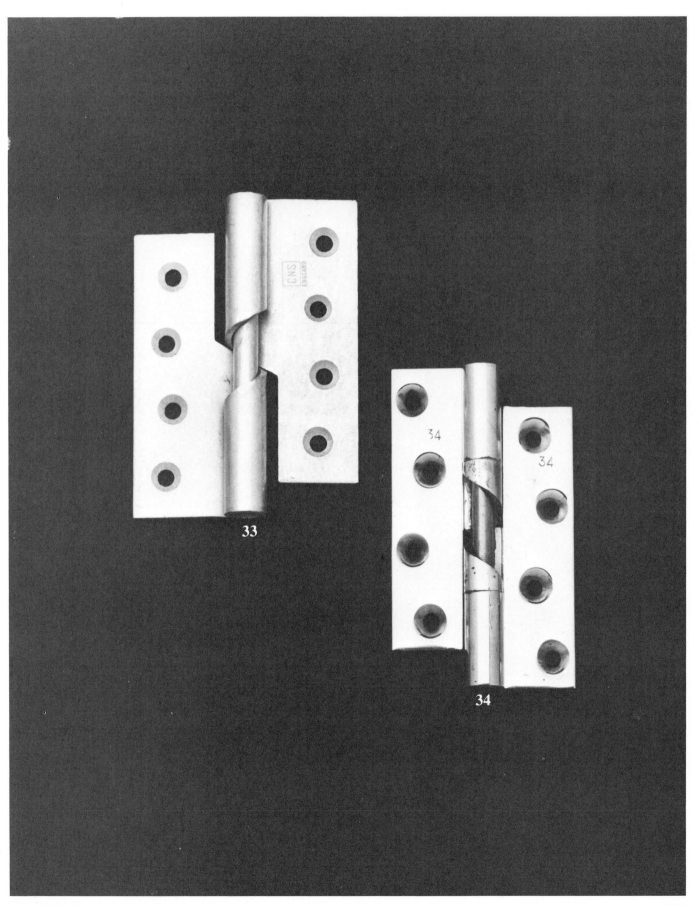

33

34

34

34

Spring Hinges

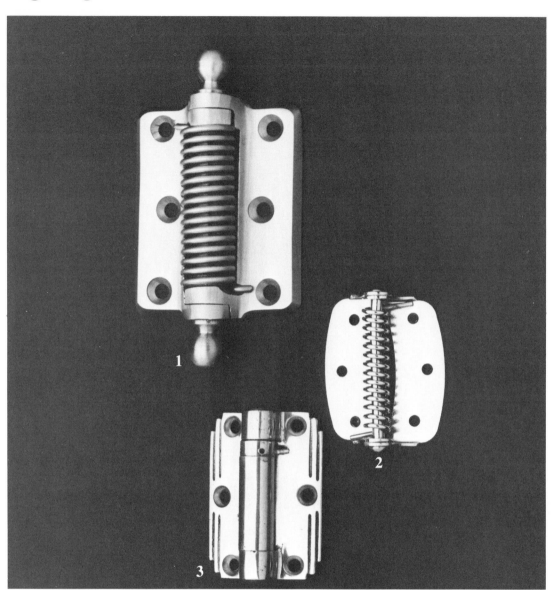

1

2

3

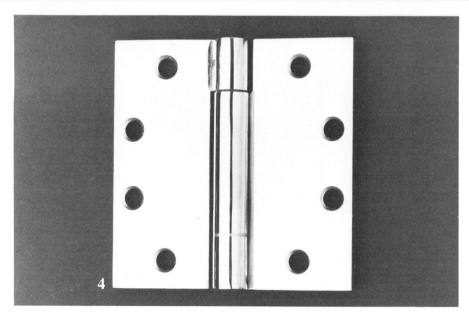

4

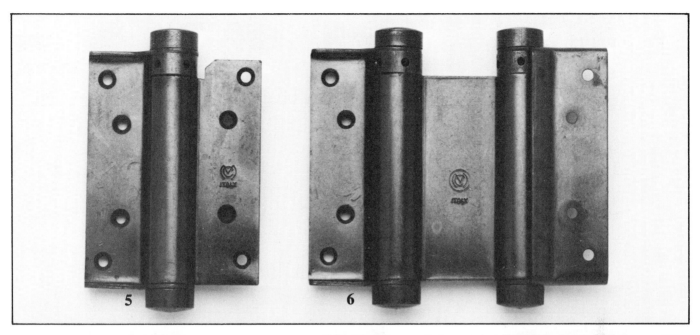

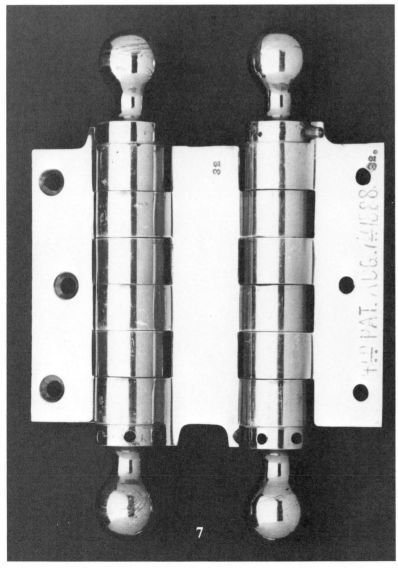

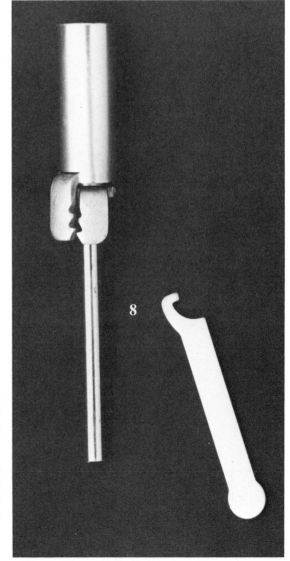

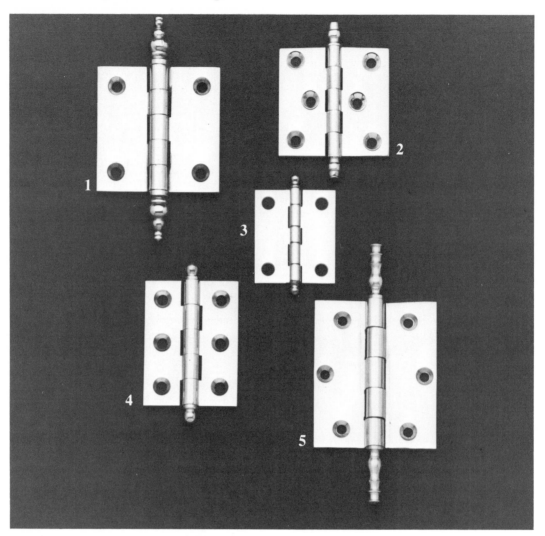

1

2

3

4

5

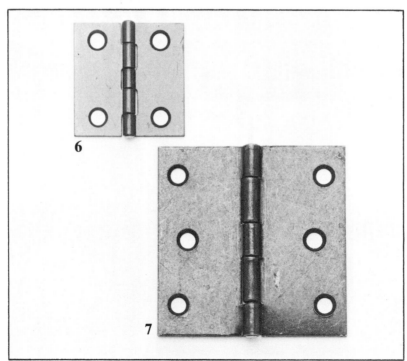

6

7

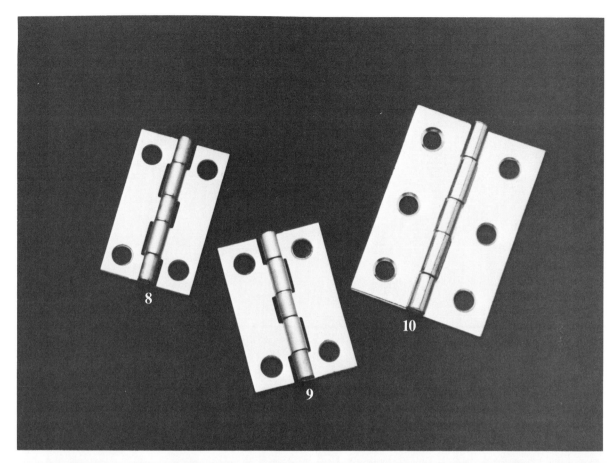

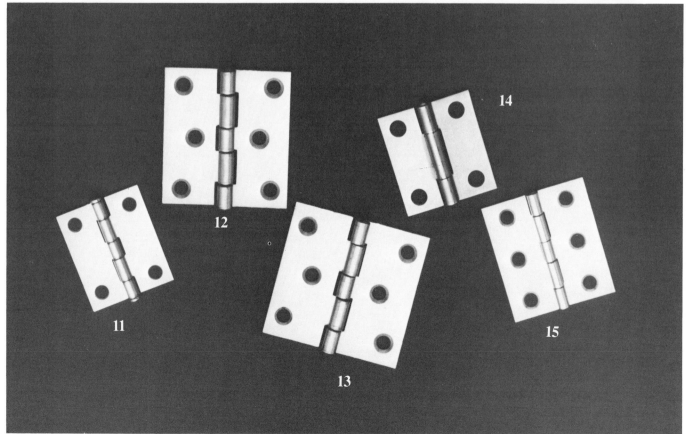

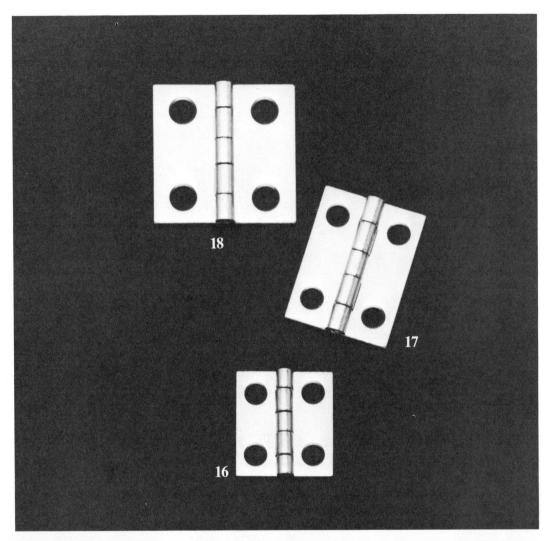

18

17

16

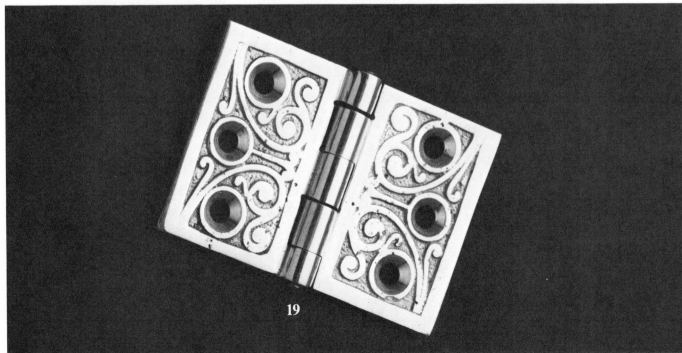

19

20

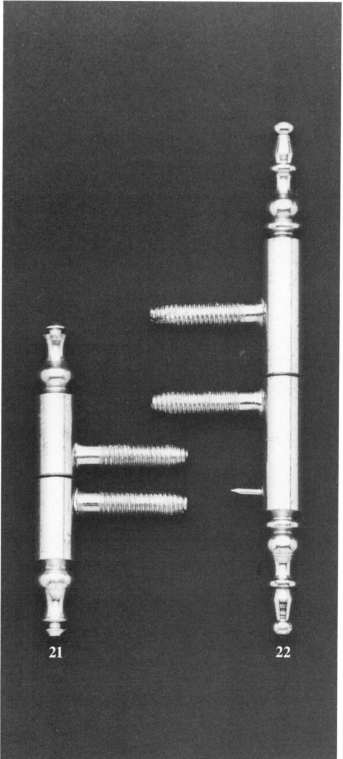

21   **22**

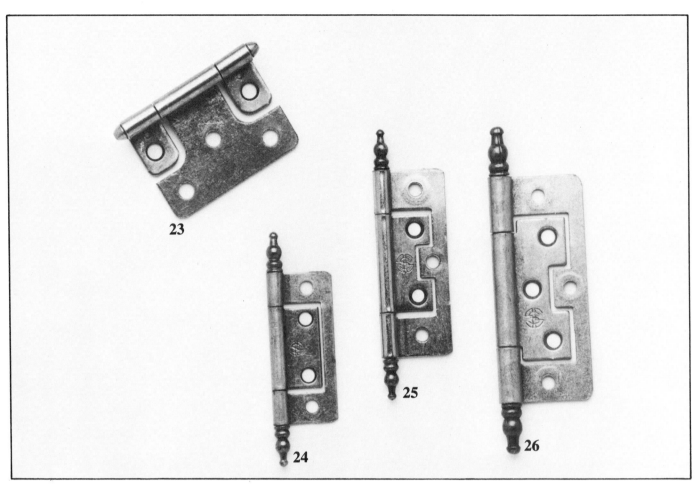

23

24

25

26

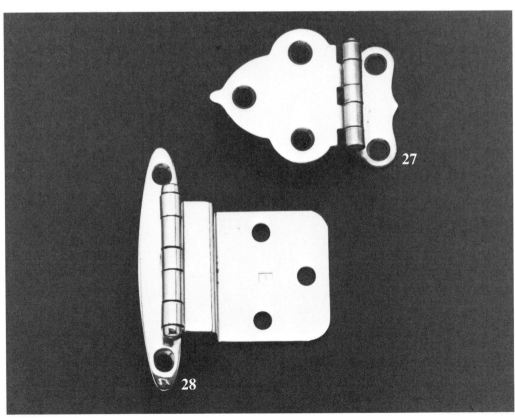

27

28

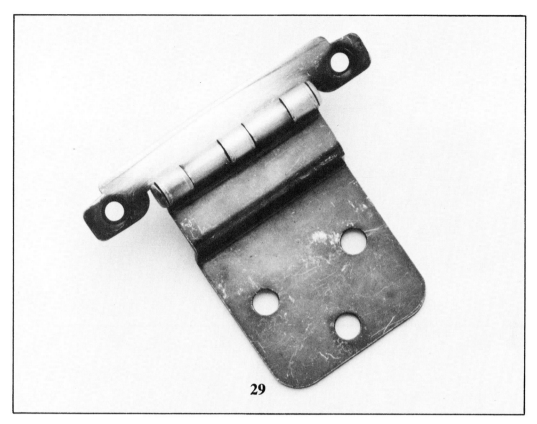

29

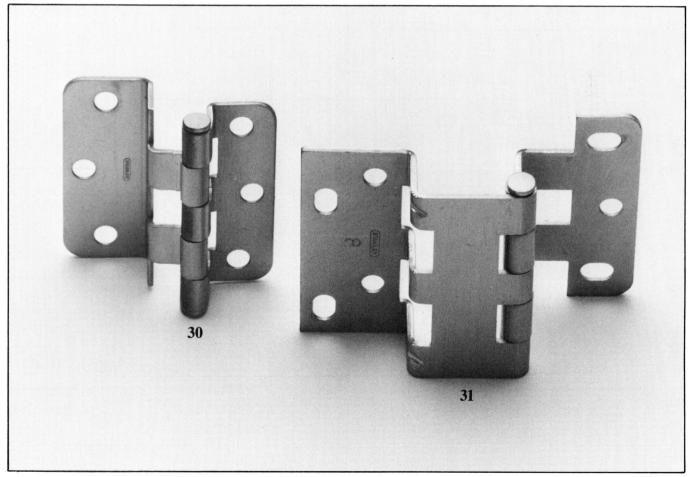

30

31

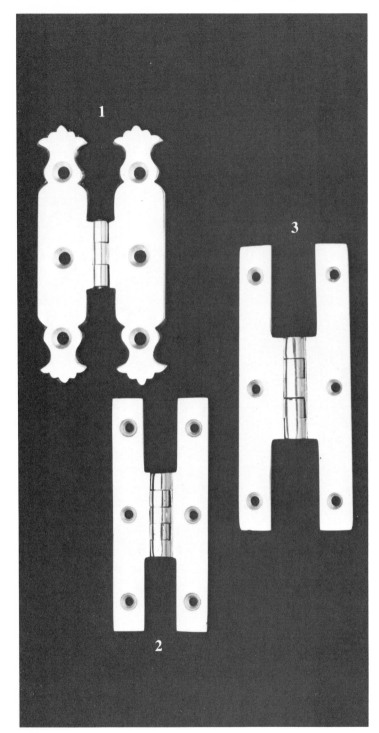

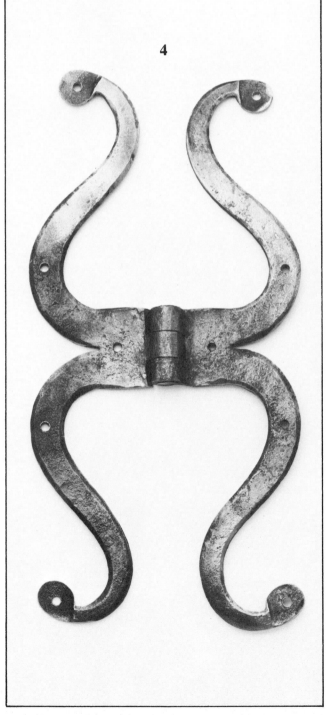

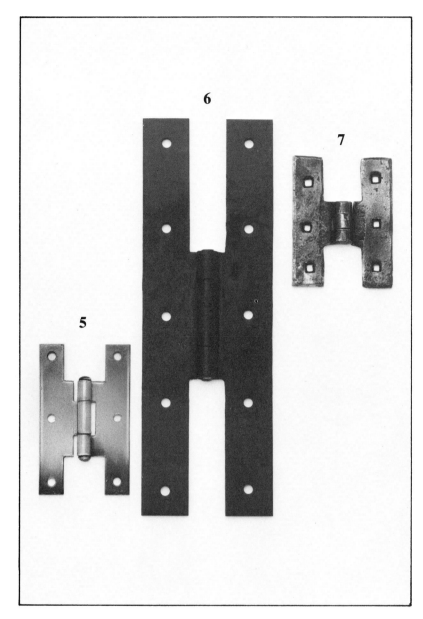

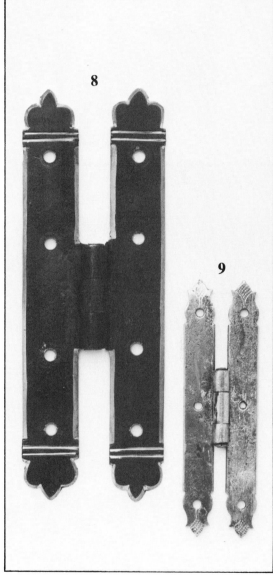

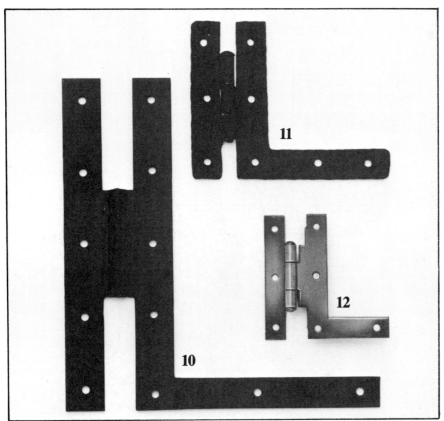

11

12

10

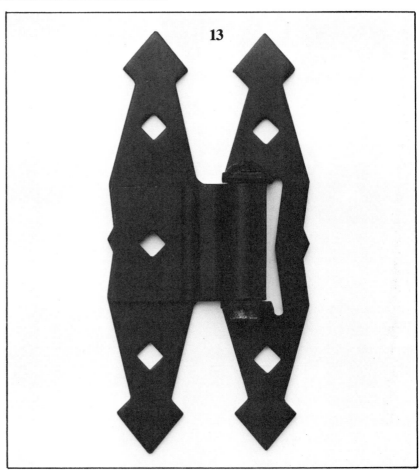

13

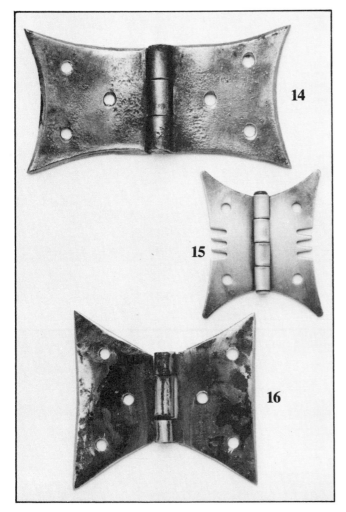

14

15

16

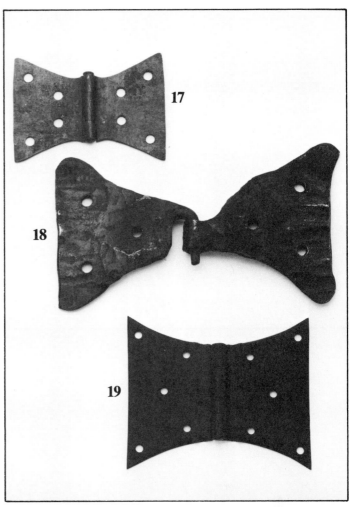

17

18

19

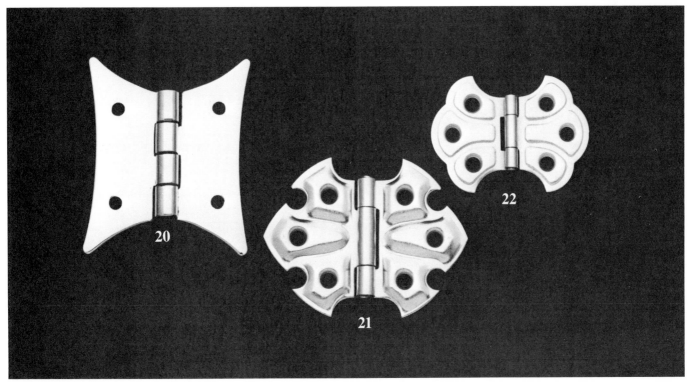

20

21

22

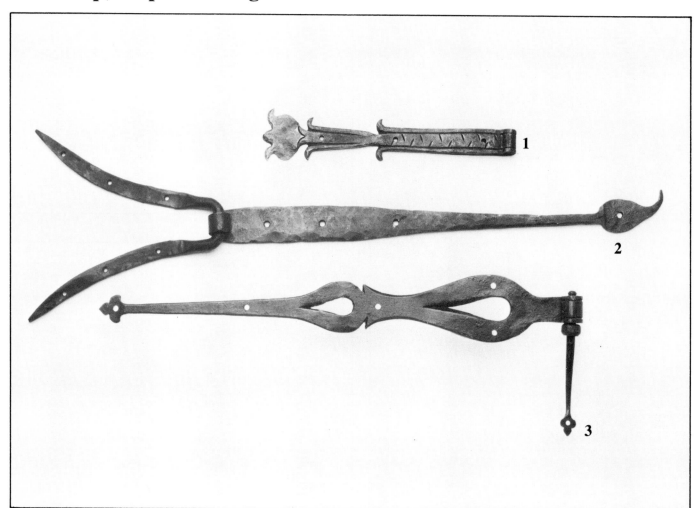

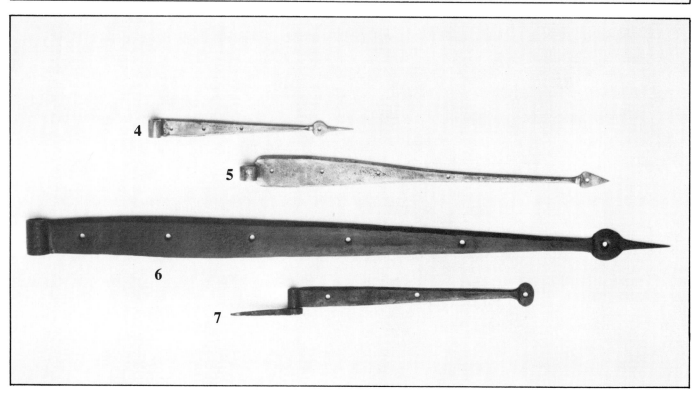

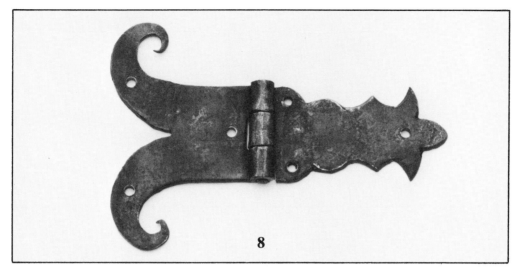

8

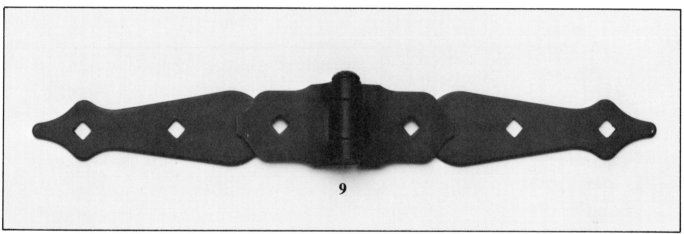

9

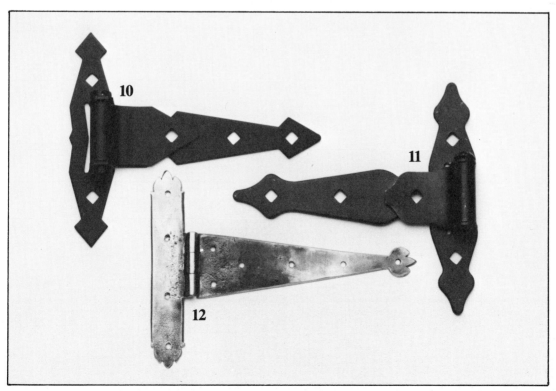

10

11

12

13

14

15

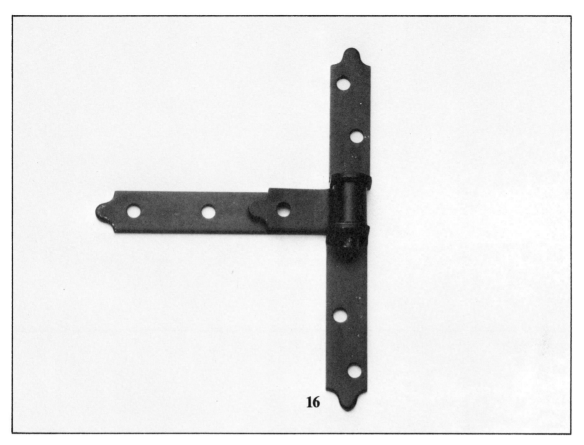

16

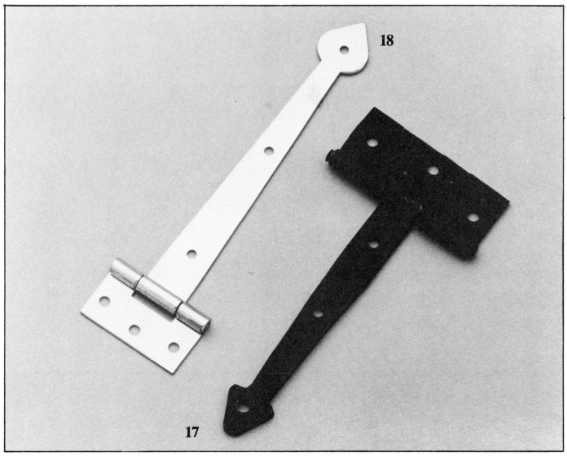

18

17

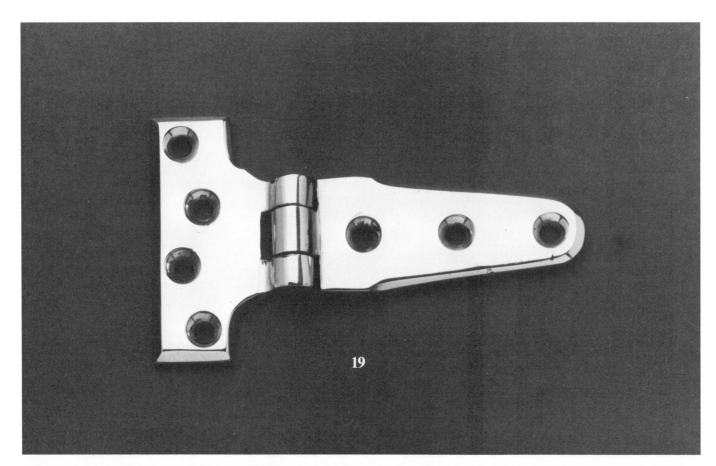

19

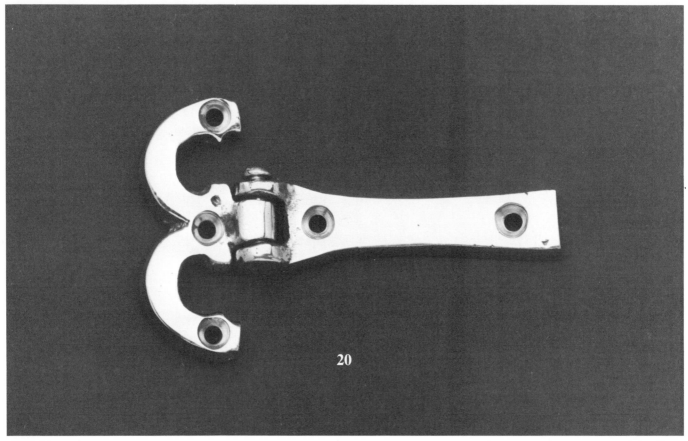

20

238

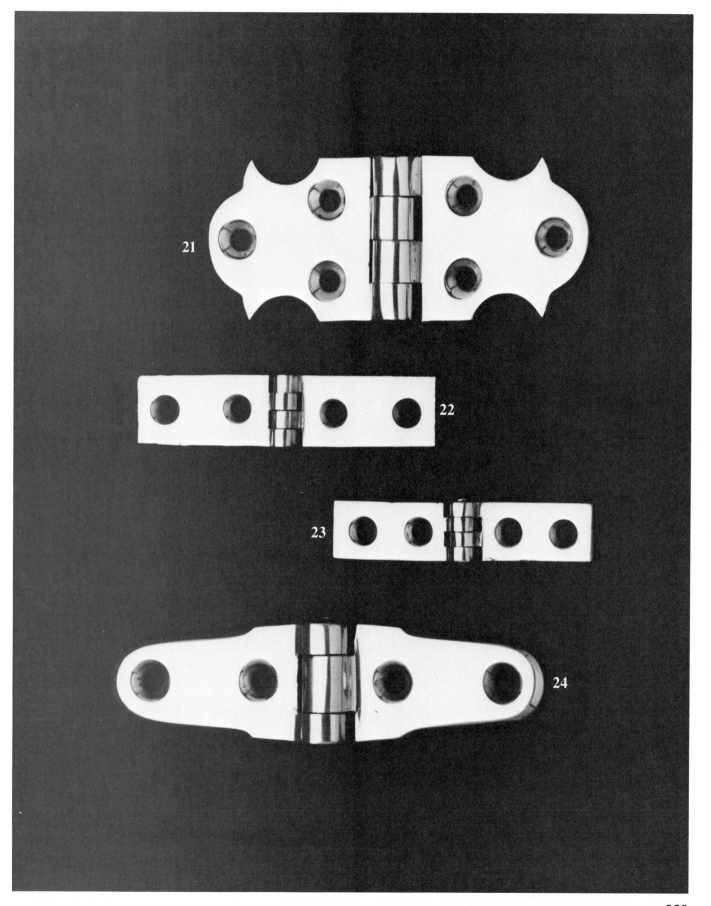

Box, Desk & Chest Hinges

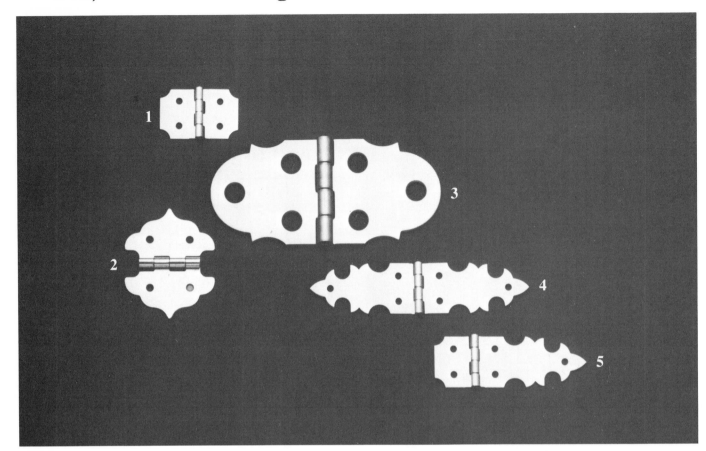

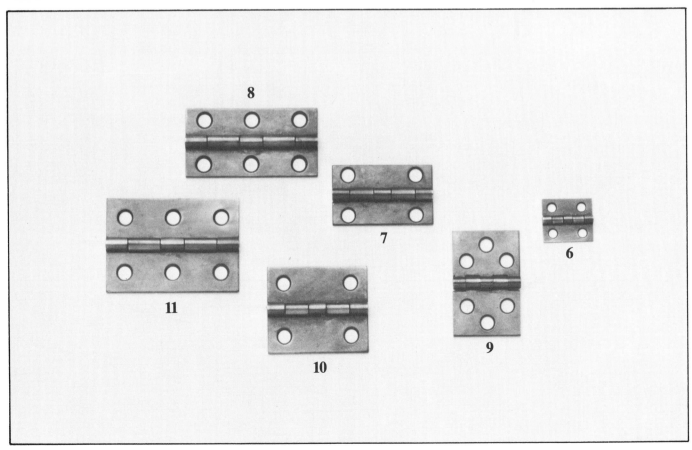

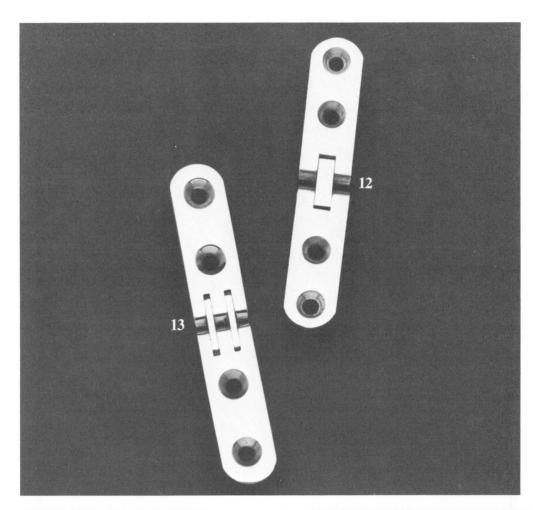

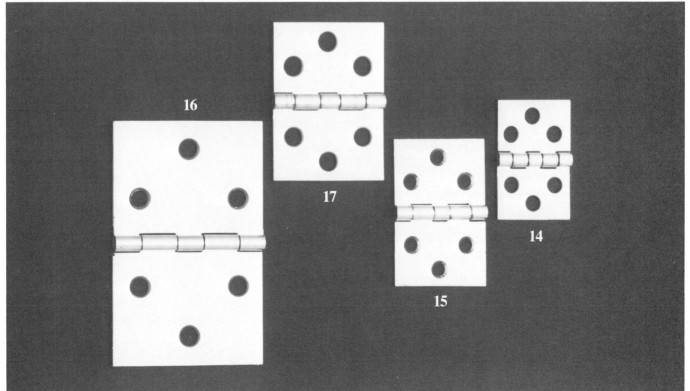

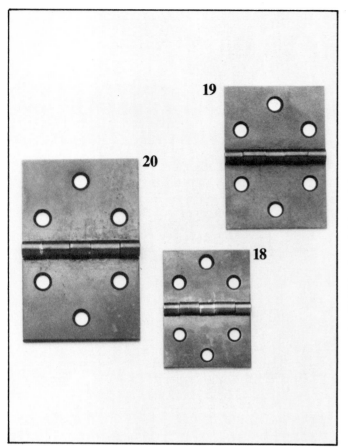

19

20

18

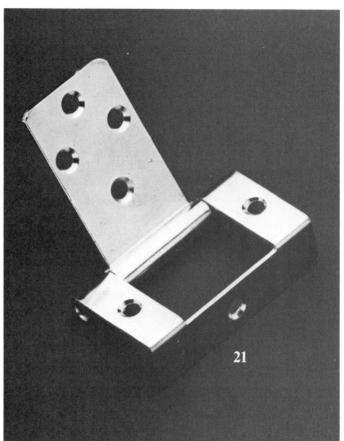

21

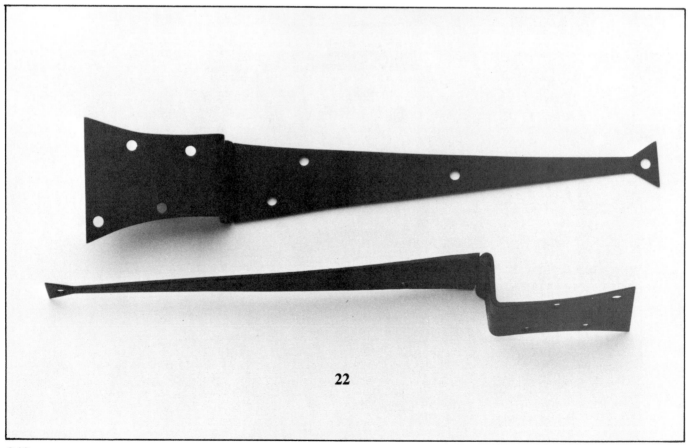

22

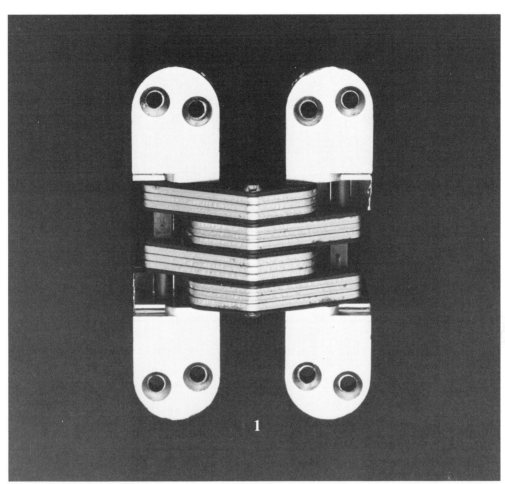

1

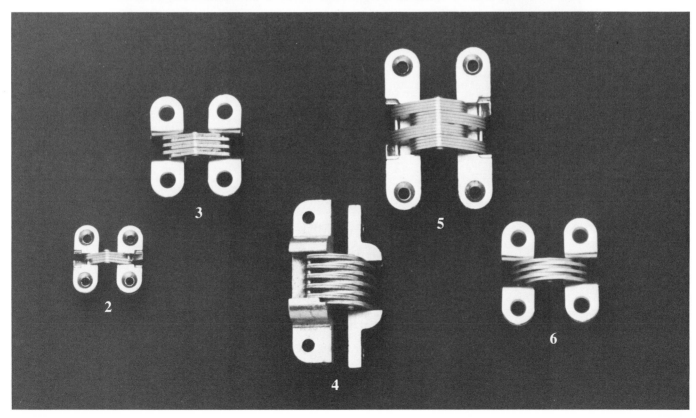

3

2

5

4

6

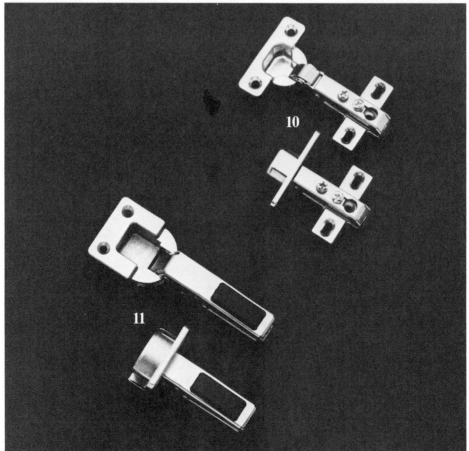

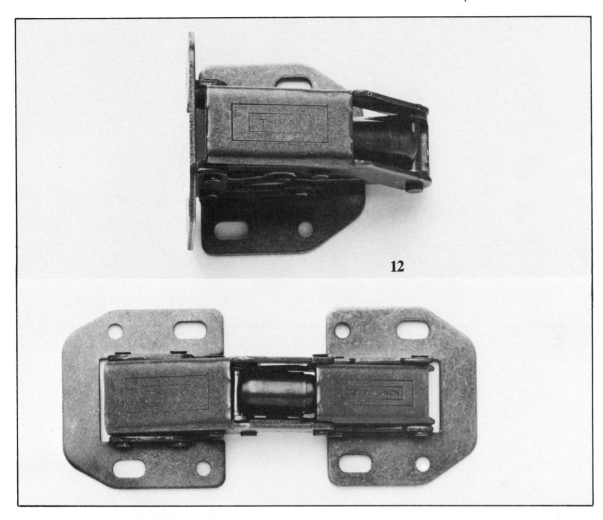

12

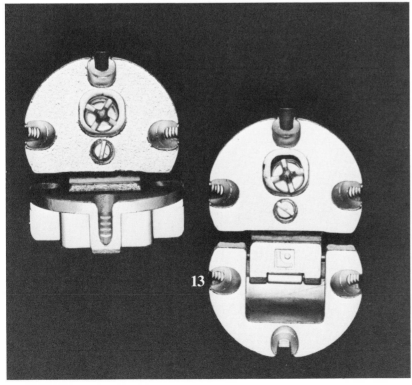

13

14

Miscellaneous Hinges

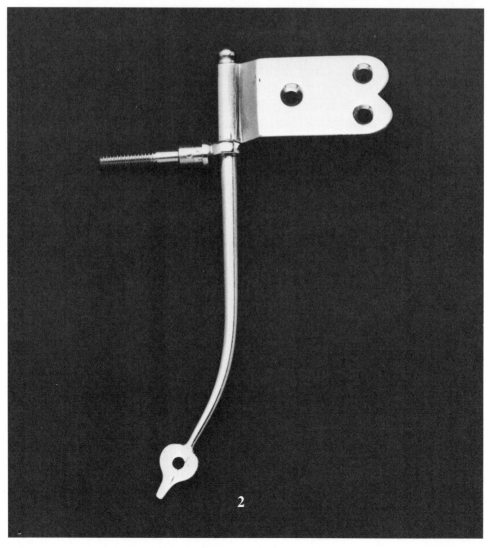

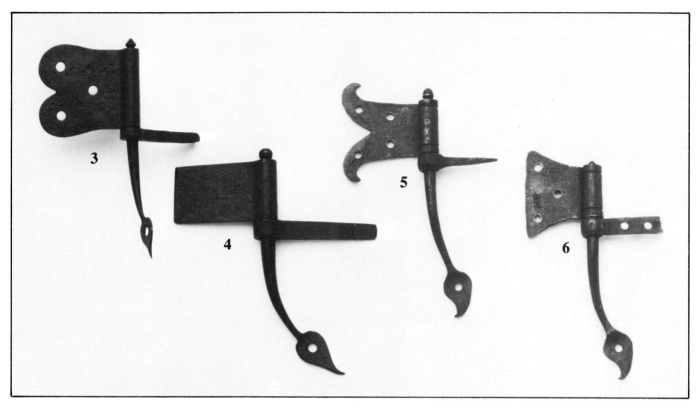

3

4

5

6

7

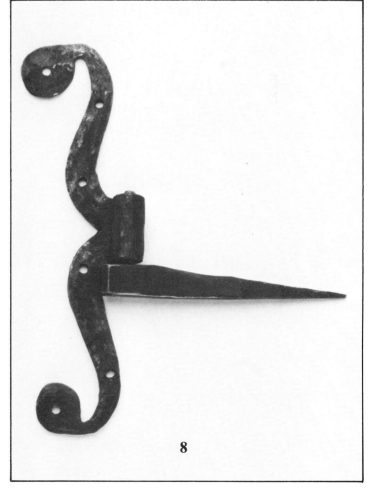

8

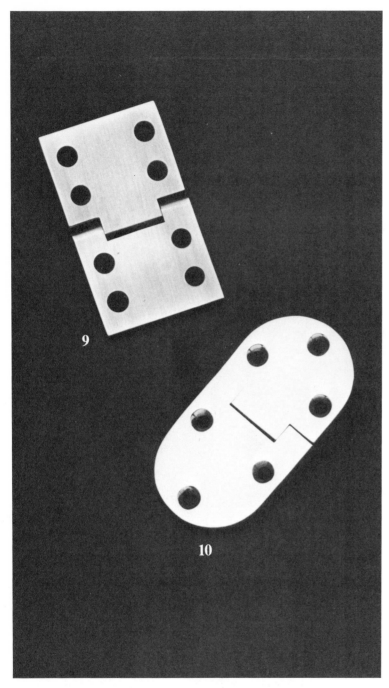

9

10

11

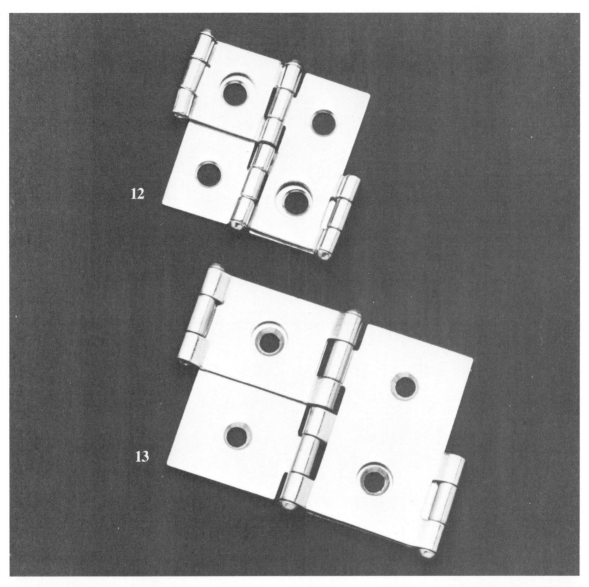

12

13

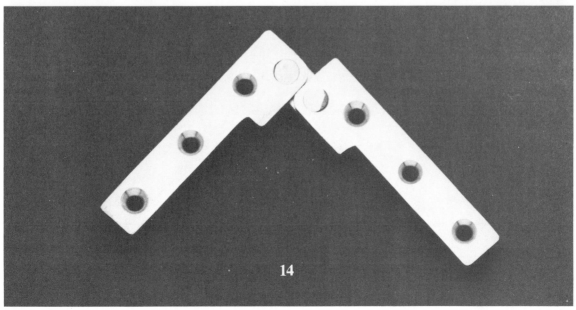

14

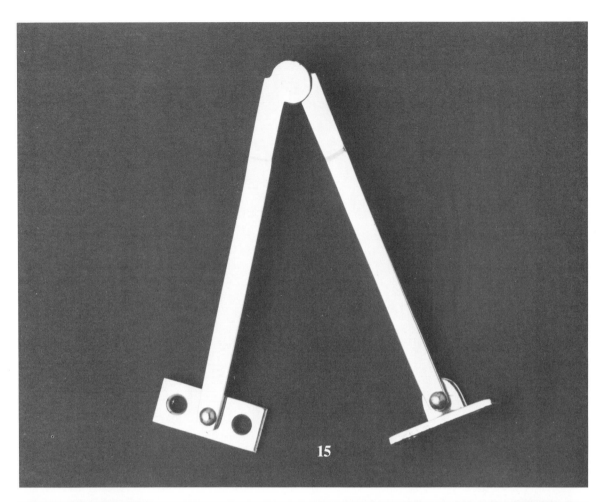

15

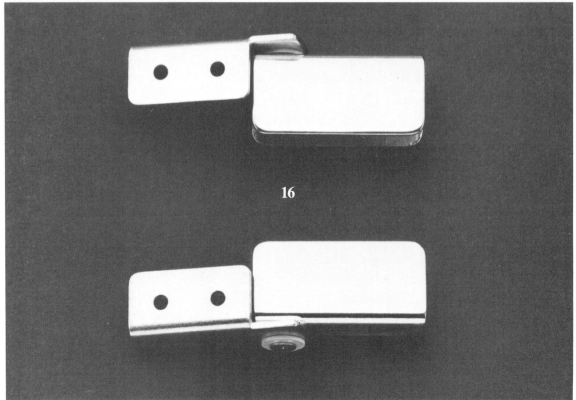

16

250

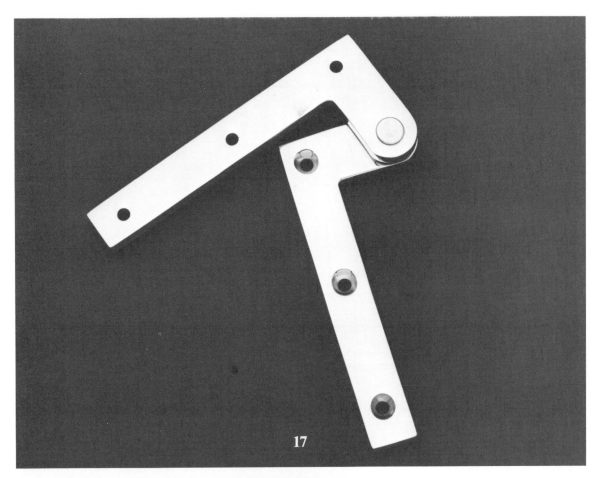

17

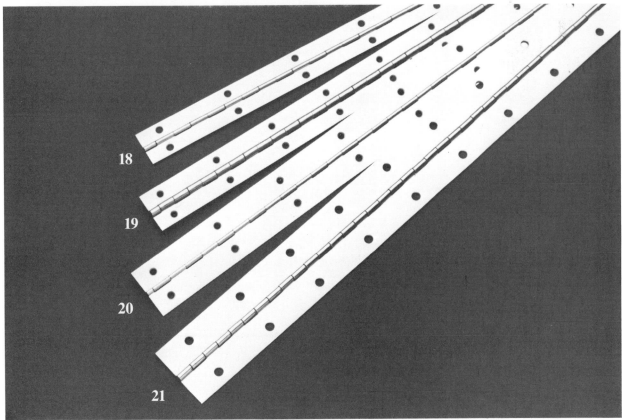

18

19

20

21

22

Butt Door Hinges

1 Butt door hinge with steeple tips
Baldwin
Extruded brass
Height and width: 4″ × 4″

2 Butt door hinge with steeple tips
Ball and Ball
Extruded brass
Height and width: 4″ × 4″

3, 4 Butt door hinges with steeple tips
Kraft Hardware
Extruded brass
Heights and widths: 3⅛″ × 2⅜″ and 4″ × 2¾″

5 Butt door hinge with steeple tips
The Merit Brass Collection
Extruded brass
Height and width: 4″ × 4″

6 Butt door hinge with ball tips
Baldwin
Extruded brass
Height and width: 4″ × 4″

7 Butt door hinge with acorn tips
Baldwin
Extruded brass
Height and width: 4″ × 4″

8, 9 Two-knuckle butt door hinges
Omnia Industries
Die-cast brass
Heights and widths: 4⅜″ × 2½″ and 7½″ × 4″
(Right-hand hinges are shown.)

10 Two-knuckle butt door hinge
Kraft Hardware
Solid brass
Height and width: 5½″ × 2¾″
(A left-hand hinge is shown.)

11 Two-knuckle butt door hinge with steeple tips
Omnia Industries
Die-cast brass
Height and width: 4″ × 2¾″
(A left-hand hinge is shown.)

12 Two-knuckle butt door hinge
Sherle Wagner International
Solid brass
Height and width: 6″ × 3⅛″
(A right-hand hinge is shown.)

13 Two-knuckle butt door hinge
Sherle Wagner International
Solid brass
Height and width: 6″ × 3″
(A left-hand hinge is shown.)

14 Two-knuckle butt door hinge
Kraft Hardware
Solid brass
Height and width: 9⅝″ × 4¾″
(A right-hand hinge is shown.)

15 Two-knuckle butt door hinge
Sherle Wagner International
Solid brass
Height and width: 6″ × 3⅛″
(A right-hand hinge is shown.)

16 Butt door hinge with button tips
Acorn
Steel, black finish
Height and width: 3″ × 3″

17 Antique butt door hinge with steeple tips (Victorian)
By-Gone Days Antiques
Cast iron
Height and width: 3″ × 3″

18 Antique two-knuckle projecting butt door hinges with steeple tips (dated 1869)
By-Gone Days Antiques
Cast bronze
Height and width: 6″ × 2¾″
(Left-hand hinges are shown.)

19 Two-knuckle butt door hinge with fancy tips (Victorian)
Ritter & Son
Lost-wax cast bronze
Height and width: 5″ × 5″
(A left-hand hinge is shown.)

20 Two-knuckle butt door hinge with fancy tips (Victorian)
Ritter & Son
Lost-wax cast bronze
Height and width: 4½″ × 4½″
(A left-hand hinge is shown.)

21 Butt door or cabinet hinge with steeple tips (Victorian)
Ritter & Son
Lost-wax cast bronze
Height and width: 3½″ × 3½″

22 Antique butt door hinge with ball tips (Victorian)
Kraft Hardware
Cast brass
Height and width: 6″ × 6″

23 Antique butt door hinges
Bob Pryor Antiques
Solid bronze
Height and width: 4″ × 4″

24 Antique two-knuckle projecting butt door hinges with steeple tips and decorative screw plates (Victorian)
Urban Archeology
Cast brass
Height and width: 6″ × 6″
(Left-hand hinges are shown.)

25 Ball bearing butt door hinge with button tips
The Merit Brass Collection
Extruded brass
Height and width: 4″ × 4″

26 Two-knuckle butt door hinge
The Merit Brass Collection
Extruded brass
Height and width: 4½″ × 4½″
(A left-hand hinge is shown.)

27 Ball bearing butt door hinge with button tips
The Merit Brass Collection
Extruded brass
Height and width: 3″ × 3″

28 Two-knuckle butt door hinge
Omnia Industries
Die-cast brass
Height and width: 2⅜″ × 3⅛″
(A left-hand hinge is shown.)

29 Two-knuckle ball bearing butt door hinge
Stanley Hardware
Forged bronze
Height and width: 5″ × 4½″
(A right-hand hinge is shown.)

30 Parliament door hinge
Ball and Ball
Solid brass
Height and width: 4″ × 4″

31 Round corner butt door hinge
Stanley Hardware
Wrought steel
Height and width: 4″ × 4″

32 Ball bearing butt door hinge
Stanley Hardware
Wrought steel
Height and width: 4½″ × 4½″

33 Rising butt door hinge
Selby Furniture Hardware
Cold-rolled steel, brass plated
Height and width: 4″ × 3″
(A left-hand hinge is shown.)

34 Rising butt door hinge
Ball and Ball
Solid brass
Height and width: 3″ × 2⅜″
(A right-hand hinge is shown.)

Spring Hinges

1 Surface-mounted spring hinge
The Merit Brass Collection
Cast brass
Height and width: 3″ × 2½″

2 Surface-mounted spring hinge
Stanley Hardware
Plated steel
Height and width: 2″ × 1¾″

3 Surface-mounted spring hinge
The Merit Brass Collection
Cast brass
Height and width: 2¼″ × 1¾″
(Tension is adjustable.)

4 Spring butt door hinge
Stanley Hardware
Steel, satin brass finish
Height and width: 4″ × 4″
(Tension is adjustable.)

5 Spring butt door hinge
Selby Furniture Hardware
Steel, dull bronze finish
Height and width: 4″ × 3″
(Tension is adjustable.)

6 Double-action spring butt door hinge
Selby Furniture Hardware
Steel, dull bronze finish
Height and width: 4″ × 5¼″
(Tension is adjustable.)

7 Antique double-action spring butt door hinge
Urban Archeology
Solid bronze
Height and width: 4″ × 5″
(Tension is adjustable.)

8 Spring hinge converter
Brookstone
Converts standard butt door hinges extending at least ⅜″ from door moulding.

Cabinet & Cupboard Hinges

1 Butt cabinet hinge with steeple tips
The Merit Brass Collection
Extruded brass
Height and width: 2″ × 2″

2 Butt cabinet hinge with steeple tips
Ball and Ball
Cast brass
Height and width: 1¾″ × 1¾″

3 Butt cabinet hinge with ball tips
Stanley Hardware
Solid brass
Height and width: 1½″ × 1¼″

4 Butt cabinet hinge with ball tips
Baldwin
Extruded brass
Height and width: 2″ × 1½″

5 Butt cabinet hinge with steeple tips
Kraft Hardware
Extruded brass
Height and width: 2⅜″ × 2″

6 Butt cabinet hinge
Selby Furniture Hardware
Steel, brass plated
Height and width: 1½″ × 1½″

7 Butt cabinet hinge
Selby Furniture Hardware
Steel
Height and width: 2½″ × 2½″

8,9 Butt cabinet hinges
Stanley Hardware
Solid brass
Heights and widths: 1½″ × ⅞″ and 1½″ × 1″

10 Butt cabinet hinge
Selby Furniture Hardware
Solid brass
Height and width: 2″ × 1⅜″

11 Butt cabinet hinge
Stanley Hardware
Solid brass
Height and width: 1½″ × 1¼″

12, 13 Butt cabinet hinges
Selby Furniture Hardware
Cold-rolled steel
Heights and widths: 2″ × 1¹¹⁄₁₆″ and 2″ × 2″

14 Butt cabinet hinge
Horton Brasses
Steel
Height and width: 1½″ × 1⅜″

15 Butt cabinet hinge
Selby Furniture Hardware
Steel, brass plated
Height and width: 1¾″ × 1⁹⁄₁₆″

16–18 Butt cabinet hinges
Ball and Ball
Solid brass
Heights and widths: ¾″ × ¹¹⁄₁₆″, 1″ × ¾″, and 1″ × 1¹⁄₃₂″

19 Butt cabinet hinge (Victorian)
Ball and Ball
Cast brass
Height and width: 1½″ × 2″

20 Lift-off parliament cabinet hinge
Paxton
Cast brass
Leaves: 1⅛″ × ¾″
(A left-hand hinge is shown.)

21, 22 No-screw lift-off cabinet hinges
Selby Furniture Hardware
Steel, bronze finish
Overall lengths: 2¾″ × 4⅜″
(Top threaded arm screws into door and bottom arm screws into cabinet. Can be used on flush, overlapping, or lipped doors.)

23 Semiconcealed flush-mounting cabinet hinge
Selby Furniture Hardware
Steel, brass finish
Overall height: 2″
(For overlapping doors.)

24–26 Semiconcealed flush-mounting cabinet hinges
Selby Furniture Hardware
Steel, brass finish
Overall heights: 2″, 2½″, and 3″
(For overlapping doors.)

27 Offset cabinet hinge
Restoration Hardware
Cast brass
Hinge leaf: 1½″ × 1½″
(Surface mounts for ⅜″ offset cabinet doors.)

28 Lipped-door cabinet hinge
The Merit Brass Collection
Wrought brass
Outside leaf: 3″
(For ⅜″ lipped doors.)

29 Lipped-door cabinet hinge
Acorn
Steel
Outside leaf: 2½″
(For ⅜″ lipped doors.)

30 Lipped- or overlay-door cabinet hinge
Stanley Hardware
Wrought steel
Oveall height: 2½″
(⅜″ inset for ¾″-thick lipped doors.)

31 Overlay-door cabinet hinge
Stanley Hardware
Wrought steel
Overall height: 2½″
(For ¾″-thick overlay cabinet doors.)

H, H/L & Butterfly Hinges

1 H hinge
Ball and Ball
Cast brass
Height and width: 4″ × 2″

2,3 H hinges
Kraft Hardware
Cast brass
Heights and widths: 3½″ × 1½″ and 4¼″
× 1¾″

4 Serpentine hinge
Mark E. Rocheford, Hammerworks
Hand-forged iron
Height and width: 12″ × 6″

5 H hinge
Acorn
Steel, pewter finish
Height and width: 3″ × 1¾″

6 H hinge
**Peter A. Renzetti, The Arden Forge
Company**
Hand-forged iron
Height and width: 8″ × 2¾″

7 H hinge
Bob Patrick, Big Anvil Forge
Hand-forged iron
Height and width: 2⅝″ × 2″

8 H hinge
Mark E. Rocheford, Hammerworks
Hand-forged iron
Height and width: 8¼″ × 2¼″

9 H hinge
Mark E. Bokenkamp, Bokenkamp's Forge
Hand-forged iron, antique tin plate finish
Height and width: 4″ × 1¼″

10 H/L hinge
**Peter A. Renzetti, The Arden Forge
Company**
Hand-forged iron
Height and width: 8″ × 8″

11 H/L hinge
Robert H. Klar, Salmon Falls Forge
Height and width: 4″ × 5¼″

12 Offset H/L hinge
Acorn
Steel, pewter finish
Height and width: 3″ × 3¼″, offset: ¾″

13 H hinge
Arrowsmith Industries
Steel, zinc plated and black enamel
painted
Height and width: 3⅝″ × 1¾″

14 Butterfly hinge
Mark E. Rocheford, Hammerworks
Hand-forged iron
Height and width: 2¼″ × 4¼″

15 Butterfly hinge
Acorn
Steel, pewter finish
Height and width: 2⅜″ × 2″

16 Butterfly hinge
Lance Cloutier, The Ram's Head Forge
Hand-forged iron
Height and width: 2¾″ × 3″

17 Butterfly hinge
Mark E. Bokenkamp, Bokenkamp's Forge
Hand-forged iron
Height and width: 2⅜″ × 3¼″

18 Butterfly hinge
**Steve Kayne, Steve Kayne Hand Forged
Hardware**
Hand-forged iron
Height and width: 3½″ × 6″
(A left-hand hinge is shown.)

19 Butterfly hinge
**Peter A. Renzetti, The Arden Forge
Company**
Hand-forged iron
Height and width: 3¼″ × 4″

20 Butterfly hinge
The Renovator's Supply
Cast brass
Height and width: 2¾″ × 2″

21, 22 Butterfly hinges
Stanley Hardware
Stamped steel, brass finish
Heights and widths: 2⅛″ × 2¾″ and 1½″
× 2⅛″

Strap, Flap & T Hinges

1 Strap hinge
Larry B. Wood, The Farm Forge
Hand-forged iron
Overall length: 11″

2 Strap hinge
Craig Kaviar, Kaviar Forge
Hand-forged iron
Overall length: 26″

3 Strap hinge
Mark E. Bokenkamp, Bokenkamp's Forge
Hand-forged iron
Overall length: 20″

4 Cupboard strap hinge
Mark E. Rocheford, Hammerworks
Hand-forged iron
Overall length: 11″

5 Strap hinge
Mark E. Rocheford, Hammerworks
Hand-forged iron
Overall length: 19½″

6 Strap hinge
Mark E. Rocheford, Hammerworks
Hand-forged iron
Overall length: 34″

7 Strap hinge with drive-in pintle
Mark E. Bokenkamp, Bokenkamp's Forge
Hand-forged iron
Overall strap length: 12½″

8 Strap hinge
Bob Patrick, Big Anvil Forge
Hand-forged iron
Height and width: 3⅛″ × 5¾″

9 Double strap hinge
PTI-Dolco/Simpson Hardware
Steel, zinc plated and black lacquer
painted
Overall length: 8″

10 Spring-loaded T hinge
Arrowsmith Industries
Steel, zinc plated and black enamel
painted
Height and width: 6½″ × 9″

11 Gate T hinge
PTI-Dolco/Simpson Hardware
Steel, zinc plated and black lacquer
painted
Height and width: 8″ × 9″

12 Cross garnet hinge
Mark E. Rocheford, Hammerworks
Hand-forged iron
Height and width: 6½″ × 9″

13–15 Large exterior door hinge plates
Erco
Hammered cast bronze
(Custom lengths available.)

16 Lift-off T hinge
PTI-Dolco/Simpson Hardware
Steel, zinc plated and black lacquer
painted
Height and width: 10″ × 8″
(A left-hand hinge is shown.)

17 Strap hinge
Richard C. Swenson, Swenson's Forge
Hand-forged iron
Strap length: 4½″

18 Strap hinge
The Renovator's Supply
Solid brass
Overall length: 6″

19 T hinge
The Merit Brass Collection
Cast brass
Overall length: 6″

20 Fancy T hinge
Custom Decor
Sand-cast brass
Overall length: 4″

21 Flap hinge
The Merit Brass Collection
Cast brass
Overall length: 4″

22, 23 Flap hinges
The Merit Brass Collection
Cast brass
Overall lengths: 2¾″ and 2⅜″

24 Flap hinge
The Merit Brass Collection
Cast brass
Overall length: 4″

Box, Desk & Chest Hinges

1 Box hinge
Stanley Hardware
Solid brass
Height and width: ⅝″ × 1″

2 Box hinge
Stanley Hardware
Solid brass
Height and width: 1⅛″ × 1½″

3 Box hinge
Stanley Hardware
Solid brass
Height and width: 1⁵/₁₆″ × 2¹⁵/₁₆″

4 Box hinge
Stanley Hardware
Solid brass
Height and width: ⅝″ × 2¹¹/₁₆″

5 Box hinge
Stanley Hardware
Solid brass
Height and width: ⅝″ × 1⅞″

6–11 Box hinges
Horton Brasses
Solid brass
Heights (along knuckles) and widths: ¾″ × ⅝″, 1½″ × ⅞″, 2″ × 1″, 1″ × 1½″, 1½″ × 1¼″, and 2″ × 1⅜″

12 Box hinge
Selby Furniture Hardware
Solid brass
Overall length: 2¾″

13 Box hinge
Ball and Ball
Cast brass
Overall length: 3″

14–16 Desk hinges
Stanley Hardware
Solid brass
Heights (along knuckles) and widths: 1″ × 1½″, 1½″ × 2″, and 2″ × 3¹/₁₆″

17 Desk hinge
Ball and Ball
Rolled brass
Height (along knuckle) and width: 1¼″ × 1⅞″

18–20 Desk hinges
Horton Brasses
Solid brass
Heights (along knuckles) and widths: 1½″ × 2″, 1¾″ × 2½″, and 2″ × 3¹/₁₆″

21 Chest hinge
Selby Furniture Hardware
Cold-rolled steel, brass finish
Knuckle: 2″

22 Blanket chest hinge
Peter A. Renzetti, The Arden Forge Company
Hand-forged iron
Strap length: 8″

Concealed Hinges

1 Invisible door hinge (Soss)
Michigan Production Grinding Company
Rust-proof zinc alloy casting
Overall height: 4⅝″, mortise depth: 1¹⁹/₃₂″
(For use on full-size doors.)

2, 3 Invisible hinges (Soss)
Michigan Production Grinding Company
Steel
Overall heights: 1″ and 1½″, mortise depths: ¹⁵/₃₂″ and ⅝″

4 Invisible hinge (Soss)
Michigan Production Grinding Company
Rust-proof zinc alloy casting
Overall height: 2⅜″
(Mounts on back of door and frame and requires no moritse. Hinge is visible on back.)

5, 6 Invisible hinges (Soss)
Michigan Production Grinding Company
Rust-proof zinc alloy casting
Overall heights: 2⅜″ and 1½″
(For use on metal cabinet doors.)

7, 8 Invisible hinges
Selby Furniture Hardware
Solid brass with brass-plated steel linkage
Diameters: ½″ and ⁹/₁₆″, mortise depths: ¹⁷/₃₂″ and ⁹/₁₆″
(Mortise is drilled.)

9 Invisible hinge
Michigan Production Grinding Company
Rust-proof zinc alloy casting
Diameter: ½″, mortise depth: ¹⁹/₃₂″
(Mortise is drilled.)

10 Concealed cabinet hinges
Selby Furniture Hardware
Steel
Overall length, extended: 3⅜″
(For use on flush or overlay doors.)

11 Concealed cabinet hinge
Stanley Hardware
Steel
Overall length, extended: 4¼″
(For use on flush or overlay doors.)

12 Concealed cabinet hinges
Selby Furniture Hardware
Steel
Overall length, extended: 3½″
(For use on flush or overlay doors.)

13 Concealed flap hinges
Selby Furniture Hardware
Steel, nickle plated
Flap diameter: 1⅜″

14 Semiconcealed pivot hinge
Michigan Production Grinding Company
Steel
Overall height: 1⅝″
(Only the pivot of the hinge is visible when door is closed.)

Miscellaneous Hinges

1 Oriental dragon cabinet hinge
Kraft Hardware
Solid brass, hand chased
Height and width: 3″ × 9½″

2 Offset rattail hinge
Ball and Ball
Cast brass
Height and width: 5″ × 2″, offset: ⅜″
(A right-hand hinge is shown.)

3 Rattail hinge
Peter A. Renzetti, The Arden Forge Company
Hand-forged iron
Overall length: 4½″
(A left-hand hinge is shown.)

4 Mortise rattail hinge
Peter A. Renzetti, The Arden Forge Company
Hand-forged iron
Overall length: 4¾″
(A left-hand hinge is shown.)

5 Rattail hinge
Mark E. Bokenkamp, Bokenkamp's Forge
Hand-forged iron
Overall length: 4¾″
(A left-hand hinge is shown.)

6 Rattail hinge
Mark E. Bokenkamp, Bokenkamp's Forge
Hand-forged iron
Overall length: 4½″
(A left-hand hinge is shown.)

7 Snipe hinge
Horton Brasses
Soft iron
Each side: 2¾″

8 Dutch stone house pintle hinge
Steve Kayne, Steve Kayne Hand Forged Hardware
Hand-forged iron
Overall height: 7¾″
(A left-hand hinge is shown.)

9 Butler's tray hinge
Horton Brasses
Solid brass
Height and width: 2½″ × 1½″

10 Butler's tray hinge
Period Furniture Hardware
Wrought brass
Height and width: 3″ × 1½″

11 Back flap hinge
Selby Furniture Hardware
Steel
Height and width: 3″ × 1¼″

12, 13 Double-acting folding screen hinges
Selby Furniture Hardware
Steel, brass plated
Heights: 1¾″ and 2″

14 Card table hinge
Paxton
Cast brass
Each leaf: 2½″

15 Lid support
The Merit Brass Collection
Drop forged cast brass
Open length: 8″

16 Glass door hinge set
Selby Furniture Hardware
Solid brass
Height and width: ½″ × 1½″
(Hinges clip on top and bottom corners of ⅛″ to ³/₁₆″ glass without cutting or drilling.)

17 Pivot door hinge
Kraft Hardware
Chrome
Overall length: 4⅜″

18–20 Continuous hinges
Selby Furniture Hardware
Steel, brass plated
Open widths: ⅞″, 1″, and 1¼″, standard and custom lengths available

21 Continuous hinge
The Merit Brass Collection
Stainless steel, brass plated
Open width: 2″, standard and custom lengths available

22 Harpsichord hinge
Ball and Ball
Cast brass
Width: 1¾″

9

Window & Shutter Hardware

WINDOWS contain a good deal of hardware. Bottom sashes have to be lifted and lowered. Top and bottom sashes at times must be kept tightly shut and unopenable to keep out the cold or calculating intruders. When the idea is to let in just a breeze and nothing more, a lower sash has to be held up just slightly while remaining unviolatably secure. For each of these simple operations there is hardware galore—some old, some reproduction, and endless supplies of new. But windows are mainly for looking out of, so whatever gets installed on them ought to be spare.

Shutters on windows take even more hardware. They need hinges of one type or another to swing on, dogs to keep them open, and some sort of bolt, latch, or catch to secure them when they're shut.

Plenty of ready-made hardware is available for shutters, too, but a less conventional and more adventurous place to begin is maybe at your blacksmith.

259

Some Window & Shutter Terms

Sash Fastener. Any locking or holding device attached to the meeting rail of a double-hung window and used to fasten the two sashes together.

Sash Lift. Any flush-mounted cup or surface-mounted bar applied to the lower sash and by which the sash is raised or lowered.

Sash Lock. Any locking device controlled by a key used to fasten a window.

Sash Pin. A narrow rod inserted through holes drilled into both upper and lower sashes so that the lower sash may be held partly opened yet immobile.

Shutter Bar. Any latching or bolting device used to fasten shutters together when they are closed.

Shutter Dog. An ornamental gravitating catch used to hold opened shutters back against the exterior surface surrounding a window. Also called a *Shutter Turn* or *Shutter Holdback*.

Sash Lifts, Locks, Bolts & Fasteners

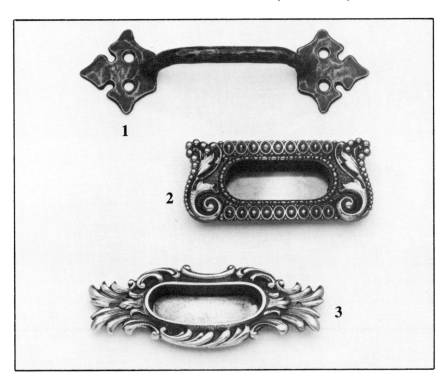

1

2

3

4

5

6

7

8

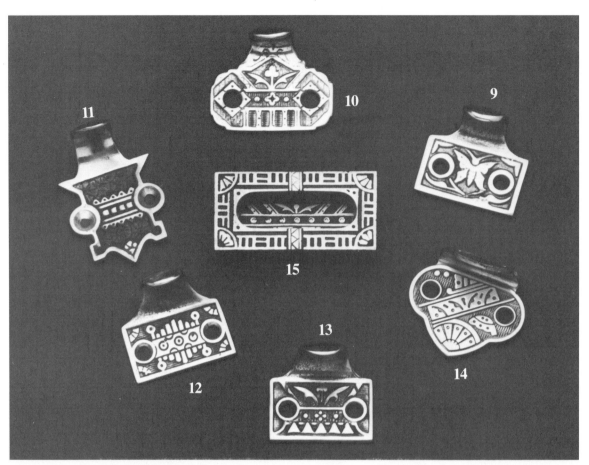

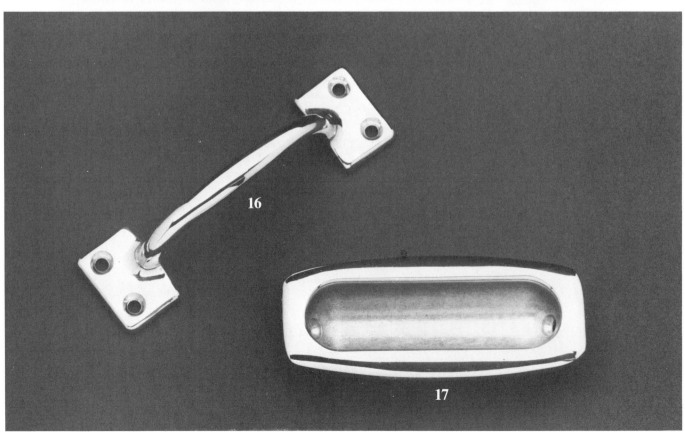

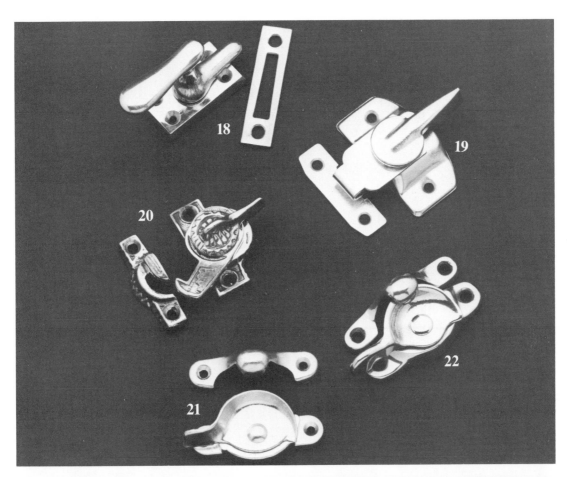

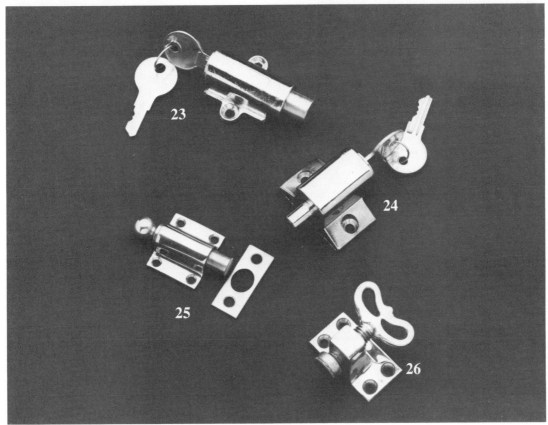

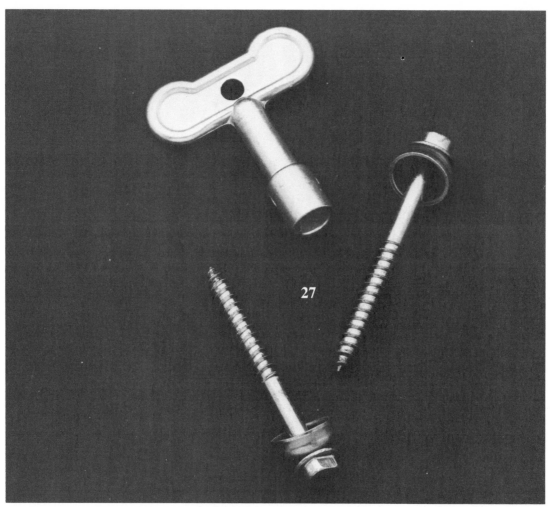

27

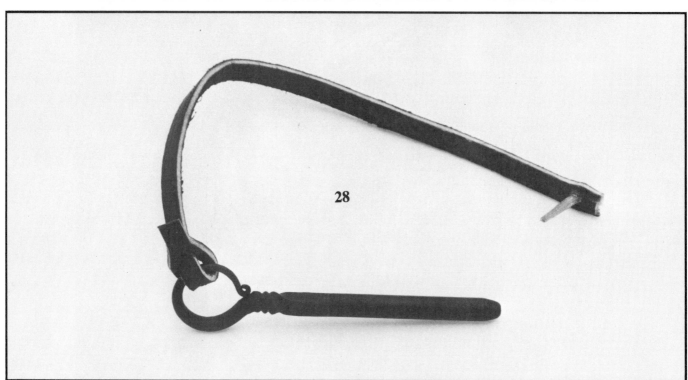

28

264

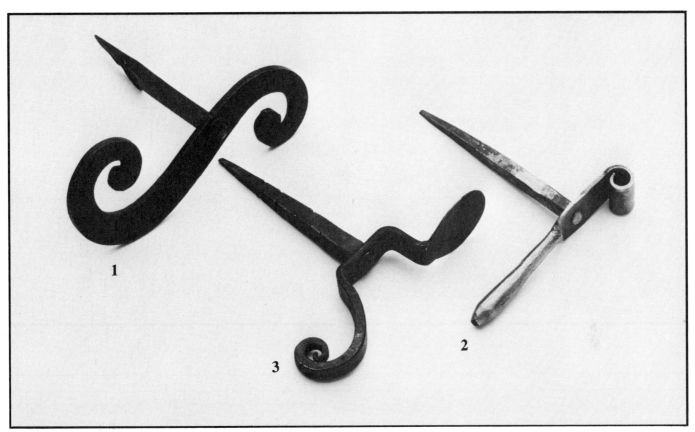

1

2

3

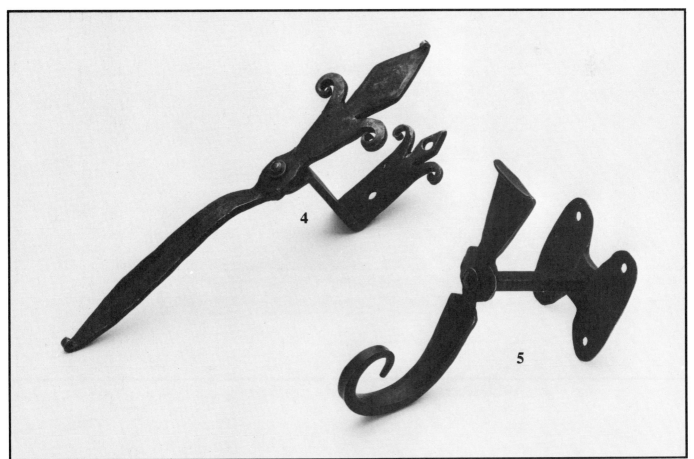

4

5

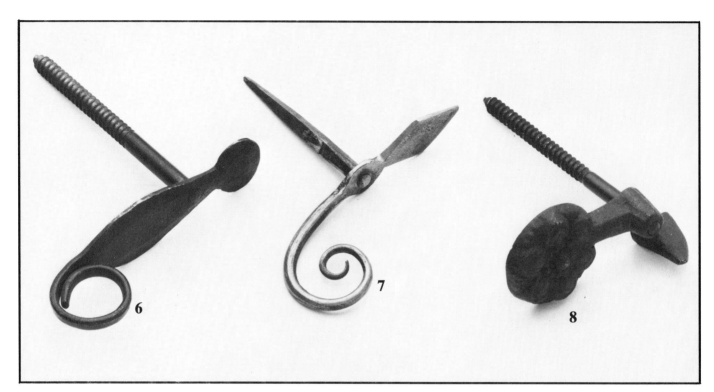

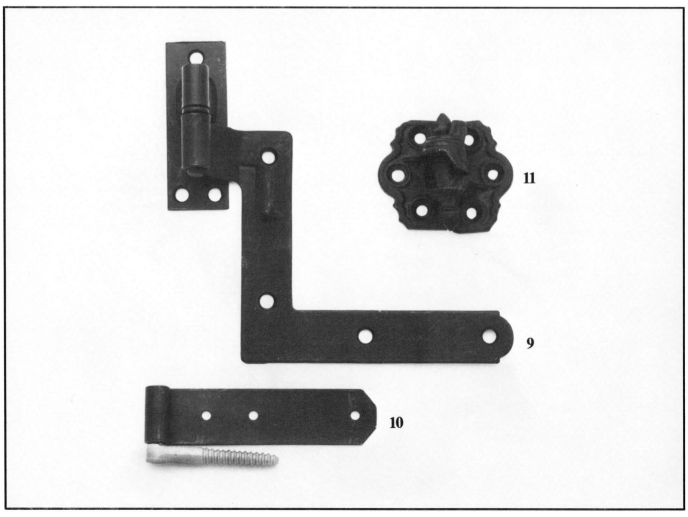

12

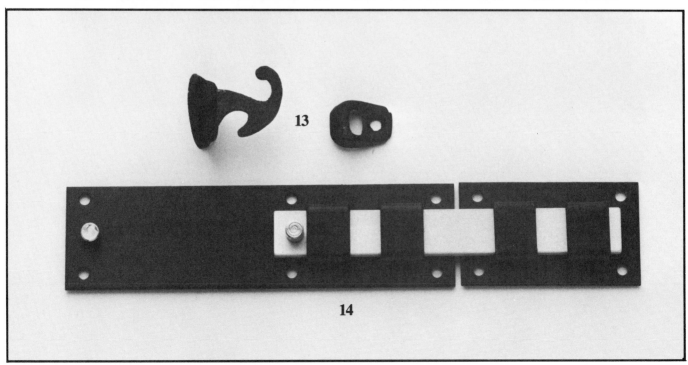

13

14

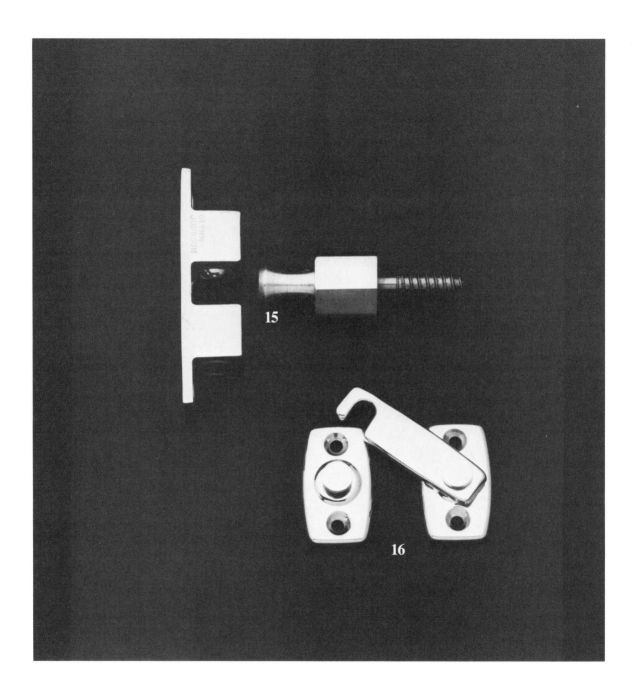

268

Sash Lifts, Locks, Bolts & Fasteners

1 Sash lift
Erco
Hammered cast bronze
Overall length: 6⅛″

2 Antique sash lift (Victorian)
Urban Archeology
Copper oxide
Overall length: 4″

3 Antique sash lift (Victorian)
By-Gone Days Antiques
Cast brass
Overall length: 4¾″

4 Antique sash lift (Art Nouveau)
By-Gone Days Antiques
Stamped brass
Overall length: 5¼″

5 Antique sash lift (Victorian)
By-Gone Days Antiques
Cast brass
Overall length: 5½″

6 Antique sash lift (Victorian)
By-Gone Days Antiques
Cast brass
Overall length: 5½″

7 Sash lift
H. Pfanstiel
Solid brass
Overall length: 4″

8 Antique sash lift (Victorian)
By-Gone Days Antiques
Stamped brass
Overall length: 3¾″

9–13 Sash lifts (Victorian)
Ritter & Son
Cast bronze
Widths: 1⁹⁄₁₆″, 1⅞″, 1⅜″, 1⁹⁄₁₆″, and 1⁹⁄₁₆″

14 Sash lift
The Renovator's Supply
Cast brass
Width: 1¾″

15 Antique sash lift (Victorian)
Urban Archeology
Cast brass
Length and width: 2⅜″ × 1³⁄₁₆″

16 Sash lift
Baldwin
Solid, hot-forged brass
Overall length: 4″

17 Sash lift
Baldwin
Solid, hot-forged brass
Overall length: 3½″

18 Antique casement fastener
(approximately 50 years old)
Garrett Wade
Solid brass
Backplate length: 1⅞″

19 Sash fastener
Selby Furniture Hardware
Steel, brass plated
Width: 2⅜″

20 Sash fastener (Victorian)
Ritter & Son
Lost-wax cast bronze
Width: 2″

21 Sash fastener
Stanley Hardware
Die-cast metal, brass finish
Width: 2⁹⁄₁₆″

22 Sash fastener
The Merit Brass Collection
Cast brass
Width: 2¾″

23 Sash lock
VSI Hardware
Die-cast Zamac, brass finish
Overall length, bolt thrown: 2⅜″

24 Sash lock
Stanley Hardware
Cast brass
Overall length, bolt thrown: 2⅛″

25 Sash lock
The Merit Brass Collection
Cast brass
Base length and width: 1¼″ × 1⅛″

26 Sash lock
The Merit Brass Collection
Cast brass
Base length and width: 1¾″ × 1″

27 Sash locking bolts and wrench
Brookstone

28 Sash locking pin with leather thong
Peter A. Renzetti, The Arden Forge Company
Hand-forged iron pin, leather thong
Pin length: 3½″

Shutter Hardware

1 Shutter dog
Steve Kayne, Steve Kayne Hand Forged Hardware
Hand-forged iron
Overall length and width: 6″ × 2½″

2 Shutter dog
Mark E. Rocheford, Hammerworks
Hand-forged iron
Overall length and width: 4½″ × ¾″

3 Shutter dog
Larry B. Wood, The Farm Forge
Hand-forged iron
Overall length and width: 5″ × 1¼″

4 Shutter dog
Larry B. Wood, The Farm Forge
Hand-forged iron
Overall length and width: 10½″ × 2½″

5 Shutter dog
Steve Kayne, Steve Kayne Hand Forged Hardware
Hand-forged iron
Overall length and width: 6″ × 1¼″

6 Shutter dog
Mark E. Rocheford, Hammerworks
Hand-forged iron
Overall length and width: 6″ × 1″

7 Shutter dog
Ball and Ball
Hand-forged iron
Overall length: 6″

8 Shutter dog
Ball and Ball
Cast iron
Overall length: 3¾″

9 Shutter hinge
Acorn
Stamped steel
Shutter leaf: 4¼″ × 5″, pintle plate: 3⅛″ × 1⅛″

10 Shutter hinge
Acorn
Stamped steel
Length: 4¼″

11 Shutter hinge (Victorian)
Ball and Ball
Cast iron
Height: 2⅛″, width: 2½″

12 Shutter latch
Mark E. Bokenkamp, Bokenkamp's Forge
Hand-forged iron, antique tin plate finish
Overall length and width: 3¾″ × 3″

13 Shutter holdback (Victorian)
Ball and Ball
Cast iron
Projection: 1¾″

14 Shutter bolt
Baldwin
Steel
Bolt plate length: 6¾″, strike plate length:
3⅛″, bolt length: 6″

15 Shutter catch
Glynn-Johnson
Extruded bronze
Strike length: 2¾″

16 Shutter bar
Baldwin
Solid brass
Overall width, shut position: 2¼″

10
Miscellaneous Decorative Hardware

HERE, finally, is a marvelous rag-tag decorative hardware army of devices assigned to some special and sometimes interesting duties.

The job of the coat and hat, wardrobe, or utility hook is to defy gravity and keep anything hangupable off the floor.

Hand rail brackets installed on a wall support a hand rail. Stair carpet holders secure a carpet zig-zagging its way up the length of a staircase.

Curtain tie-backs and drapery holdbacks do what their names imply, as do card holders, which identify what's filled or stashed away out of sight inside a drawer.

Numbers and name plates are also information providers, telling the world who and where you are.

Wall plates hide something common: the unsightly scramble of wires residing inside an electrical outlet or switch box.

Bed bolt covers hide something somewhat

more exotic: the heads of bolts holding four-poster bed frames together.

Ice box hinges and latches can operate in the way they always have—but now on a piece of furniture that can be anything other than an ice box.

Chest lifts and campaign trim provide both handles and decoration.

Furniture castors and foot sockets help to protect your furniture.

And all sorts of interesting nails can be used in innumerable ways.

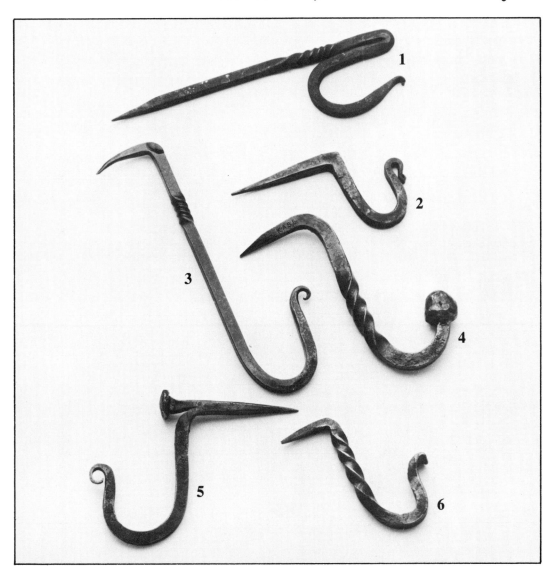

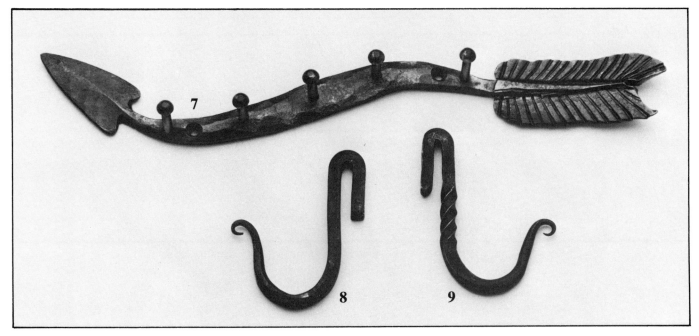

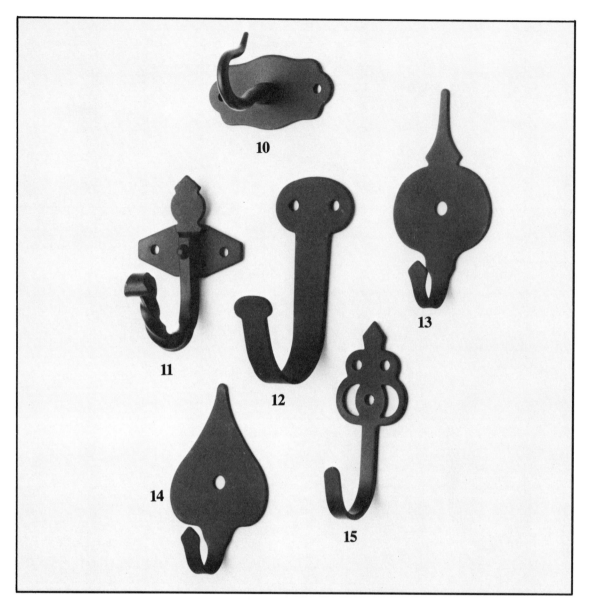

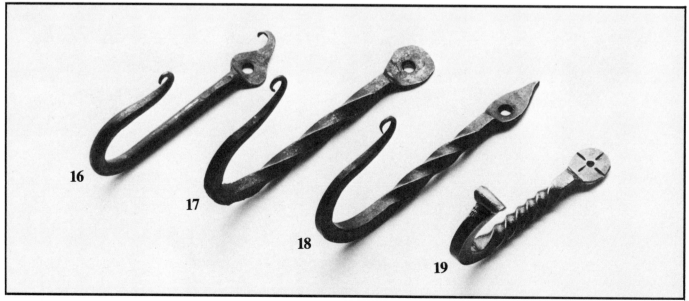

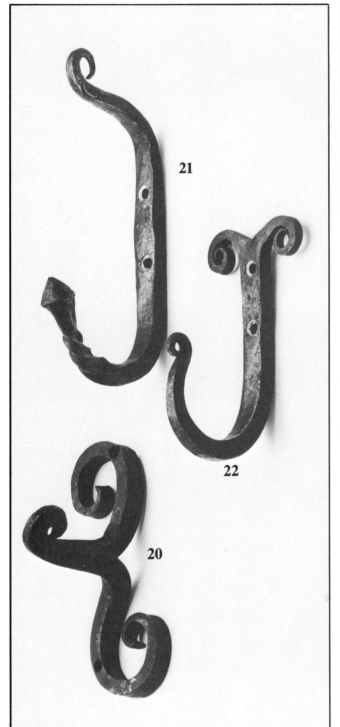

21

20

22

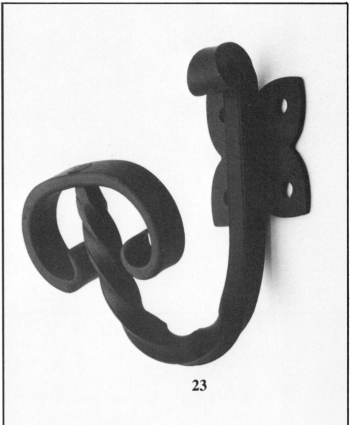

23

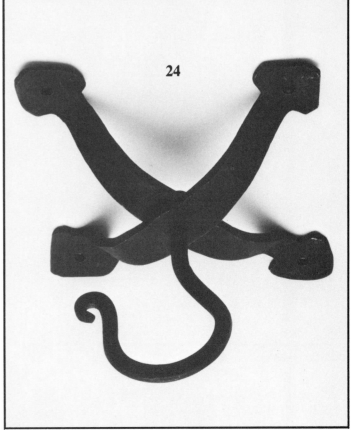

24

275

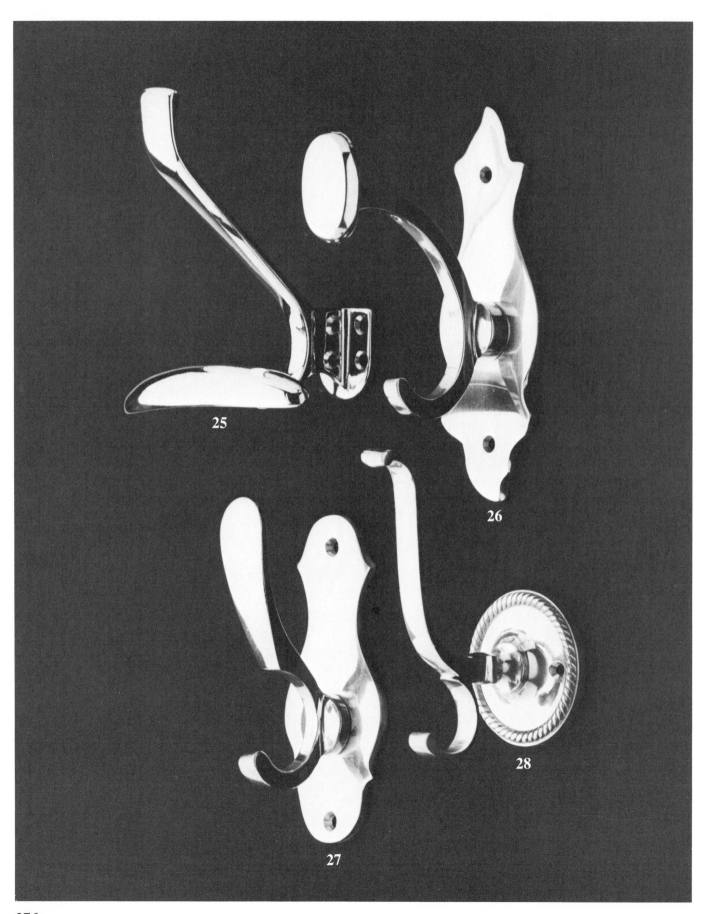

25

26

27

28

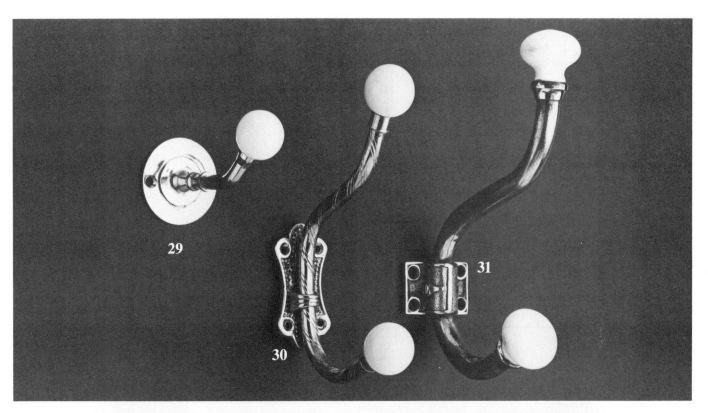

29

30

31

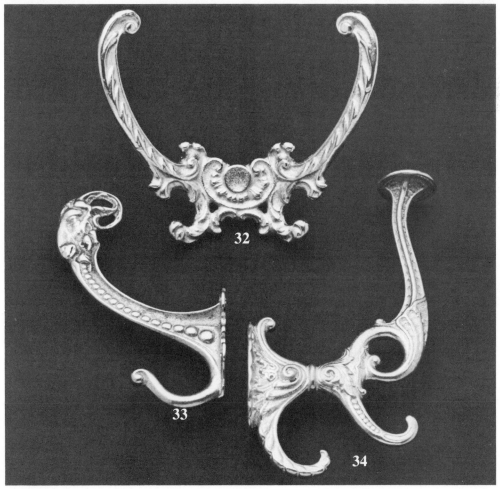

32

33

34

277

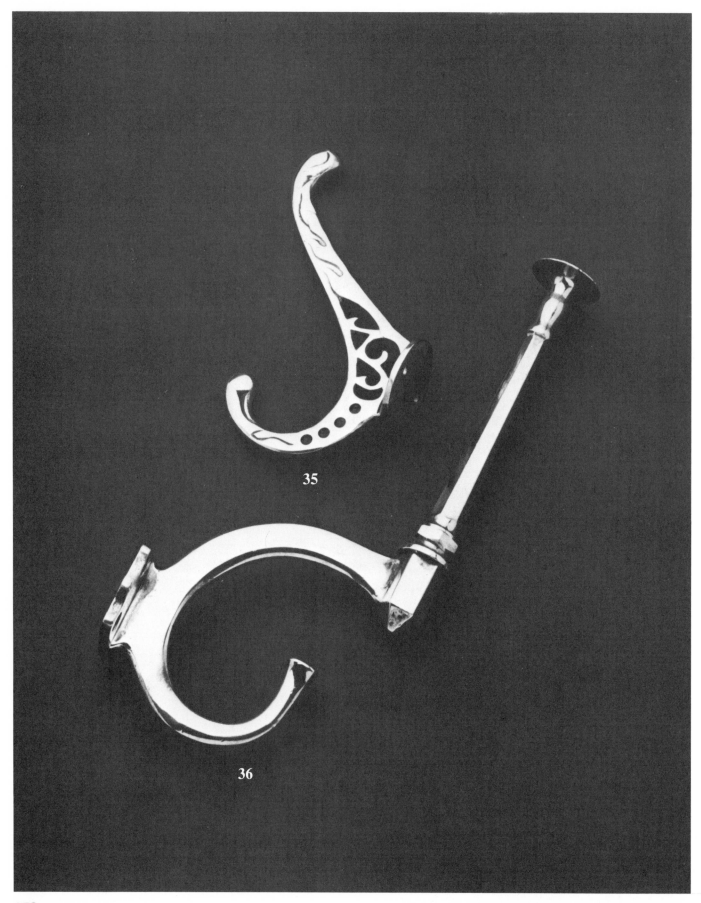

35

36

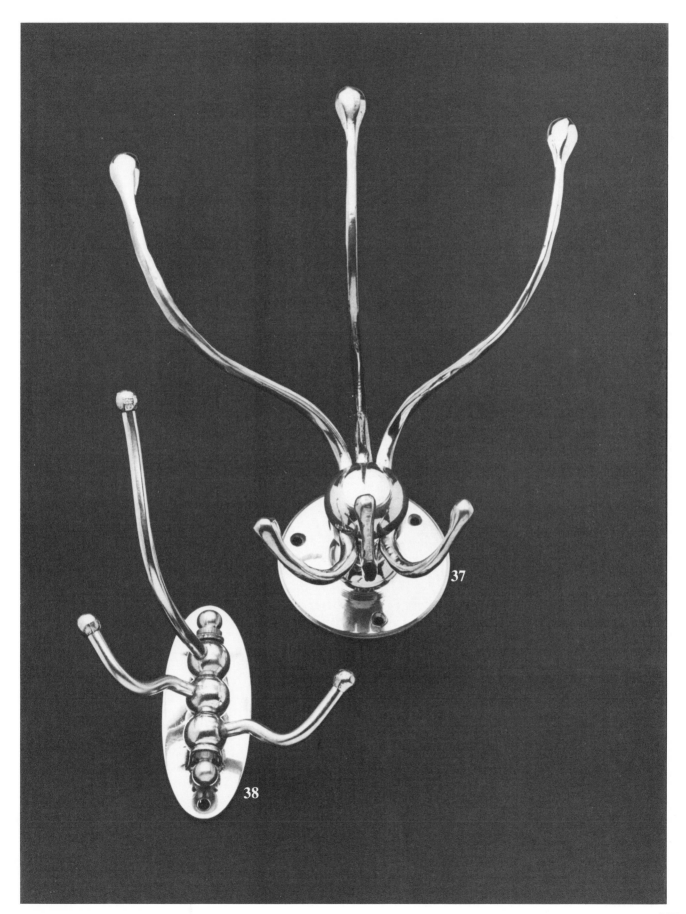

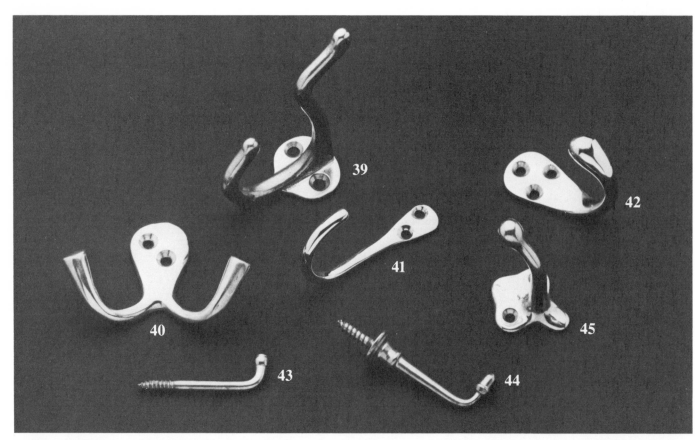

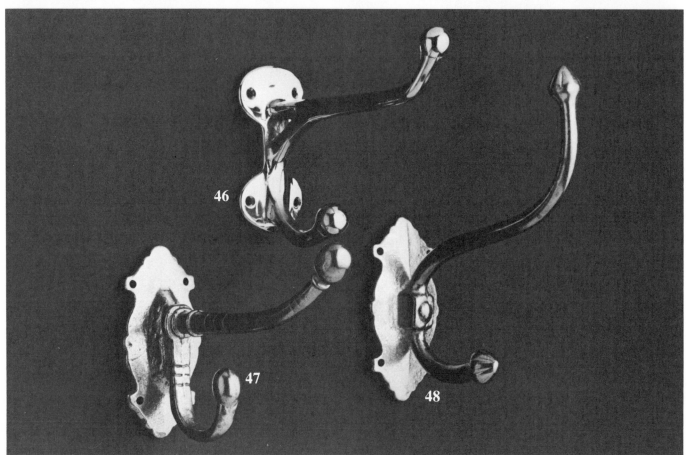

280

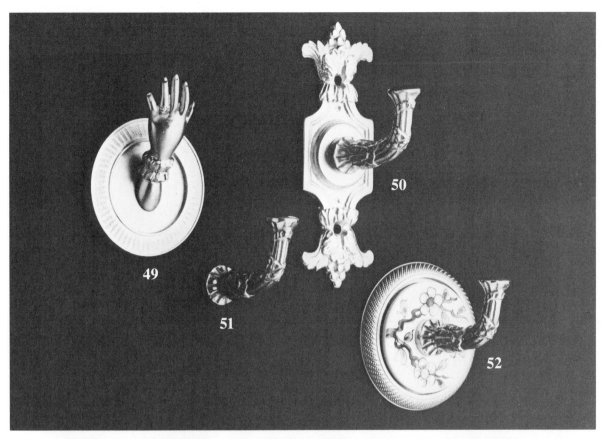

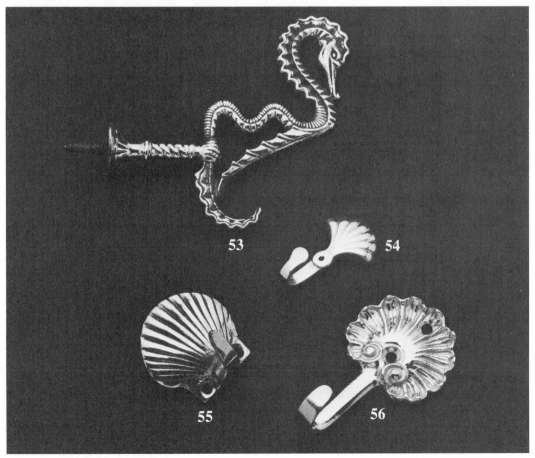

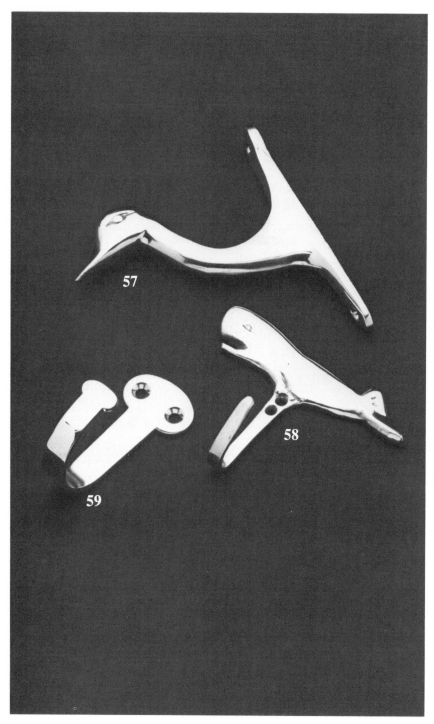

57

58

59

60

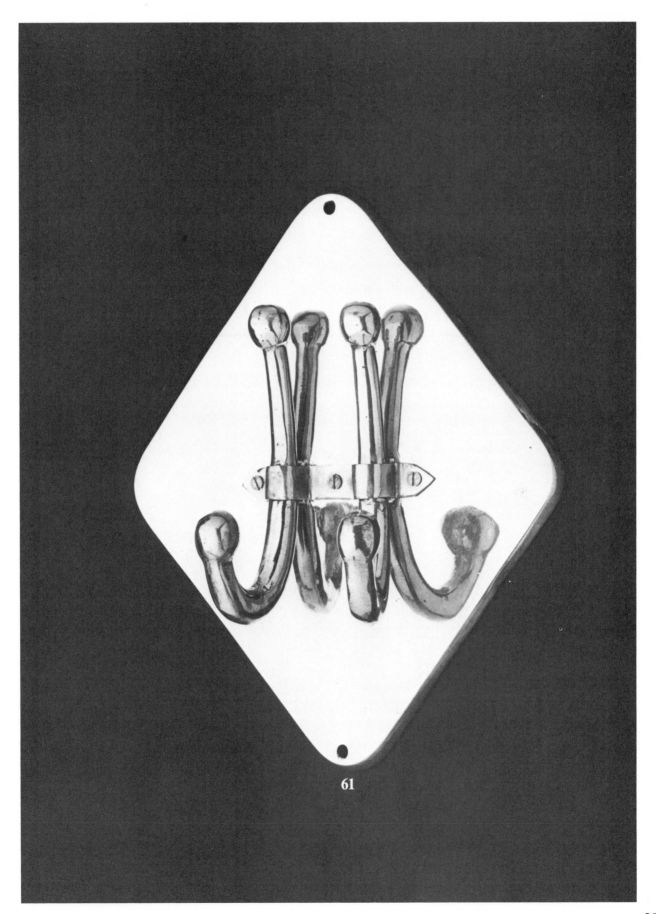

61

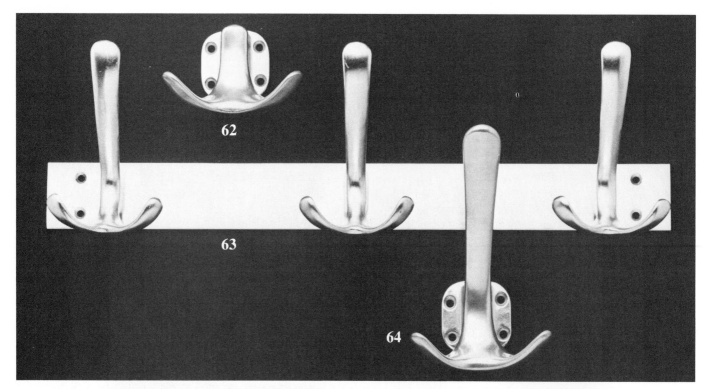

62

63

64

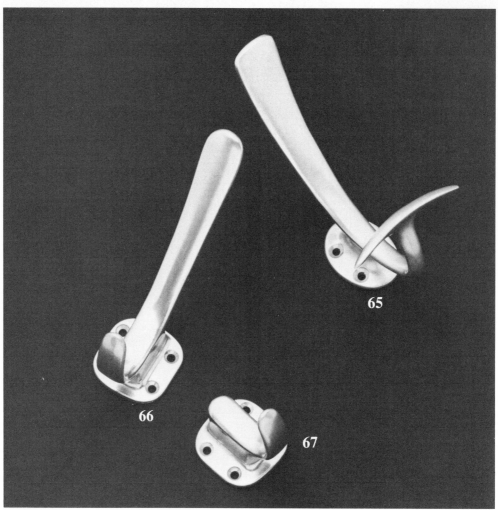

65

66

67

284

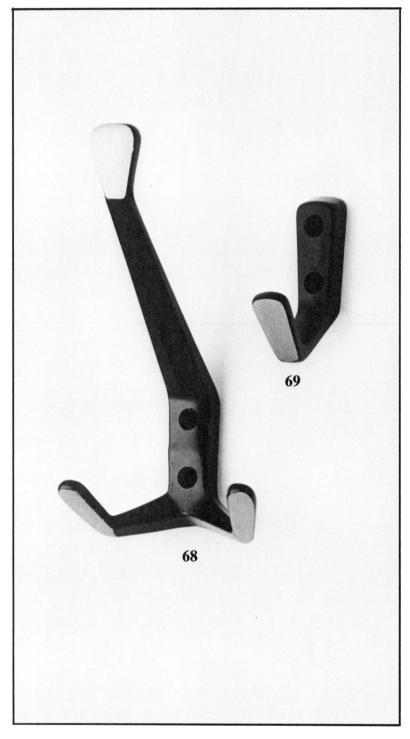

68

69

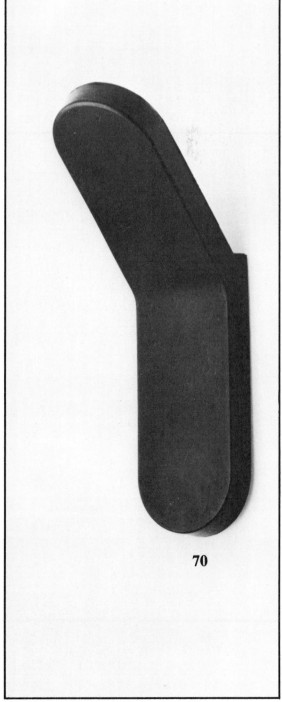

70

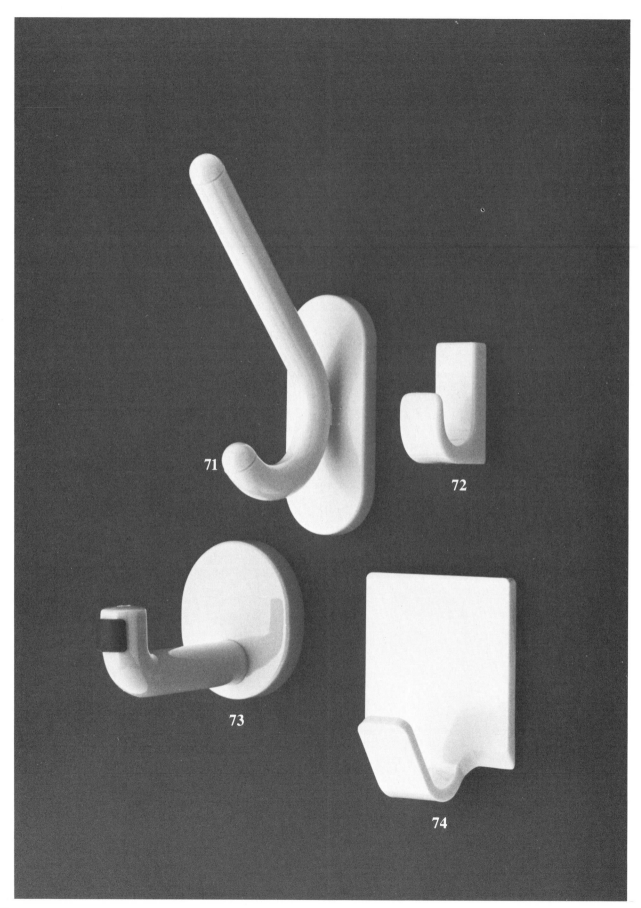

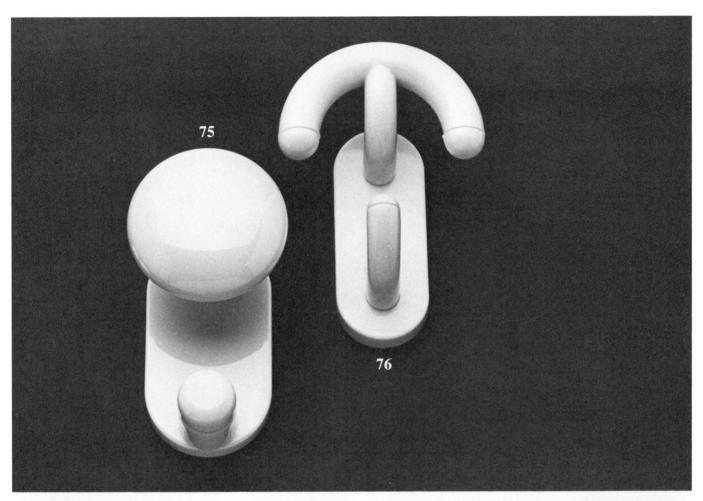

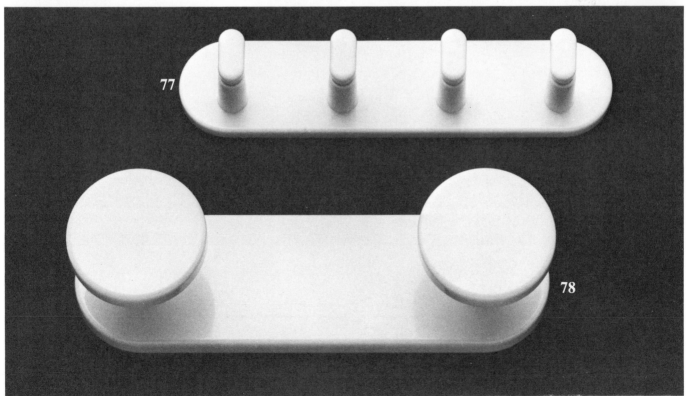

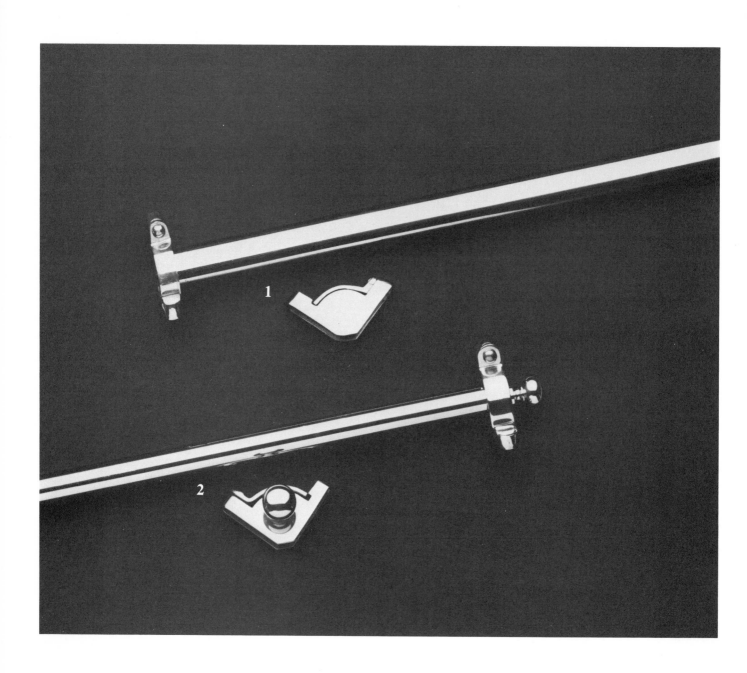

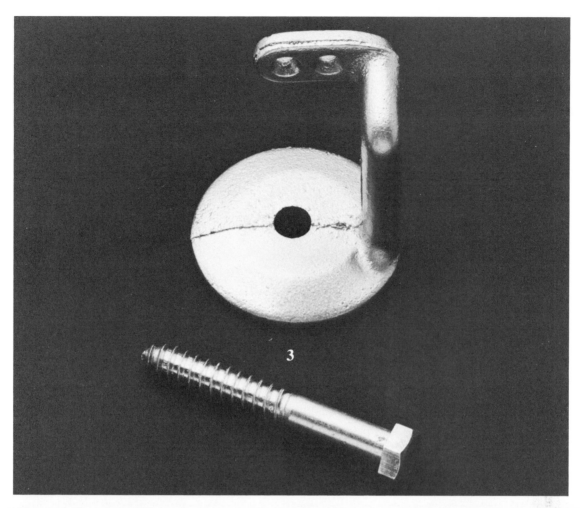

3

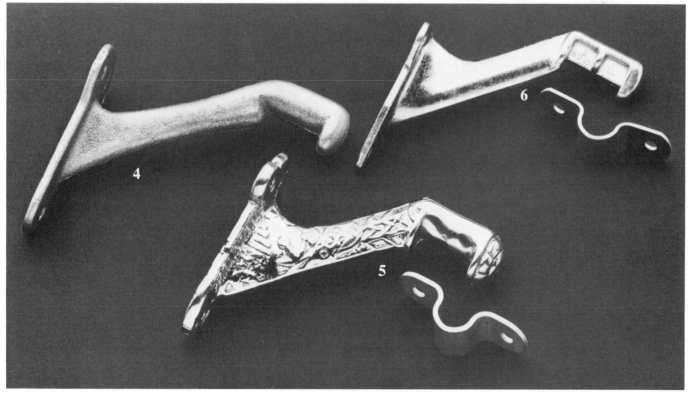

4

5

6

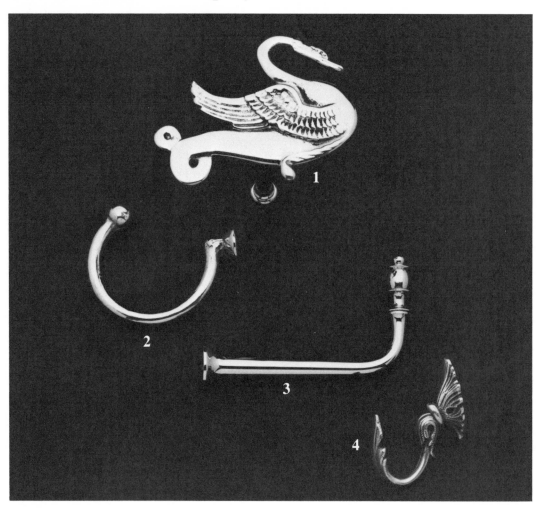

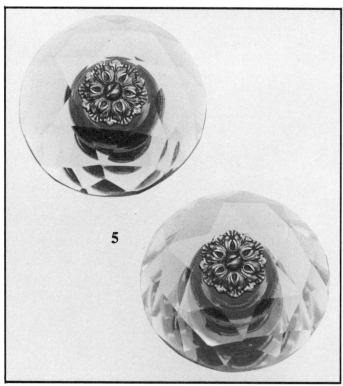

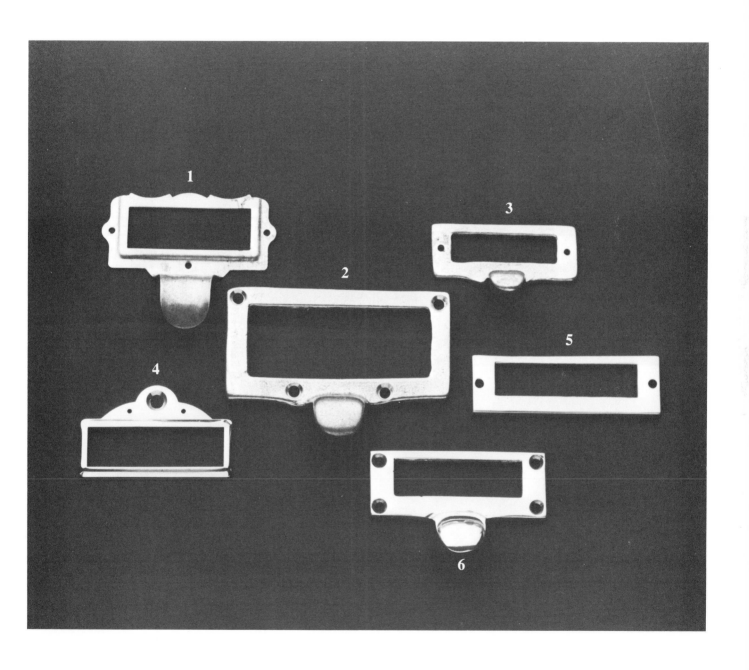

1

2

6

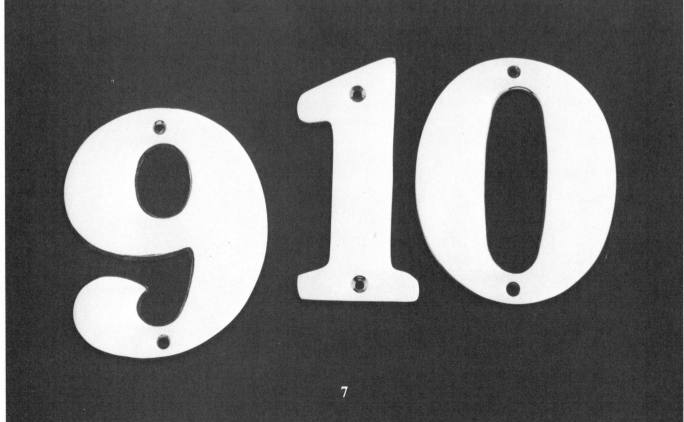

7

8

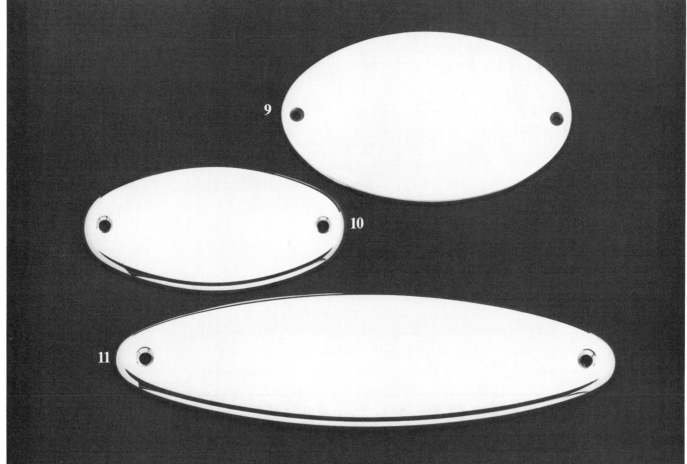

9

10

11

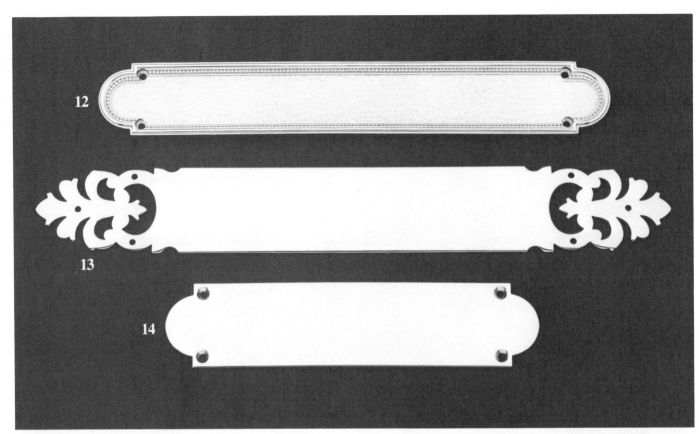

12

13

14

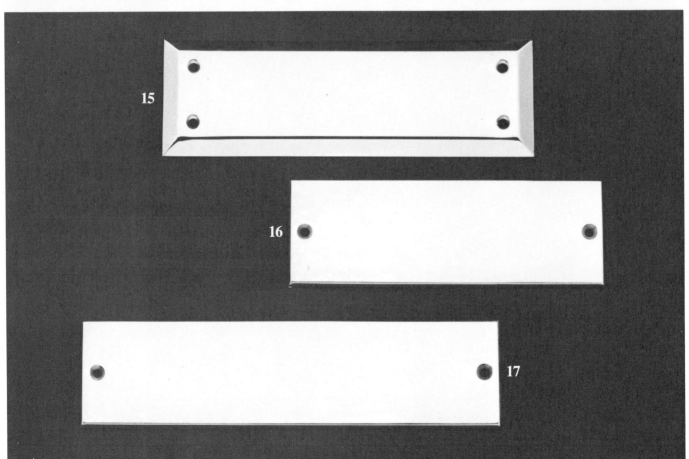

15

16

17

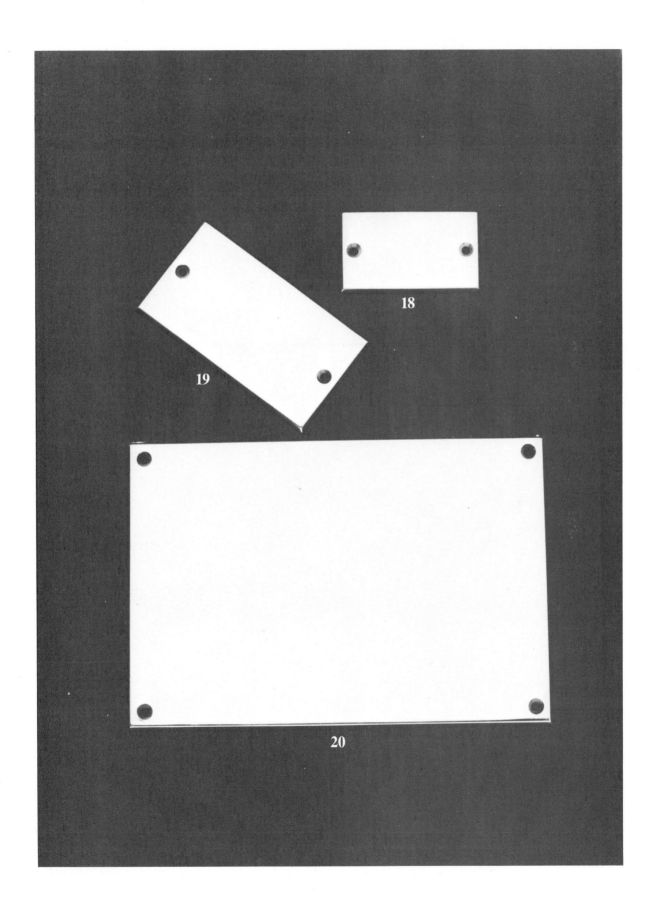

18

19

20

Wall Plates

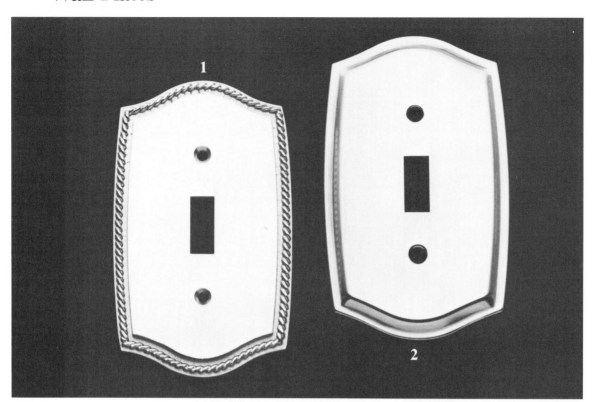

5

6

7

8

13

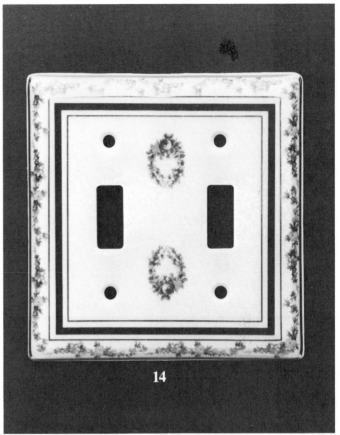

14

15

16

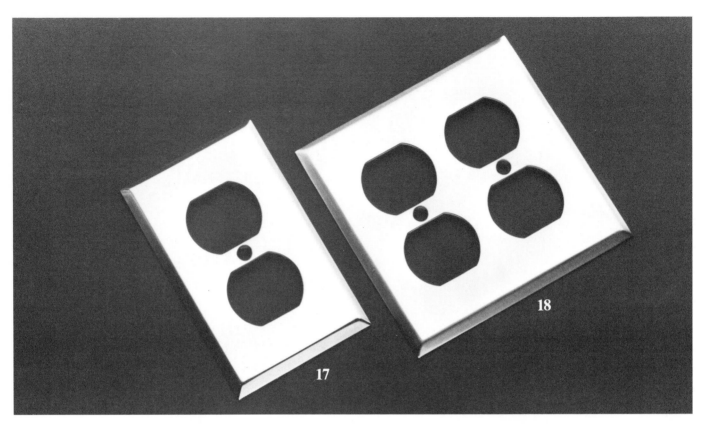

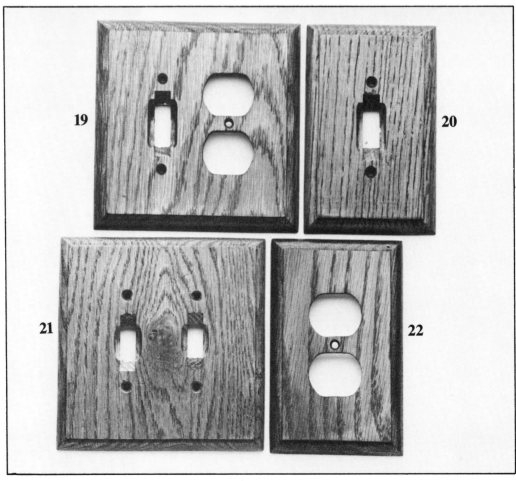

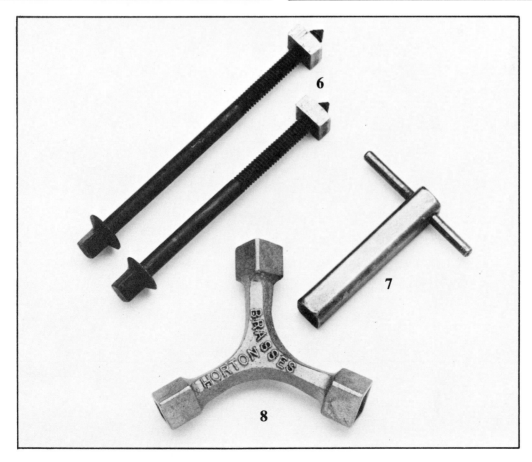

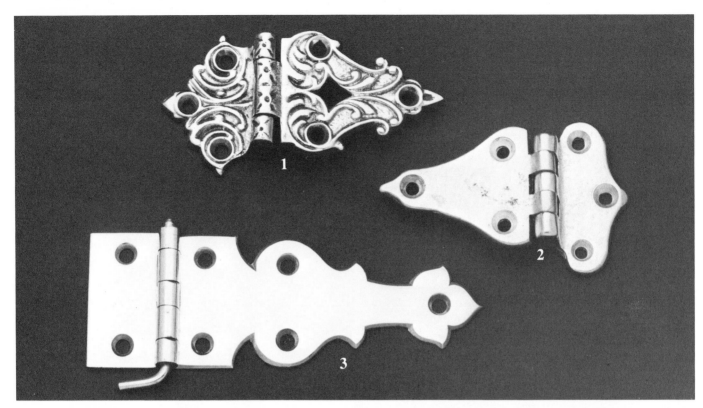

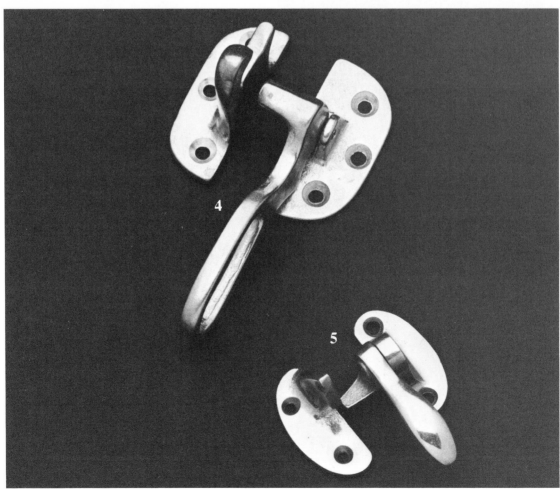

6

Chest Lifts & Campaign Hardware

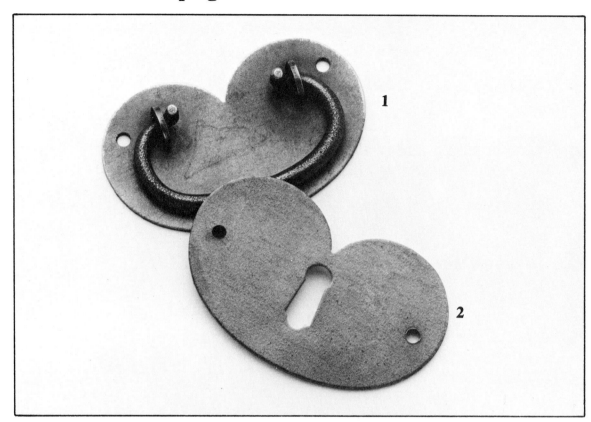

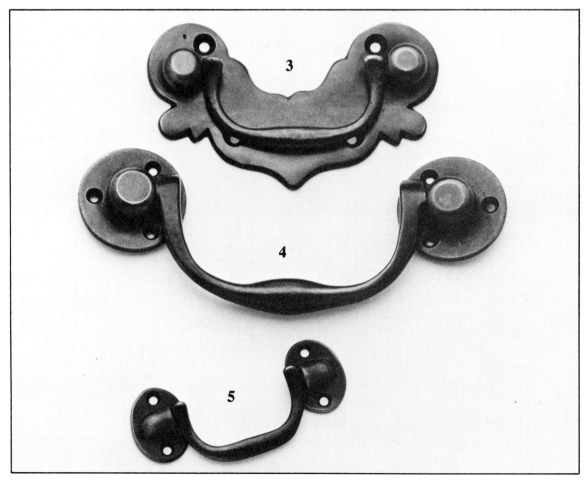

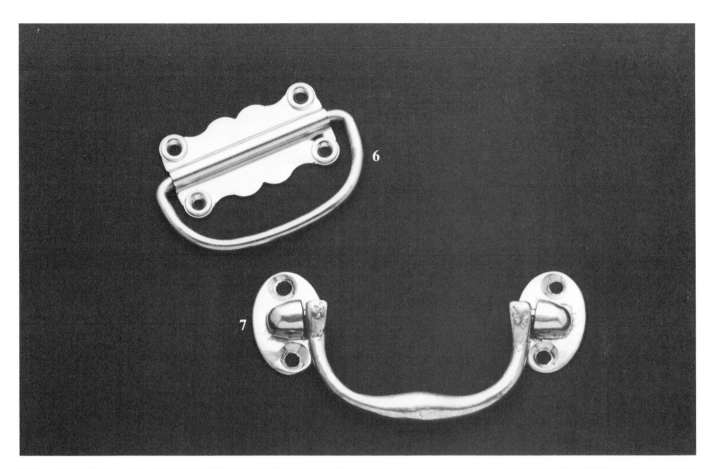

6

7

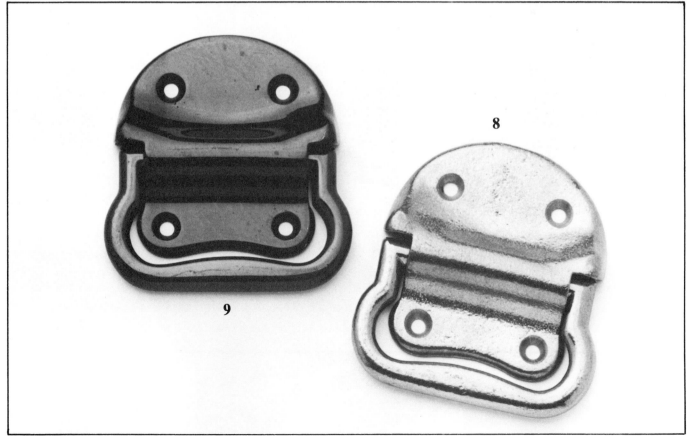

8

9

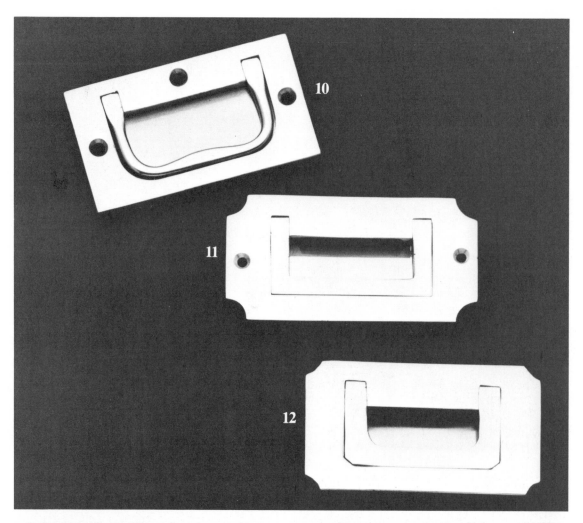

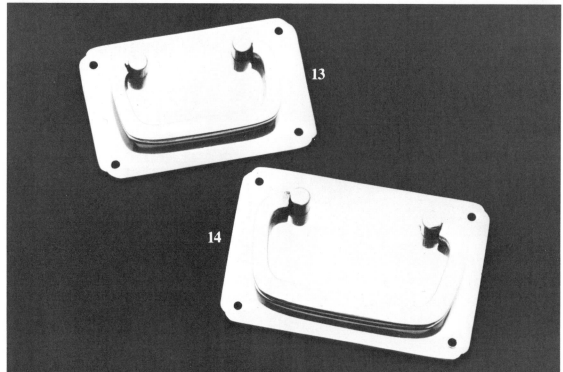

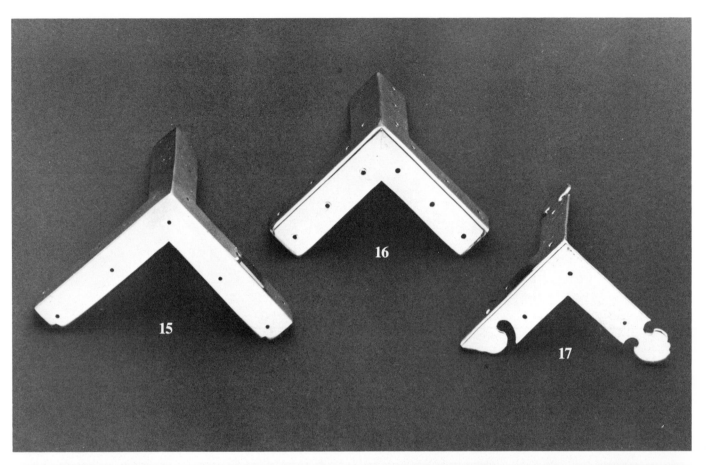

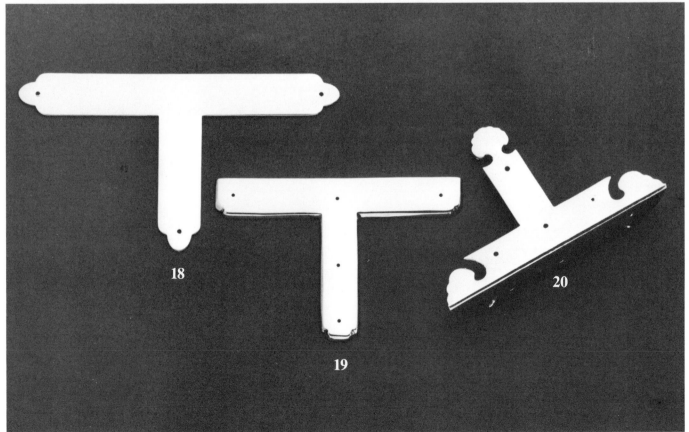

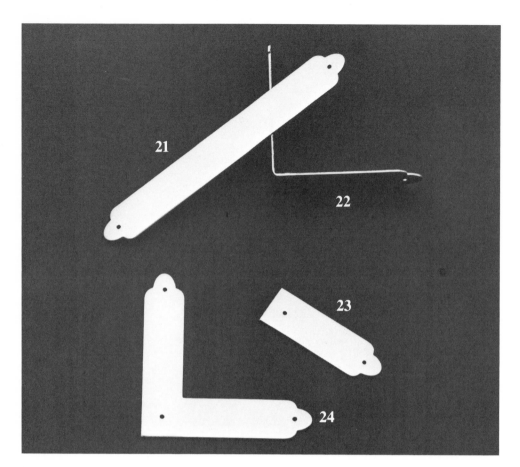

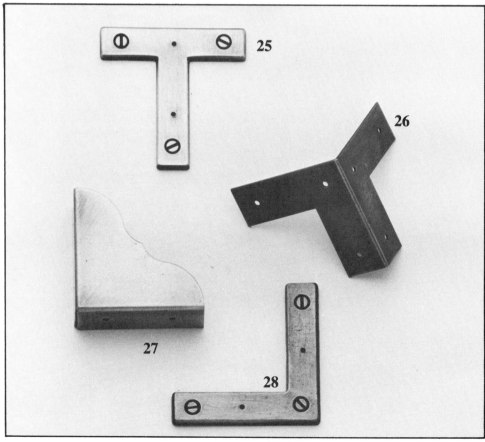

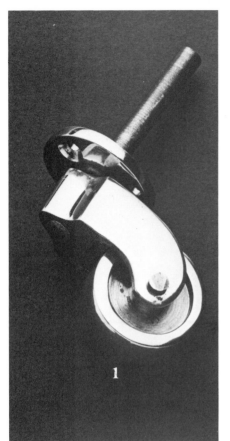

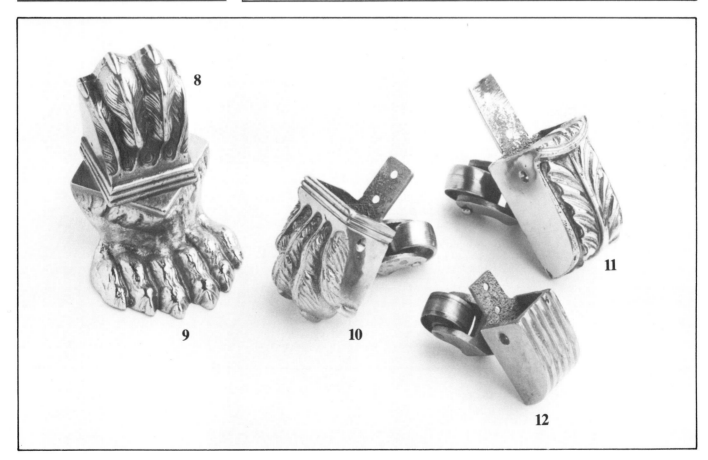

Decorative Fasteners

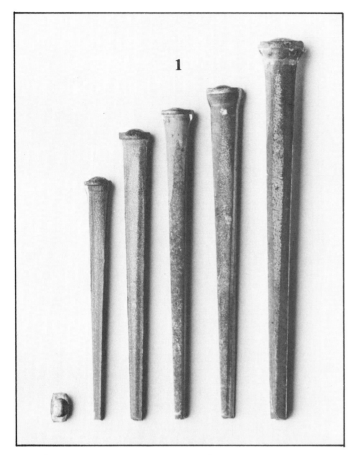

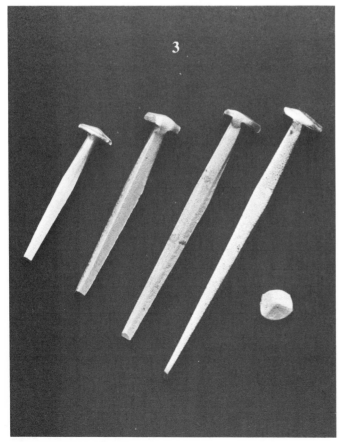

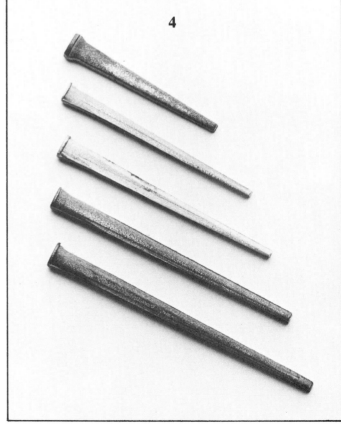

5

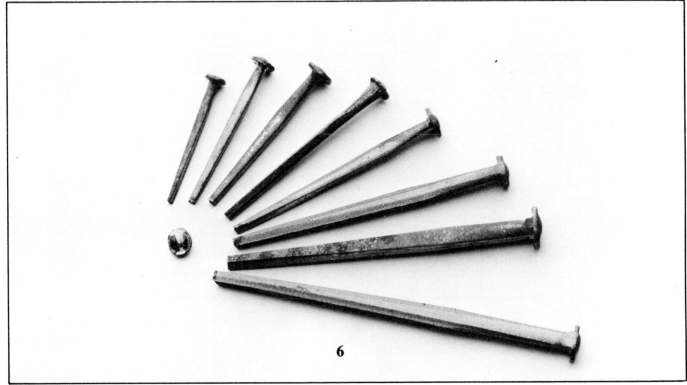

6

7

8

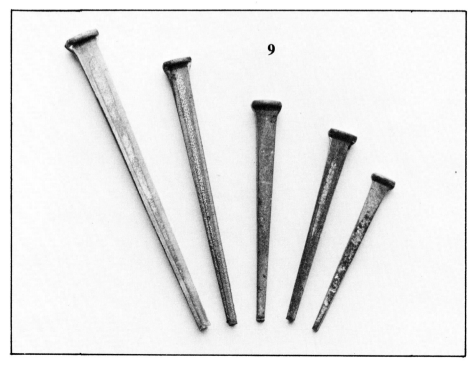

9

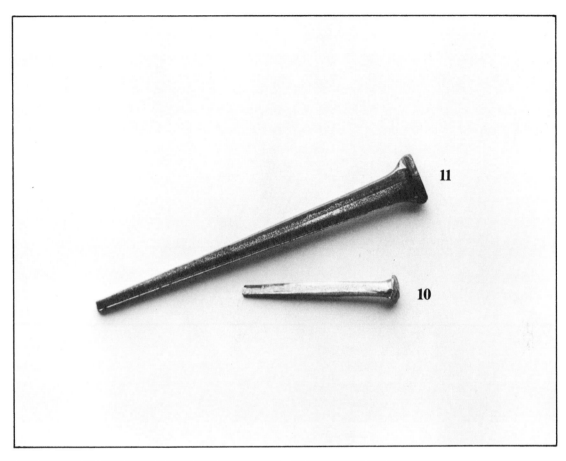

11

10

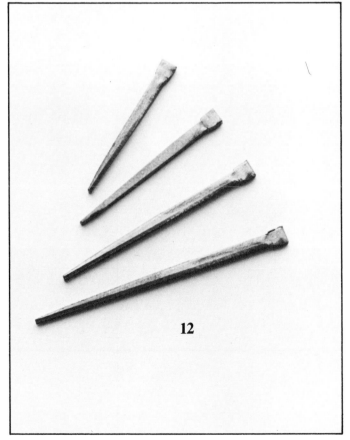

12

13   14

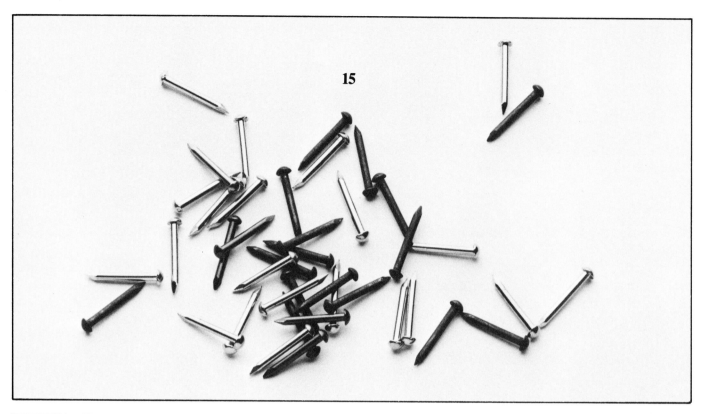

15

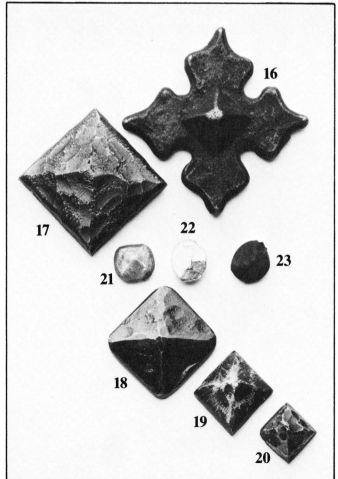

16

17

22

21

23

18

19

20

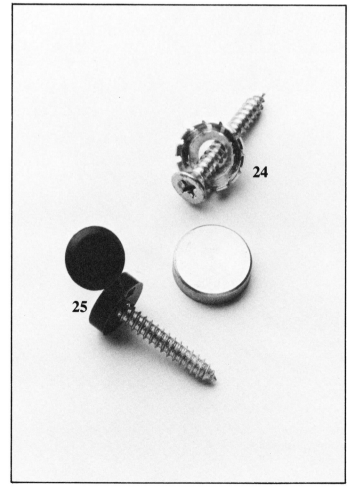

24

25

Coat & Hat, Wardrobe, & Utility Hooks

1 Drive-in utility or wardrobe hook
Barry Berman, Valley Forgeworks, Ltd.
Hand-forged iron
Spike length: 4½″, projection: 2″

2 Drive-in utility or wardrobe hook
Bob Patrick, Big Anvil Forge
Hand-forged iron
Height: 2″, projection: 1½″

3 Drive-in utility or wardrobe hook
Lance Cloutier, The Ram's Head Forge
Hand-forged iron
Height: 6½″, projection: 2″

4 Drive-in utility or wardrobe hook
Ronald H. Kass, Ronald H. Kass Forge
Hand-forged iron
Height: 4¼″, projection: 2″

5 Drive-in utility or wardrobe hook
Bob Patrick, Big Anvil Forge
Hand-forged iron
Height: 3″, projection: 2″

6 Drive-in utility or wardrobe hook
Ronald H. Kass, Ronald H. Kass Forge
Hand-forged iron
Height: 2¾″, projection: 1¾″

7 Arrow key holder
Ronald H. Kass, Ronald H. Kass Forge
Hand-forged iron
Length: 12″

8 Hang-up utility hook
Steve Kayne, Steve Kayne Hand Forged Hardware
Hand-forged iron
Height: 3¼″, projection: 2″

9 Hang-up utility hook
Steve Kayne, Steve Kayne Hand Forged Hardware
Hand-forged iron
Height: 3½″, projection: 2¼″

10 Utility hook
Baldwin
Black painted steel
Height: 1⅜″, projection: 1²³/₃₂″

11 Utility or wardrobe hook
Baldwin
Black painted steel
Height: 2⅝″, projection: 1⅝″

12 Gun hook
Horton Brasses
Black painted brass
Height: 3″

13 Utility or wardrobe hook
Acorn
Steel, black finish
Height: 3″

14 Utility or wardrobe hook
Acorn
Steel, black finish
Height: 3″

15 Utility or wardrobe hook
Baldwin
Black painted steel
Height: 2½″, projection: 1¼″

16 Utility or wardrobe hook
Mark E. Bokenkamp, Bokenkamp's Forge
Hand-forged iron
Height: 4″, projection: 1½″

17 Utility or wardrobe hook
Steve Kayne, Steve Kayne Hand Forged Hardware
Hand-forged iron
Height: 5″, projection: 2¼″

18 Utility or wardrobe hook
Steve Kayne, Steve Kayne Hand Forged Hardware
Hand-forged iron
Height: 5″, projection: 2″

19 Utility or wardrobe hook
Ronald H. Kass, Ronald H. Kass Forge
Hand-forged iron
Height: 3¼″, projection: 1½″

20 Wardrobe hook
Bob Patrick, Big Anvil Forge
Hand-forged iron
Width: 4″, projection: 2½″

21 Wardrobe hook
Bob Patrick, Big Anvil Forge
Hand-forged iron
Height: 5¼″, projection: 2⅜″

22 Wardrobe hook
Bob Patrick, Big Anvil Forge
Hand-forged iron
Height: 3½″, projection: 2″

23 Coat hook
Baldwin
Forged steel
Height: 3¾″, projection: 3¼″

24 Ceiling beam hook
Richard C. Swenson, Swenson's Forge
Hand-forged iron
Height: 4″

25 Coat and hat hook
Baldwin
Solid brass
Height: 4⅝″, projection: 4⅛″

26 Coat and hat hook
Impex
Solid brass
Height: 5¾″

27 Coat and hat hook
Impex
Solid brass
Height: 5¼″

28 Coat and hat hook
Urfic
Solid brass
Height: 4½″, projection: 2″

29 Wardrobe hook
The Renovator's Supply
Brass and porcelain
Projection: 3⅜″

30 Coat and hat hook (Victorian)
The Renovator's Supply
Brass and porcelain
Height: 6″, projection: 4⅛″

31 Antique coat and hat hook (Victorian)
Urban Archeology
Brass and porcelain
Height: 7″, projection: 5″

32 Coat and hat hook (Victorian)
Ritter & Son
Solid brass
Projection: 3½″

33 Coat and hat hook (Victorian)
Ritter & Son
Solid brass
Projection: 3½″

34 Coat and hat hook (Victorian)
Ritter & Son
Solid brass
Projection: 4⅜″

35 Coat and hat hook (Victorian)
Restoration Hardware
Cast brass
Projection: 3½″

36 Antique coat and hat hook (Victorian)
Urban Archeology
Bronze
Height: 9¼″

37 Coat and hat hook
Kraft Hardware
Solid brass
Height: 6½″, projection: 6½″

38 Coat and hat hook
The Renovator's Supply
Solid brass
Overall height: 5¾″, projection: 4¼″

39 Coat and hat hook
The Merit Brass Collection
Cast brass
Height: 3¼″

40 Wardrobe hook
Custom Decor
Sand-cast brass
Height: 1¾″

41 Wardrobe hook
The Broadway Collection
Solid brass
Height: 2¾″

42 Wardrobe hook
The Broadway Collection
Solid brass
Height: 1¾″

43 Utility hook
Horton Brasses
Solid brass
Projection: 1½″

44 Fireplace pipe tong hook
Ball and Ball
Solid brass
Projection: 2¼″

45 Wardrobe hook
The Merit Brass Collection
Cast brass
Height: 1¼″

46 Coat and hat hook
Custom Decor
Sand-cast brass
Height: 5″

47 Coat and hat hook (Victorian)
Ritter & Son
Solid brass
Projection: 6″

48 Coat and hat hook (Victorian)
Ritter & Son
Solid brass
Projection: 5¼″

49 Wardrobe hook
Sherle Wagner International
Solid brass
Backplate diameter: 2¼″

50 Wardrobe hook
Sherle Wagner International
Solid brass
Height: 4½″

51 Wardrobe hook
Sherle Wagner International
Solid brass
Height: 2″

52 Wardrobe hook
Sherle Wagner International
Solid brass and porcelain insert
Projection: 2⅛″

53 Antique coat and hat hook (Victorian)
Urban Archeology
Solid brass
Height: 4″, projection: 4¼″

54 Picture hook
Ball and Ball
Solid brass
Height: 2″

55 Wardrobe hook
Custom Decor
Sand-cast brass
Height: 1½″

56 Wardrobe hook
The Broadway Collection
Solid brass
Height: 3⅛″

57 Gun hook
Custom Decor
Sand-cast brass
Height: 4½″

58 Wardrobe hook
Custom Decor
Sand-cast brass
Height: 4″

59 Gun hook
Horton Brasses
Solid brass
Height: 3″

60 Picture hook
Ball and Ball
Solid brass
Height: 5″

61 Wardrobe hook
Unique Handicraft
Cast brass
Height: 10″

62 Wardrobe hook
H. Pfanstiel
Chrome
Projection: 2¼″

63 Multiple coat and hat hook
Simon's Hardware
Aluminum
Backplate length and width: 15″ × 1½″,
hook projection: 3″

64 Coat and hat hook
H. Pfanstiel
Chrome
Height: 5¾″, projection: 3½″

65 Coat and hat hook
Simon's Hardware
Aluminum
Height: 5½″, projection: 4″

66 Coat and hat hook
H. Pfanstiel
Chrome
Height: 5¼″, projection: 3¾″

67 Wardrobe hook
H. Pfanstiel
Chrome
Projection: 2½″

68 Coat and hat hook
H. Pfanstiel
Anodized aluminum
Height: 6″, projection: 3″

69 Wardrobe hook
H. Pfanstiel
Anodized aluminum
Height: 2″

70 Wardrobe hook
Forms and Surfaces
Soft neoprene
Height: 4″, projection: 1⅞″

71 Coat and hat hook
IDG Marketing
ABS plastic (white, red, yellow, brown,
or blue)
Height: 6½″

72 Wardrobe hook
IDG Marketing
ABS plastic (white, red, yellow, brown,
or blue)
Height: 2″

73 Wardrobe hook/door bumper
Kraft Hardware
Nylon
Projection: 3½″

74 Wardrobe hook
IDG Marketing
Styrene (white, red, yellow, brown, or
blue)
Height and width: 3¾″ × 2¹⁵/₁₆″

75 Coat and hat hook
IDG Marketing
ABS plastic (white, red, yellow, brown,
blue or chrome)
Height: 5¼″

76 Coat and hat hook
IDG Marketing
ABS plastic (white, red, yellow, brown,
or blue)
Height: 5⅜″

77 Multiple wardrobe hook
IDG Marketing
ABS plastic (white, red, yellow, brown, or blue)
Overall: 7¾″ × 1¾″ × 1½″

78 Double coat hook
IDG Marketing
ABS plastic (white, red, yellow, brown, or blue)
Overall: 8³⁄₁₆″ × 2⁵⁄₁₆″ × 2″

Hand Rail Brackets & Stair Carpet Holders

1 Stair carpet holder
Kraft Hardware
Solid brass
Quarter round rod radius: ¾″; length: cut to length required; bracket height: 1¼″

2 Stair carpet holder
Baldwin
Forged brass
Rod diameter: ⅝″; length: cut to length required; bracket height: 1¾″

3 Hand rail bracket and fastener
Baldwin
Cast iron
Base diameter: 3″, base to rail center: 3⅛″

4 Hand rail bracket
Baldwin
Cast iron
Base length and width: 2¾″ × 1½″, base to rail center: 2¾″

5 Hand rail bracket (Victorian)
The Renovator's Supply
Cast brass
Base length and width: 3″ × 1⅜″, projection: 3½″

6 Hand rail bracket
Stanley Hardware
Die-cast brass
Base length and width: 2¼″ × 1⅜″, base to rail center: 2⁷⁄₁₆″

Curtain Tie-backs & Drapery Holdbacks

1 Drapery holdback
Period Furniture Hardware
Solid brass
Height: 3″, width: 4⅛″, projection: 2⅝″

2 Drapery holdback
The Renovator's Supply
Cast brass
Projection: 3¼″

3 Curtain tie-back
Baldwin
Solid brass
Projection: 4⅛″

4 Curtain tie-back
Baldwin
Solid brass
Projection: 2″

5 Antique drapery holdbacks (Victorian)
By-Gone Days Antiques
Amethyst glass and brass
Diameter: 3″

6 Drapery holdback
Baldwin
Solid brass
Base diameter: 1¾″, head diameter: 3¹⁷⁄₃₂″, projection: 4″

Card Holders

1 Card holder
Ritter & Son
Stamped brass
Width: 2¼″

2 Card holder
Ritter & Son
Solid brass
Width: 3⅛″

3 Card holder
Ritter & Son
Solid brass
Width: 2¼″

4 Card holder
Baldwin
Wrought brass
Width: 2¼″

5 Card holder
The Merit Brass Collection
Cast brass
Width: 2⅞″

6 Card holder
The Merit Brass Collection
Cast brass
Width: 2½″

Numbers & Name Plates

1 Numbers
Erco
Hammered cast bronze
Height: 4″

2 Numbers
Urfic
Solid brass
Height: 3½″

3 Numbers
Custom Decor
Sand-cast brass
Height: 3½″

4 Numbers
Baldwin
Solid brass
Height: 3¼″

5 Numbers
Restoration Hardware
Solid brass
Height: 4″

6 Numbers
The Renovator's Supply
Cast brass
Height: 3⅞″

7 Numbers
Custom Decor
Sand-cast brass
Height: 4″

8 Numbers
Stanley Hardware
Cast Zamac
Height: 4″

9 Name plate
Simon's Hardware
Solid brass
Overall: 6″ × 3⅝″

10 Name plate
Baldwin
Forged brass
Overall: 5⅜″ × 2¹¹⁄₁₆″

11 Name plate
Baldwin
Solid brass
Overall: 11″ × 2¾″

12 Name plate
Baldwin
Forged brass
Overall: 11⅜″ × 1¾″

13 Name plate
Baldwin
Forged brass
Overall: 11¼″ × 1⅞″

14 Name plate
Baldwin
Forged brass
Overall: 8″ × 1²⁵⁄₃₂″

15 Name plate
Baldwin
Solid brass
Overall: 7¼″ × 2¼″

16 Name plate
Simon's Hardware
Solid brass
Overall: 6″ × 2″

17 Name plate
Simon's Hardware
Solid brass
Overall: 8″ × 6″

18 Name plate
Simon's Hardware
Solid brass
Overall: 2¾″ × 1⅝″

19 Name plate
Simon's Hardware
Solid brass
Overall: 4″ × 2¼″

20 Name plate
Simon's Hardware
Solid brass
Overall: 8″ × 5½″

Wall Plates

1 Single switch plate
The Broadway Collection
Solid brass
Height: 5⅛″, width: 3″

2 Single switch plate
Baldwin
Solid brass
Height: 5⅛″, width: 3″

3 Single switch plate
Sherle Wagner International
Solid brass
Height: 6¼″, width: 2¼″

4 Single switch plate
Sherle Wagner International
Solid brass
Height: 6″, width: 3″

5 Single switch plate
Sherle Wagner International
Porcelain, hand painted, and cast brass, gold plated
Height: 5¼″, width: 3⅛″

6 Double switch plate
Restoration Hardware
Cast brass
Height: 4½″, width: 4½″

7 Single switch plate
Restoration Hardware
Cast brass
Height: 4½″, width: 2¾″

8 Double outlet
Restoration Hardware
Cast brass
Height: 4½″, width: 2¾″

9 Single switch plate
The Broadway Collection
Porcelain
Height: 4½″, width: 2¾″

10 Double outlet
Baldwin
Limoges porcelain
Height: 4½″, width: 2¾″

11 Single switch plate
Restoration Hardware
Porcelain
Height: 4½″, width: 2¾″

12 Double switch plate
Plexacraft Metals
Porcelain
Height: 5⅞″, width: 5⅞″

13 Combination wall plate
Baldwin
Limoges porcelain, applied design
Height: 4½″, width: 4½″

14 Double switch plate
Baldwin
Limoges porcelain, applied design with gold trim
Height: 4½″, width: 4½″

15 Single switch plate
Baldwin
Limoges porcelain, applied design
Height: 4½″, width: 2¾″

16 Double switch plate
The Broadway Collection
Porcelain, applied design
Height: 4½″, width: 4½″

17 Double outlet
Baldwin
Solid brass
Height: 4½″, width: 2¾″

18 Multiple outlet
Baldwin
Solid brass
Height: 4½″, width: 4½″

19 Combination wall plate
VSI Hardware
Solid oak
Height: 4½″, width: 4½″

20 Single switch plate
VSI Hardware
Solid oak
Height: 4½″, width: 2¾″

21 Double switch plate
VSI Hardware
Solid oak
Height: 4½″, width: 4½″

22 Double outlet
VSI Hardware
Solid oak
Height: 4½″, width: 2¾″

Bed Bolts & Bed Bolt Covers

1 Bed bolt cover
Ball and Ball
Cast brass
Length: 2½″, width: 1½″

2 Bed bolt cover
Ball and Ball
Cast brass
Diameter: 1¾″

3 Bed bolt cover
Horton Brasses
Stamped brass
Length: 2¼″, width: 1⅞″

4 Bed bolt cover
Horton Brasses
Stamped brass
Diameter: 1⅞″

5 Bed bolt cover
Horton Brasses
Stamped brass
Diameter: 1⅝″

6 Bed bolts
Horton Brasses
Steel
Lengths: 6″ and 7″

7 Bed bolt wrench
Ball and Ball

8 Cast iron bed bolt wrench
Horton Brasses

Ice Box Hardware

1 Icebox hinge
Steve Kayne, Steve Kayne Hand Forged Hardware
Cast brass
Overall length and width: 4¼″ × 2¼″

2 Ornamental strap icebox hinge
Garrett Wade
Nickel-plated brass
Overall length and width: 6¼″ × 2¼″

3 Icebox hinge
Ritter & Son
Cast brass
Overall length and width: 4″ × 2⅝″,
offset: ⅜″

4 Offset icebox latch
Ritter & Son
Solid brass
Length and width of each base: 2⅛″ ×
³⁄₁₆″, offset: ⅜″

5 Icebox latch
Garrett Wade
Nickel-plated brass
Length and width of each base: 1⅝″ × ¾″

6 Icebox nameplate
Ritter & Son
Cast brass

Chest Lifts & Campaign Hardware

1, 2 Chest lift and matching escutcheon
Horton Brasses
Cast iron
Each overall: 2¼″ × 3½″

3 Chest lift
Horton Brasses
Cast brass
Overall length: 4″

4 Chest lift
Horton Brasses
Cast brass
Overall length: 6¼″

5 Chest lift
Horton Brasses
Cast brass
Overall length: 3⅛″

6 Chest lift
Stanley Hardware
Solid brass
Overall length: 2″

7 Chest lift
Ball and Ball
Cast brass
Boring: 3″

8 Old chest lift
Urban Archeology
Cast bronze
Overall length: 3½″

9 Old chest lift
Urban Archeology
Nickle oxide finish
Overall length: 3½″

10 Flush chest lift
The Merit Brass Collection
Cast brass
Overall: 2″ × 3½″

11 Campaign chest pull
Ball and Ball
Cast brass
Overall: 2″ × 3⅝″

12 Campaign chest pull
Kraft Hardware
Cast brass
Overall: 2″ × 3⅜″

13, 14 Campaign chest pulls
Kraft Hardware
Cast brass
Overall: 2⅝″ × 3⅞″ and 3½″ × 4¼″

15 Corner trim
Kraft Hardware
Solid brass
Overall: 4″ × 4″ × 4″

16 Corner trim
Period Furniture Hardware
Solid brass
Overall: 2½″ × 2½″ × 2½″

17 Bottom trim
Period Furniture Hardware
Solid brass
Overall: 2½″ × 2½″ × 2½″

18 T trim
Paxton
Wrought brass
Overall: 5¼″ × 2⅞″

19 T trim
Kraft Hardware
Solid brass
Overall: 4″ × 2⅝″

20 Side trim
Period Furniture Hardware
Solid brass
Overall: 2½″ × 4″ × ¾″

21 Strap trim
Paxton
Wrought brass
Overall length: 5³⁄₁₆″

22 Corner trim
Paxton
Wrought brass
Overall: 2⁹⁄₁₆″ × 2⁹⁄₁₆″

23 Strap trim
Paxton
Wrought brass
Overall length: 2¼″

24 Angle trim
Paxton
Wrought brass
Overall: 3″ × 3″

25 T trim
Harris Hardware
Cast Zamac
Overall: 2⁷⁄₁₆″ × 2⅜″

26 Corner trim
Harris Hardware
Wrought steel
Overall: 2″ × 2″ × 2″

27 Corner trim
Harris Hardware
Wrought steel
Overall: 2″ × 2″

28 Angle trim
Harris Hardware
Cast Zamac
Overall: 2½″ × 2½″

Furniture Foot Hardware

1 Caster
Kraft Hardware
Cast brass
Wheel diameter: 1⅛″

2–5 Square ferrules
Kraft Hardware
Cast brass
Top inside openings: 1⅜″, 1⅛″, ⅞″, and ½″

6 Square ferrule
Paxton
Solid brass
Top inside opening: 1¼″

7 Round ferrule
Paxton
Solid brass
Top inside opening: 1⅛″

8 Claw foot socket
Paxton
Solid brass
Inside width: 1⅜″, height and length: 1½″ × 2⅜″

9 Lion claw caddy
Kraft Hardware
Cast brass
Overall width: 3″

10 Claw socket caster
Kraft Hardware
Cast brass
Inside width: 1⅛″

11 Socket caster
Kraft Hardware
Cast brass
Inside width: 1⅛″

12 Socket caster
Kraft Hardware
Cast brass
Inside width: ⅞″

Decorative Fasteners

1 Common rosehead nails
Tremont Nail Company
Hot-rolled carbon sheet steel
Lengths: 2″, 2½″, 3″, 3¼″, 3½″, and 4″

2 Wrought head cut nails
Tremont Nail Company
Hot-rolled carbon sheet steel
Lengths: 1″, 1½″, 2″, 2½″, and 3″

3 Wrought head cut nails
Tremont Nail Company
Hot-rolled carbon sheet steel
Lengths: 1″, 1½″, 2″, 2½″, and 3″

4 Fine finish nails
Tremont Nail Company
Hot-rolled carbon sheet steel
Lengths: 1¼″, 1½″, 1¾″, 2″, and 2¼″

5 Cut spikes
Tremont Nail Company
Hot-rolled carbon sheet steel
Lengths: 3″, 3½″, 4″, 4½″, 5″, 5½″, 6″, 7″, and 8″

6 Clinch rosehead nails
Tremont Nail Company
Hot-rolled carbon sheet steel
Lengths: 1¼″, 1½″, 1¾″, 2″, 2¼″, 2½″, 3″, 3½″, and 4″

7 Hinge nails
Tremont Nail Company
Hot-rolled carbon sheet steel
Lengths: 1″, 1¼″, 1½″, 1¾″, 2″, 2¼″, 2½″, 3″, 3½″, and 4″

8 Clout nails
Tremont Nail Company
Hot-rolled carbon sheet steel
Lengths: ¾″, ⅞″, 1″, 1⅛″, 1¼″, 1½″, 1¾″, 2″, and 2¼″

9 Box nails
Tremont Nail Company
Hot-rolled carbon sheet steel
Lengths: 1¾″, 1½″, 2″, 2½″, and 3″

10 Cut brad
Tremont Nail Company
Hot-rolled carbon sheet steel
Length: 1″

11 Common siding nail
Tremont Nail Company
Hot-rolled carbon sheet steel
Length: 2¼″

12 Fine cut headless brads
Tremont Nail Company
Hot-rolled carbon sheet steel
Lengths: ⅞″, 1″, 1¼″, and 1½″

13 Pyramid head screws
Acorn
Steel
Lengths: ¾″, ⅝″, 1″, 1¼″, 1½″, and 2″

14 Pyramid/Phillips head screw
Acorn
Steel
Length: ⅝″

15 Escutcheon pins
Horton Brasses
Brass, antique finish and bright finish
Length: ½″

16 Fancy stud
Erco
Hammered cast bronze
Head: 1¼″

17–20 Studs
Erco
Hammered cast bronze
Heads: 1″, ¾″, ⅝″, and ⅜″

21 Decorative nail
Tremont Nail Company
Hot-rolled carbon sheet steel, matte black finish
Length: ⅝″

22 Decorative nail
Tremont Nail Company
Hot-rolled carbon sheet steel, brass plated
Length: ⅝″

23 Double-pointed decoration tack
Tremont Nail Company
Copper
Head: ⅜″

24 Snap-on screw head cover
Selby Furniture Hardware
Brass
Fits #8 to #14 wood screws and ⅛″ to ¼″ machine screws

25 Snap-on screw head cover
Selby Furniture Hardware
Plastic
Fits #6 to #10 flat-head screws

A Directory of Sources for Decorative Hardware

For more information about where to find, or just learn more about, the decorative hardware presented in this book (and, of course, a whole lot more) the reader may consult the list of sources, including manufacturing companies, retail stores, mail-order supply houses, importers, antique dealers, and forges, provided below. In most cases a catalog, brochure, or some sort of descriptive literature is available and provided on request, either gratis or for a modest price. For your convenience (and theirs) a source's preference or preferences regarding how an inquiry should be made—by calling, writing, or visiting—has been noted.

Acorn Manufacturing Company
P.O. Box 31
School Street
Mansfield, MA 02048
617-339-4500

A catalog is available for $2.00. Write or call.

Albert Constantine and Son Incorporated
2050 Eastchester Road
Bronx, NY 10461
212-792-1600

A mail-order catalog is available for $1.00. For a copy, write or call. Visit the store to see their full line of products.

The Arden Forge Company, Peter A. Renzetti
301 Brinton's Bridge Road
West Chester, PA 19380
215-399-1530

A catalog is available for $4.00. Write for more information about his custom hand-forged hardware, reproduction, and restoration work.

Arrowsmith Industries, Inc.
9700 Bellanca Avenue
Los Angeles, CA 90045
213-776-0890

A catalog is not available to the retail customer. Free descriptive literature is provided on request. Write or call; ask for the hardware division.

Baldwin Hardware Manufacturing Corporation
841 Wyomissing Boulevard
P.O. Box 82
Reading, PA 19603
215-777-7811

A catalog is not available to the retail customer. Individual brochures on rim locks (brochure #9980), mortise locks (brochure #9981), narrow backset locks (brochure #9982), and decorative hardware in general (brochure #9984) are provided on request. Write only. Each brochure is 95¢. Also ask for the list of retail Baldwin Brass Centers. Visit their flagship store in New York City at 210 East 60th Street (212-421-0090).

323

Ball and Ball
463 West Lincoln Highway
Exton, PA 19341
215-363-7330

Write for more information about the availability of a catalog.

Big Anvil Forge, Bob Patrick
Box 205
Bethel, MO 63434
816-284-6610

A catalog is available for $1.00. Write or call for more information about his custom hand-forged hardware, reproduction, and restoration work.

Bob Pryor Antiques
1023 Lexington Avenue (at 73rd Street)
New York, NY 10021
212-688-1516

A catalog is not available. Visit the store to see a fine collection of antique decorative hardware.

Bokenkemp's Forge, Mark E. Bokenkamp
10132 Liberty Road
Powell, OH 43065
614-889-0819

A catalog is in the works. Write or call for more information about his custom hand-forged hardware, reproduction, and restoration work.

The Broadway Collection
250 North Troost Street
Olathe, KS 66061
913-782-6244

A catalog is not available to the retail customer. Free descriptive literature is provided on request. Write only.

Brookstone Company
651 Vose Farm Road
Peterborough, NH 03458
603-924-7181

A mail-order catalog is available free of charge. Write only. Ask for the locations of their nine retail outlets; there might be one nearby to visit.

By-Gone Days Antiques
P.O. Box 30864
Charlotte, NC 28230
704-372-7032

A brochure is available free of charge. For a copy, write or call. Visit the store to see an outstanding collection of antique architectural hardware. Ask for Mr. Dothan R. Boothe.

Custom Decor, Inc.
P.O. Box 538
Dover, DE 19901
302-734-9414

A catalog is not available to the retail customer. Write for more information about The Windcurrent Collection.

Erco Manufacturing Company
2368 North Elston Avenue
Chicago, IL 60614
312-278-7302

A catalog is available. Write or call.

The Farm Forge, Larry B. Wood
6945 Fishburg Road
Dayton, OH 45424
513-233-6751

A catalog is available for $1.00. Write or call for more information about his custom hand-forged hardware, reproduction, and restoration work.

Forms & Surfaces
P.O. Box 5215
1170 Coast Village Road
Santa Barbara, CA 43108
805-969-4767

A catalog is available only through distributors and retail outlets. Kraft Hardware, 300 East 64th Street, New York, NY 10021 (212-838-2214), is a major outlet for Forms & Surfaces products. Write, call, or visit Kraft Hardware for more information.

Garrett Wade Company, Inc.
161 Avenue of the Americas (at Vandam Street)
New York, NY 10013
212-807-1155

A mail-order catalog with 3 supplements issued throughout the year is available for $3.00. For a copy, write or call. Regular customers automatically receive the latest catalog and supplements.

Glynn-Johnson Corporation
4422 North Ravenswood Avenue
Chicago, IL 60640
312-878-5500

A brochure is available free of charge. Write or call.

Hammerworks, Mark E. Rocheford
75 Webster Street
Worcester, MA 01603
617-755-3434

A catalog is available for $1.00. Write or call for more information about his custom hand-forged hardware, reproduction, and restoration work.

Harris Hardware Sales Corporation
4 Harbor Park Drive
Port Washington, NY 11050
516-484-4440

A catalog is available for $2.00. Write only.

Home Hardware, a division of Hammit Industries, Inc.
16205 Distribution Way
Cerritos, CA 90701
213-404-1414

A catalog is available free of charge. Ask for retail price list. Write or call (toll-free) 1-800-854-6275.

Horton Brasses
Nooks Hill Road
P.O. Box 95
Cromwell, CT 06416
203-635-4400

A mail-order catalog is available for $1.50. Write only.

IDG Marketing Limited
1100 Slocum Avenue
Ridgefield, NJ 07657
201-941-2700

Free descriptive literature is available on request. Write or call. The Optimist, a mail-order supply house, P.O. Box 394, Ridgefield, NJ 07657 (201-941-2701), carries IDG's full line of products. Contact them for more information.

Impex Associates Limited, Inc.
25 North Dean Street
Englewood, NJ 07631
201-568-2243

A catalog is available for $2.50. Write or call.

Jaybee Manufacturing Corporation
P.O. Box 54110
Los Angeles, CA 90054
213-223-3121

A catalog is not available to retail customers. Write or call for more information about their products.

Kaviar Forge, Craig Kaviar
P.O. Box 52
Harvard, MA 01451
617-456-8651

A catalog is in the works. Write or call for more information about his custom hand-forged hardware, reproduction, and restoration work.

Kraft Hardware
300 East 64th Street
New York, NY 10021
212-838-2214

A catalog is not available. Write, call, or visit the store for more information about their large selection of cabinet and architectural hardware.

Medeco Security Locks, Inc.
P.O. Box 1075
Salem VA 24153
703-387-0481

A catalog is not available to the retail customer. For more information about Medeco Security Locks visit your local locksmith.

The Merit Brass Collection
242 Valley Road
Warrington, PA 18976
215-342-2500

A catalog of The Merit Brass Collection is available free of charge. For more information, write to Merit Metal Products at the address above; phone inquiries are very welcome. The Merit Brass Collection is sold through major distributors of quality hardware, mail order houses, and retailers throughout the United States.

Michigan Production Grinding Company
Soss Invisible Hinge
P.O. Box 628
Pioneer, OH 43554
419-737-2324

A catalog is available free of charge. Write or call.

Omnia Industries, Inc.
49 Park Street
P.O. Box 263
Montclair, NJ 07042
201-746-4300

A catalog is not available to the retail customer. Write for more information.

PTI-Dolco/Simpson Hardware
851 East Walnut Street
Carson, CA 90746
213-538-2710

A catalog is available free of charge. Write or call.

Paxton Hardware
7818 Bradshaw Road
Upper Falls, MD 21156
301-592-8505

A mail-order catalog is available for $1.50. Write or call. Visit their retail store in Upper Falls, where there is a full stock of cabinetmaker's hardware and where, they say, orders are filled and shipped in 24 hours.

Period Furniture Hardware Company, Inc.
123 Charles Street
Boston, MA 02114
617-227-0758

A mail-order catalog is available for $3.50. Write only.

H. Pfanstiel Hardware Company, Inc.
Route 52
Jeffersonville, NY 12748
914-482-4445

A catalog is available. Write or call for more information.

Plexacraft Metals
5406 San Fernando Road
Glendale, CA 91203
213-246-8201

A catalog is available for $3.50. Write only.

Quincy Manufacturing Company, Inc.
263 Boerum Street
Brooklyn, NY 11206
212-386-9668

A catalog is available for 50¢ (to cover the cost of postage and handling). Mail and telephone inquiries are welcome.

The Ram's Head Forge, Lance Cloutier
RR #34A
Fish Street
Fryeburg, ME 04037
207-697-2011

A catalog is not available. Write or call for more information about his custom hand-forged hardware, reproduction, and restoration work.

The Renovator's Supply
171 Northfield Road
Millers Falls, MA 01349
413-659-3961

A mail-order catalog is available for $2.00. Write only.

Restoration Hardware
438 Second Street
Eureka, CA 95501
707-443-3152

A mail-order catalog is available for $3.00. For a copy, write or call. Visit the retail store in Eureka to see their complete line of products.

Ritter & Son Hardware
P.O. Box 578
Gualala, CA 95445
707-884-3363

A catalog is available for $1.00. Write or call.

Ronald H. Kass Forge, Ronald H. Kass
183 South Main Street
Yardley, PA 19067
215-493-8598

A catalog is not available. Write or call for more information about his custom hand-forged hardware, restoration, and reproduction work.

Salmon Falls Forge, Robert H. Klar
Route 4A
Hollis, ME 04042
207-929-3275

A catalog is not available. Write or call for more information about his custom hand-forged hardware, reproduction, and restoration work.

Selby Furniture Hardware Company
15-19 East 22nd Street
New York, NY 10010
212-673-4097

A catalog is not available to the retail customer. Albert Constantine and Son Incorporated, 2050 Eastchester Road, Bronx, New York (212-792-1600), carries a complete line of Selby Furniture Hardware products. Write, call or visit Albert Constantine and Son for more information.

Sherle Wagner International
60 East 57th Street
New York, NY 10022
212-758-3300

A full-color catalog is available for $5.00. For a copy, write or call. Sherle Wagner's products are sold primarily through architects and interior decorators.

Simon's Hardware
421 Third Avenue
New York, NY 10016
212-532-9220

A catalog is not available. Write, call, or visit their store for more information.

Stanley Hardware, a division of The Stanley Works
P.O. Box 1800
New Britain, CT 06050
203-225-5111

A catalog is not available to the retail customer. Free descriptive literature is provided on request. Write or call.

Steve Kayne Hand Forged Hardware, Steve Kayne
17 Harmon Place
Smithtown, NY 11788
516-724-3669

A catalog is available for $2.00. Write or call for more information about his custom hand-forged hardware, reproduction, and restoration work.

Swenson's Forge, Richard C. Swenson
RD #1
Box 137
Ulster, PA 18850
717-358-3949

A brochure is available free of charge. Write or call for more information about his custom hand-forged hardware, reproduction, and restoration work.

Terra Sancta Guild
858 Sussex Boulevard
Broomall, PA 19008
215-544-9900

A brochure is available free of charge. Write only.

Tremont Nail Company
P.O. Box 111
Wareham, MA 02571
617-295-0038

A catalog is available free of charge. Write or call.

Unique Handicraft Corporation
Space 1033
225 Fifth Avenue
New York, NY 10010
212-696-9730

A catalog is not available to the retail customer. Write or call for more information.

Urban Archeology
137 Spring Street
New York, NY 10012
212-431-6969

A catalog is not available. Write, call, or visit the store for more information about their fascinating collection of antique architectural hardware.

Urfic, Inc.
1000 South Broadway
Salem, OH 44460
216-332-9500

A catalog is available free of charge. Write or call.

VSI Hardware, a Fairchild Industries Company
12930 Bradley Avenue
Sylmar, CA 91342
213-367-2131

The Fortress Security Products catalog is available free of charge. Write or call.

Valley Forgeworks, Ltd., Barry Berman
2491 South Refugio Road
Goleta, CA 93117
805-688-1501

A full-color brochure is available free of charge. Write or call for more information about his custom hand-forged hardware, reproduction, and restoration work.

Valli and Colombo (USA), Inc.
1540 Highland Avenue
Duarte, CA 91010
213-359-2569

A catalog is available free of charge. Write or call.

Waddell Manufacturing Company, Inc.
1115 Taylor Avenue NW
Grand Rapids, MI 49503
616-454-8328

A catalog is available free of charge. Write only.